TO SLEEP WITH THE ANGELS

TO
SLEEP
WITH
THE
ANGELS

The Story of a Fire

DAVID COWAN
AND
JOHN KUENSTER

Elephant Paperbacks
IVAN R. DEE, PUBLISHER, CHICAGO

Photo credits (page numbers refer to pages of the photo section following
page 144): page 1—top, *Chicago Tribune*; page 1—bottom, page 2—top,
page 3—bottom, page 5—top, Stephen Lasker; page 8—top, Bill Rowe;
page 8—bottom, *New World.*

Maps by Victor Thompson

Library of Congress Cataloging-in-Publication Data:
Cowan, David, 1963–
To sleep with the angels : the story of a fire / David Cowan and
John Kuenster.
p. cm.
Includes index.
ISBN 1-56663-217-x
1. Our Lady of the Angels School (Chicago, Ill.)—Fire, 1958.
2. Elementary schools—Fires and fire prevention—Illinois—Chicago—
History—20th century. I. Kuenster, John. II. Title.
LD7501.C434C68 1996
372.9773′11—dc20   95-46795

*So that they not be forgotten, this book is
dedicated to the memory of the ninety-two
children and three nuns who perished in the
fire at Our Lady of the Angels School on
December 1, 1958;
to the families of the fire victims and to the
survivors of the fire, all of whom have quietly
passed through life bearing grief and
memories;
and to those members of the Chicago Fire
Department who battled the blaze and who, in
the face of great personal danger, performed
unselfishly in the highest traditions of the
American fire service.*

Foreword

THIS BOOK IS about the fire at Our Lady of the Angels School in Chicago, one of the most tragic in the nation's history, and about how it affected the people and the community it touched. What happened on December 1, 1958, and after is much more than a story of sorrow and death. It is also a story of hope and survival. Through taped interviews with former students who survived the fire, parents of those who died, teachers, firefighters, clergy, police, investigators, hospital personnel, news reporters, and others—many of them talking publicly for the first time—we have tried to construct a narrative of courage, perseverance, compassion, and professional dedication. The stories of these lives testify to the resiliency and essential goodness of the human spirit, and deserve to be remembered.

Our Lady of the Angels was not the worst school disaster in American history. That dubious distinction belongs to Consolidated School in rural New London, Texas, where on March 18, 1937, a natural gas explosion demolished the building and killed 427 pupils and teachers. The nation's second worst school tragedy occurred March 4, 1908, when fire swept the Lakeview Elementary School in Collinwood, Ohio, killing 178. Although the death toll at Our Lady of the Angels was not as great, it remains more than a defining episode in the colorful and tragic history of a great city, for it led to a complete overhaul of school fire safety laws in the United States, thereby changing the manner in which schoolchildren are housed.

The fire at Our Lady of the Angels School brought crushing grief to those who lost loved ones, inflicted terrible physical and emotional suffering on survivors and their families, sickened firefighters, police officers, and news reporters who responded to the scene, and literally destroyed the school's neighborhood. It brought angry denunciations of the archdiocese of Chicago, school personnel, and the city of Chicago.

We have often been asked why we decided to write this book. The question has never been an easy one to answer. For both of us, what began as genuine curiosity soon turned into outright obsession. The deeper we dug, the more attached we became to the subject. In many respects the Our Lady of the Angels fire remains as much a mystery as it did the day news of the disaster appeared on the front page of virtually every newspaper in the country. After several years of working independently, in 1990 we decided to combine our efforts and work together as partners. By doing so we hoped finally to set straight the record on the fire, perhaps to give voice to those who still grieve, and to provide a sense of closure to an historical void that has remained open for nearly four decades.

Outside of government and the official church, many people helped make this book a reality. It is their story, not ours; we simply put it together for them. We relied on numerous sources in the Chicago Police and Fire Departments, the Cicero, Illinois, Police and Fire Departments, the Cook County State's Attorney's office, the Cook County Medical Examiner's office, and the Illinois State Fire Marshal's office who provided us with documents, reports, photographs, and other materials. The Catholic Archdiocese of Chicago allowed us access to its archives, but the information it had collected on the fire was skimpy. There was not even a specific file on the fire, and missing were any personal papers from former Archbishop Albert Meyer pertaining to the fire. Other, more abundant sources of relevant information include the National Fire Protection Association, the International Association of Firefighters, Chicago Fire Department annual reports, and news reports published in the *Chicago Daily News, Chicago American, Chicago Tribune*, and *Chicago Sun-Times*.

At the time of the fire more than sixteen hundred pupils were enrolled in the school. Many of them had riveting stories to tell. The time, energy, and logistics involved in researching and writing a history of this fire were enormous. We sought out as many survivors as possible. Most were willing to talk with us about their experience, as unpleasant as this may have been for them, and we are deeply grateful for their candor. In most cases there was one constant: people remembered the fire as if it occurred yesterday, and they carried many unresolved feelings about it.

In the final manuscript we chose to include those recollections we thought best represented all who were involved. We made no attempt to create a "pecking order" of those who endured the worst trauma or whose lives were most deeply affected by the fire. Because there are too many people to mention, and because we fear we might inadvertently omit a name or two, we simply wish to extend a heartfelt "thank you" to everyone who gave of themselves. We would, however, like to recognize the parents of fire victims who shared their recollections with us: Lydia and John Trotta, Nick and Mary Malinski, Mario and Della Maffiola, Nick and Emma Jacobellis, Mary Stachura, and Josephine Jajkowski.

Many other men and women contributed important information or opened doors that enabled us to complete this book. The late Fire Commissioner Robert J. Quinn authorized access to the Chicago Fire Department's files on the school fire and granted us permission to interview department personnel. Among many Chicago firefighters who spoke with us were the officers of the first three fire companies to reach the scene: Lieutenants Stanley Wojnicki, Charles Kamin, and Jack McCone. Chief George Schuller, an original member of the Fire Department's arson squad, offered invaluable assistance. We are also grateful to Richard Scheidt, Salvatore Imburgia, Henry Holden, Walter Romanczak, Tony Pilas (whose daughter died in the fire), Thomas O'Donnell, Anthony Reilly, James Neville, Albin Anderson, William Mueller, Thomas Powers, and other Fire Department personnel. Ken Little, the Chicago Fire Department's unofficial historian, provided helpful information about Fire Department history, statistics, and organization.

Sergeant Drew Brown of the Chicago Police bomb and arson unit, the lead police investigator assigned to the case, provided details of his personal findings. So too did private fire investigator John A. Kennedy, who offered his extensive report on the origin and cause of the fire. Polygraph examiner John Reid turned over to us his complete files. George Lindberg, Reid's former associate, was equally helpful. Maurice Door and Ed Rothchild were patient and gracious in explaining Illinois juvenile laws and juvenile court procedures. We are grateful to former youth officer Ron Richards of the Cicero (Illinois) Police Department, and to Cornelius J. Harrington, attorney for the Chicago archdiocese. Several others deserve mention but wish to remain anonymous. They know who they are.

Many in the religious community helped us. Sisters Mary Davidis Devine and Andrienne Carolan, BVM, teachers who were in the building when the fire started, gave generously during personal interviews. Clergy stationed at OLA at the time of the fire who offered information included the Reverends Joseph Ognibene, Charles Hund, Alfred Corbo, and Monsignor John Egan. Monsignor Ed Pellicore, former OLA associate pastor, and Bishop William McManus, former Catholic school superintendent in Chicago, were especially candid in responding to our questions. So too was the Reverend Patrick McPolin, who served as Chicago Police chaplain at the time of the fire. Personnel at St. Anne's Hospital who spoke with us include Sister Mary Almunda Klaus, the hospital's administrator, and Sisters Judian Brietenbach and Stephen Brugeman, PHJH, and Henriette Rocks, RN, all nursing supervisors at the hospital when the fire occurred.

We thank several members of the news media who covered the disaster and its investigation: Hal Bruno, formerly of the *Chicago American*, one of the first reporters at the scene; Charles Cleveland of the *Chicago Daily News*, who covered the Cook County Morgue; William Braden of the *Chicago Sun-Times*; George Bliss and Weldon Whisler of the *Chicago Tribune*; Steve Lasker, former photographer with the *Chicago American*; and Jimmy Kilcoyne, photographer for *The New World* Catholic weekly. Sister Rita Benz, BVM; Alex Burkholder of WLS-TV; Dick Fitzpatrick and Bill Burnham of the Chicago Fire Department photo lab; and Jay Copp, news editor of *The New World*, also provided information and photographs.

Social workers Terri Schmidt and David Plaggemars were especially helpful in providing background information on posttraumatic stress disorder, and we are equally grateful to social worker Carolen King, herself a survivor of the fire, for sharing with us her expertise. Linda K. Maffiola graciously made available to us her many contacts in the Our Lady of the Angels community and served as a source of inspiration and encouragement.

We are particularly indebted to our editor and publisher, Ivan Dee, whose demanding editorial criticisms and suggestions made this a better book.

Lastly, we can never adequately acknowledge the support and helpful suggestions we received from our families and close friends, who never gave up on us, especially during those times when we ourselves were the greatest doubters.

DAVID COWAN
JOHN KUENSTER

Chicago, Illinois
January 1996

Contents

TO SLEEP WITH THE ANGELS

Suffer the little children to come unto me,
and forbid them not: for of such is the
kingdom of God.

—MARK, 10:14

Though the young have experienced few joys,
at least they have suffered few sorrows.

—A GREEK POET

Well has it been said that there is no grief like
the grief which does not speak.

—LONGFELLOW

One

SETTING

SCHOOLS WERE NOT ALWAYS made of concrete and steel. There was a time when they were built of wood and plaster, encased by façades of exterior brick walls. To the naked eye the buildings seemed permanent, indestructible, and when parents sent their children off to learn in such structures, they usually did so without a second thought to safety, assured by routine that their youngsters would return home safely at the end of each school day.

So it was in most American cities, no more and no less than in the city of Chicago, not only in the public schools but also in the Roman Catholic school system.

In 1958 Chicago was filled with a mixture of human integrity and the transgressions for which it had become known the world over, very much the "Toddlin' Town" that Frank Sinatra exalted in song and Al Capone and his mobster protégés had defamed with evil deeds. Under the new leadership of Mayor Richard J. Daley, a neatly groomed, ambitious former county clerk with slicked-back hair and piercing blue eyes, the city was poised to grow in stature and influence. Daley was a hard man to define. He could be immovable at times, sentimental at others. He had been elected mayor in 1955 and was busy constructing his legacy as the last political machine boss to dominate a major American city, forging alliances with business and labor, pushing forward with expansive civic projects. There was

3

much work to do, and Daley knew how to pull people together to get it done.

A new airport, expressways, and skyscrapers needed building. Slums were torn down, replaced by featureless brick high-rises that in time would evolve into even greater slums. The heart of the city's old Taylor Street Italian neighborhood was bulldozed to make way for the University of Illinois at Chicago, an arguably ugly urban campus spreading across several square blocks of city landscape.

Like the two Chicago mayors who preceded him—Edward J. Kelly and Martin Kennelly—Daley was of Irish Catholic stock and came from Bridgeport, a South Side working-class neighborhood heavily inhabited by Irish immigrants. Bridgeport's homes sat near the sprawling, malodorous Union Stockyards, the slaughter-place that prompted Carl Sandburg to christen Chicago "Hog Butcher for the World," and that Upton Sinclair exposed in less romantic prose in his 1906 muckracking novel *The Jungle*. As mayor, Daley was never far from these humble roots or the deep Catholicism he had inherited from his mother. He would remain in Bridgeport his entire life, living out his twenty-one years as mayor in a simple brick bungalow on South Lowe Avenue, less than a block from where he was born, worshiping his god a few blocks away in the same Nativity of Our Lord Church where he had been baptized as an infant.

The mayor took enormous pride in the city and wanted Chicagoans to feel likewise. Most did. He was a stickler for cleanliness, and during his administration the block-long City Hall and adjoining County Building were sandblasted of the grime that had accumulated for years. The cleansing job exemplified Daley's paternal stewardship and symbolized the city's defiant "I will" spirit.

Chicago has always been an action town, a place where the locals work hard and play hard, where good and bad happen in equal proportion. It was chartered as a city in 1835, and thanks to the railroads and Lake Michigan—the inland sea on which it sits—it boomed. The city grew with the pace of a speeding bull until one evening in October 1871 when a fire started behind Kate O'Leary's barn in the Irish ghetto on West DeKoven Street and sparked a roaring blaze that—fanned by fierce winds—traveled north for three miles, destroying everything in its path, including the heart of the old downtown and Near North Side. Three days after the fire began, the skies turned grey and the heavens opened up. It started to rain and the flames died out. Chicago rose from the ashes, licked its wounds, buried its dead, then built itself anew. Before long it was booming again.

By the 1950s it had grown into the nation's transportation hub, the crossroads of the country. Though its image and reputation had been smeared by bootleggers and machine guns, it nevertheless survived to become a center of business and industry, a nucleus of sophistication and culture that spawned some of the leading writers and academics of the twentieth century, and home to one of the great universities of the world. No longer a rebellious teenager, it had matured into a worldly adult. Yet it was still so unpredictable that it would clobber anyone who crossed it. It was the nation's Second City, and it didn't mind being so. Inside its 224 square miles lived 3.5 million residents; the greater metropolitan area held twice as many. Almost half of all Chicagoans—1.5 million—were members of the Roman Catholic church, either in name or in practice.

In May 1958 Cardinal Samuel Stritch, the archbishop of Chicago, died in Rome after suffering a stroke. Stritch was an elderly, soft-spoken Southerner who had administered the largest archdiocese in the United States, including a massive system of churches and schools, most of them closely associated with the flow of neighborhood life in the city. His prelature covered the expanse of two counties and included 424 parishes, 399 elementary schools, 37 high schools, and 21 hospitals, as well as numerous service centers, orphanages, and other charitable institutions, involving a tremendous force of priests, 2,300 in all, as well as many religious brothers, nuns, and lay people. It was a vast operation indeed, one woven tightly into the city's cultural fabric.

In September that year Archbishop Albert G. Meyer of Milwaukee was named Stritch's successor. The youngest son of a second-generation German-American grocery store owner, Meyer took up residence in a red-brick mansion owned by the Chicago archdiocese on November 15, 1958, and was enthroned in Holy Name Cathedral the next day. He was fifty-five years old, a tall, reserved, scholarly man, a keen administrator who was good at detail. He was conscientious and perhaps more sensitive than Stritch had been to the urgency of preparing for the many social changes then impending.

As the youngest archbishop in the country, Meyer faced a number of problems. He had to resolve questions of forming new parishes or redrawing the boundaries of existing parishes. He had to act on several major building projects. It would take some time before he could familiarize himself with his new and many responsibilities, not the least of which was tending to Chicago's large Catholic school enrollment, then listed at 270,299 elementary and high school students.

Meyer retained the superintendent of schools, Monsignor William E. McManus, who had been appointed by Stritch in 1957. One of the challenges facing them was the need, as pointed out by McManus, to build more elementary and high schools outside Chicago, where parishes were being formed to take care of the waves of Chicagoans leaving their old neighborhoods for the greener pastures of the suburbs.

The exodus of residents from the city, which had been going on for some time, had many causes, not the least of which was race—the movement by blacks into once all-white neighborhoods, especially those on the city's West and South sides. Just the day after Meyer was installed as archbishop, Edwin Berry, executive director of the Chicago Urban League, called Chicago "the most segregated city in the nation." To a degree it was. Even though the word "catholic" means "universal," to embrace and tolerate all people, some Catholic pastors and parishioners in Chicago were openly and bitterly opposed to any sort of integration. They did not want blacks moving into their neighborhoods, and they were ready to battle to protect their "turf."

As archbishop, Meyer was sensitive to the festering antagonisms brewing inside the archdiocese, but almost a year would pass before he admitted that the racial situation in Chicago was far worse than in Milwaukee, and that direct episcopal action was needed to diffuse animosities against blacks in many Catholic parishes and in the city at large. Still, not until 1961 would he see the end of segregation in all Catholic institutions.

Even as blacks moved into previously all-white neighborhoods, Chicago retained a rich pluralism of residents whose heritage defined them as Irish, Polish, Jewish, German, Italian, Czech, Lithuanian, Swedish, Greek, or Asian. Hispanics had not yet migrated in large numbers to the city, though they maintained sizable communities in South Chicago and on the Southwest Side. But with Mayor Daley at the controls, despite a varied electorate many key

city positions were dotted with Irish names, including that of Fire
Commissioner Robert J. Quinn, a boyhood friend of the mayor's.
Both had belonged to the Hamburg Social and Athletic Club, a
group of young men better known for their antagonism toward unwanted strangers—especially those with dark skin—who happened
to stray into the neighborhood, than for organized sportsman-
ship.

In keeping with his loyalty to old friends, especially Bridgeport
Irish, in 1957 Daley appointed Quinn commissioner of the nation's
second largest fire department. The new fire commissioner was
fifty-three years old, a rough-hewn character who kept his head
shaved bald and preferred business suits over a Fire Department uniform. He had been as good a choice as any to head the department.
Highly regarded as a firefighter in the early days of his career, he
had once climbed eight floors to the roof of the Stock Exchange
building to rescue three persons during a fire that heavily damaged
the Union Stockyards. The exploit earned him the Lambert Tree
Medal, the city's highest award for valor. During World War II he
had risen to the rank of navy commander in charge of firefighting
and prevention for the entire Atlantic Fleet. The navy had also decorated him for his part in a daring, three-day battle against a raging
fire aboard the tanker *Montana*, loaded with 100,000 barrels of avia-
tion fuel.

As fire commissioner, Quinn commanded a department that in
1958 responded to more than 65,000 fire and special duty alarms
and included a force of 4,278 men who worked twenty-four hours
on duty followed by forty-eight hours off. He was a stickler for discipline within the ranks, and he demanded that personnel assigned to
individual fire companies stay in good physical shape. A committed
bachelor, he neither smoked nor drank and stayed fit by playing
handball at the Fire Department gymnasium near Navy Pier on the
city's lakefront. His first-floor office in City Hall was filled with
photographs and memorabilia; he also kept a set of exercise weights
there.

Quinn liked nothing better than to show up at extra-alarm fires
in his battered white fire helmet and take command. He had his de-
tractors who claimed he was a poor administrator, but no one questioned his firefighting credentials or his dedication to the job. He
could be brusque with people, but there was a sentimental side to

him. He looked after the department's rank and file like a big brother.

One of Quinn's priorities upon being named fire commissioner was fire prevention, particularly for schools. Chicago had more than 800,000 buildings, including 404 public, 354 Catholic, 90 Jewish, and 49 Lutheran schools. Through the end of October 1958, the Fire Department had responded to 89 emergency calls from schools—60 public, 17 parochial, and 12 private. Like many large cities, Chicago faced serious problems not only of providing adequate classroom space for its burgeoning young student population, but also in making sure that fire-prevention standards were being observed in older educational buildings. Catholic elementary schools in particular were fully occupied, and it was not uncommon to find classrooms in the city's parochial schools jammed with more than fifty to sixty pupils. Typical of such structures was Our Lady of the Angels School on the city's West Side.

An ordinary parochial school virtually indistinguishable from hundreds like it in the Chicago archdiocese, OLA, as it was known, did its work quietly and was barely known beyond the confines of the city and the order of sisters that administered it. But though no one paid much attention—not even a fire inspector who reviewed the premises that October—part of a deadly formula was in place at Our Lady of the Angels that would make it famous the world over: crowded classrooms and an aging school building.

WITH 4,500 REGISTERED FAMILIES, Our Lady of the Angels in the late 1950s was a thriving parish, one of the largest in the Chicago archdiocese. It was spread over 150 blocks about five miles west of the downtown Loop. Within its confines was a tree-lined, working-class enclave that featured modest, well-kept homes interspersed with two- and three-flat apartment buildings.

In the early days of the parish, the Irish had been the dominant ethnic group in the community. Gradually the neighborhood around Our Lady of the Angels changed, and by 1958 it was about 60 percent Italian and 30 percent Irish, with the remaining 10 percent Polish and other Eastern European extraction. Many residents, both young and old, had immigrated to the United States, and many spoke an English tinged with the dialects of their native homelands.

The neighborhood was close-knit and boasted a convivial spirit, like an overgrown family. Its residents were proud to say they were from OLA. Their religious faith was deeply rooted in the teachings of the Catholic church, and the parish church and social hall were centerpieces of the neighborhood. On Sundays ten prayer services were held, with Masses and confessions conducted both in English and Italian.

Parishioners for the most part were ordinary hardworking people who cared deeply about their families and took pride in their community. The men were chiefly blue collar and made their livings with their hands, as carpenters, electricians, and plumbers, or in various jobs in factories, warehouses, on construction sites, or with the railroads. Some held city jobs—policemen, firemen, or sanitary workers—while others owned and operated many of the neighborhood's small shops and businesses. Most of the women were housewives and mothers; some held small jobs that helped bring in a few extra dollars. A good number of the adults had witnessed the horrors of World War II, either as Allied or Axis servicemen or civilian refugees forced from their homes; more than a decade later they had settled comfortably into the neighborhood, striving daily to provide their families with a good life.

Unlike Hyde Park, Edgewater, or Roseland, other well-known Chicago neighborhoods, the community around Our Lady of the Angels had no special name. Yet it enjoyed a sense of place, what Italians call *compagnismo*, a feeling of permanency that tied each family to the community. People were entrenched; they were not transients. They maintained their homes, produced homemade wine in their basements, tinkered with small gardens, and in general stayed put. When the evening was warm, they would often take to their front porches and chat with neighbors or passersby.

Like most others in Chicago, the neighborhood had all the ingredients of an urban village, a small town in the big city. The main street for shopping was Chicago Avenue, an east-west artery that cut through the heart of the area. Chicago Avenue was known throughout the city as a bustling, eclectic commercial strip that had the feel and smell of a European high street. Its many storefronts included a mix of businesses sprinkled with Italian names. Bakeries and butcher shops, cafés and produce stands were jammed among an array of small grocery stores, dime stores, drugstores, clothing stores, tailor shops, barber shops, pool halls, social clubs, restaurants, taverns, bowling alleys, and two movie houses. There were doctor and dentist offices for the living, funeral parlors for the dead. It was a place where women pulled shopping carts and bartered with merchants, where soda fountains and corner saloons stayed open late, and where the scents of baked bread, sweet confectioner's sugar, pungent garlic, and fresh produce filled the air.

Vice was represented mainly by gambling and booze. Bets could be placed in many a back room, and if a loan was needed to pay off a bookie, juice could be squeezed from defaulters in unpleasant ways. Still, for the most part the neighborhood was safe. A person could walk the streets at any hour of the night without fear. No one was malicious. The cops bothered few because they had nothing to bother them about. There were no strangers. Persons who walked the street would "hello" everyone.

It was a good neighborhood for growing up, a place where a kid could still be a kid. Parents expected their youngsters home when the streetlights came on. During the day, alleys behind the homes and apartments were crowded with milkmen, junkmen, and fruit peddlers, all competing for space with neighborhood boys playing softball on the narrow concrete surface.

Kells Field at Kedzie and Chicago avenues was the site of hotly competitive softball games involving older players from the neighborhood who belonged to such teams as the Bobcats, Stompers, and Shotwells. The field was named after George Kells, a former alderman and Democratic committeeman of the Twenty-eighth Ward. In the 1951 aldermanic elections, organized-crime figures decided Kells should retire, so he bowed out of politics and left Chicago the same year, claiming his wife had taken ill. He was replaced by Patrick Petrone, brother of State Representative Robert "Happy" Petrone, a close associate of syndicate boss Tony Accardo. Both Petrones were members of the city's West Side Bloc, a group of elected officials who were under the tight control of the Chicago mob.

To the young men who played softball at Kells Field, such weighty matters were of little concern; no one paid much attention to the "made guys." Instead they had their own heroes who wore steel spikes and carried wooden bats. One of these was a muscular kid named Bill Skowron who did what no one had done before: he smacked a home run out of Kells that flew clear across Chicago Avenue, soaring to the third floor of the Rockola Building across the street. The news spread fast, and Skowron became known. He later made a name for himself slugging homers in the major leagues, mostly with the New York Yankees.

THE BIRTH OF Our Lady of the Angels coincided with the massive European immigration to America late in the nineteenth century. It was chartered as a parish in 1894 when Archbishop Patrick Feehan found the need to open a church west of Humboldt Park. Feehan sent Reverend James Hynes to establish the new church, which Hynes named after his alma mater, Our Lady of the Angels Seminary in Niagara, New York.

For the first few years of its existence, religious services were conducted in a store building. The first church building was erected in 1900 on the northwest corner of Hamlin Avenue and Iowa Street, later the site of the present-day church, whose cornerstone was laid in 1939. In 1903 a parish school was built next door to the west, on the northeast corner of Iowa Street and Avers Avenue. The school featured four classrooms on the first floor while the second floor contained a chapel and living quarters for the nuns, whose order was the Sisters of Charity of the Blessed Virgin Mary (BVM).

In September 1904 Our Lady of the Angels School began educating children. Due to the rapid growth of the parish, the next year the chapel on the school's second floor was converted into two more classrooms to accommodate the seventh and eighth grades. In June 1906 the school saw its first graduating class, consisting of seventeen students.

Further growth made it necessary to expand parish facilities. In 1908 a six-flat apartment building at the southeast corner of Iowa and Avers was purchased and converted into a convent to house the nuns, whose numbers had grown to twenty-two. In 1910 a combination church and school was built just north of the original school, at 909 North Avers Avenue, increasing the number of classrooms to eighteen.

In 1939 construction began on a new church and rectory under the direction of Monsignor Joseph F. Cussen. Following the death of Father Hynes in 1936, Cardinal George Mundelein named Cussen parish pastor and commissioned him to erect the two new buildings at a cost of $220,000. The Italian-Romanesque church was designed with a large parish in mind; it would seat more than eleven hundred and featured colorful marble columns behind the altar and a high, wood-plank roof. The three-story brick rectory was built on Iowa Street between the church and south wing of the school. When the two structures were completed in April 1941, the chapel on the first floor of the school's north wing was converted into classrooms, and a new chapel was built in its basement. The school's two wings were connected in 1951 with construction of the annex, giving the building a U shape. At the front of the U, abutting the Avers Avenue sidewalk, was a seven-foot-high iron picket fence, designed to keep out trespassers.

In keeping with the architecture of its day, the two-and-a-half-story school was built of ordinary brick and timber joist construction. Its interior, including all but the stairway in the annex, was made of wood, wood lathe, and plaster. Ceilings were finished with acoustical tile, and the entire structure featured wood trim throughout. The building was of the "Old English" style, where the basement stood a half-story above street level. It was 125 feet long by 105 feet wide.

In the fall of 1958 classroom space at the school was jammed to capacity. Enrollment stood at 1,668 kindergarten to eighth-grade pupils. Two hundred of these children in kindergarten and first grade were accommodated in two separate buildings around the corner on Hamlin Avenue.

The main school building contained twenty-four classrooms with high ceilings from which hung round electric globe lights. Classroom doorways were six and a half feet high, over which were eighteen-inch-high inward-opening glass transoms. The building had six exits, and its only fire escape was located at the rear of the annex. The north wing faced Avers Avenue while the south wing fronted on Iowa Street. The school was heated by a series of radiators fueled by a coal-burning boiler located in the basement of the north wing. The coal supply was kept in an adjacent room.

All second-floor stairway landings were open; on the first floor, fire doors were in place. Although Chicago's 1949 municipal code required that all new school buildings be constructed of noncombustible materials and contain enclosed stairways and fire doors, the law was not retroactive and did not affect existing buildings. Our Lady of the Angels School had no sprinkler system. Save for the first-floor fire doors, a series of pressurized-water fire extinguishers, and a local fire alarm that rang inside the school but did not transmit a signal to the Fire Department, the school, like many of its contemporaries, was without an adequate fire-protection system.

THE PARISH SCHOOL was Monsignor Cussen's pride and joy. "Father Joe" loved kids, and he liked to stand outside the school's front doors each morning to greet the youngsters as they arrived for classes. He knew virtually every child in the school by name and had married many of their parents.

As pastor, Cussen was a levelheaded, unpretentious man whose personality was probably best mirrored by the type of food served in the rectory—a basic meat-and-potatoes fare which rarely aspired to haute cuisine. A priest for forty years, he was sixty-six years old, a large, imposing, good-hearted man who stood over six feet tall and weighed more than two hundred pounds. He wore a wry, almost sardonic look, and his black hair was just starting to show signs of grey.

When the new Our Lady of the Angels Church and rectory were being constructed between 1939 and 1941, Cussen watched every brick put in place, and it was not uncommon for him to return home at the end of the day covered with plaster dust. Outside of his own family, the parish and its people were all that mattered to him. He was a watchful, concerned shepherd, completely devoted to his flock. Unlike most pastors, he never hounded parishioners for money; instead he nickel-and-dimed his way to keep the parish running. He led a limited social life and, unlike some pastors, rarely accepted dinner invitations at people's homes. He had a cool reserve about him that sometimes bordered on piety, yet he remained extremely popular among parishioners and never lacked for friends. In the evenings he enjoyed taking walks through the neighborhood, often stopping to chat with residents sitting outside their homes.

For the other priests who lived in the rectory, a large, fortresslike structure, Cussen provided convivial, fraternal accommodations. The pastor was a hospitable man with a remarkable tolerance for newly ordained priests. He was referred to by his peers as the Babysitter, because the archdiocese liked to send him recently graduated priests straight from the seminary. Cussen liked the nickname as much as he did the opportunity to train young priests.

In 1958 two other monsignors lived in the rectory—John Egan, who would go on to become a social crusader known throughout Chicago, and Joseph Fitzgerald, who later would die after choking on a toothpick. Their presence in the house caused Cussen to joke about how "red" the upstairs bedrooms had become. Together the three elders shared the residence with four younger associate pastors: Joseph Ognibene, Joseph McDonnell, Alfred Corbo, and Charles Hund, men in their late twenties to early thirties. The priests in the house enjoyed one another's company, and at dinner, a meal that was rarely missed, they would gather around the long oak dining room table, talk about goings-on in the parish, and share jokes.

When it came to dealing with troubled marriages and other domestic difficulties, Cussen often would delegate such matters to his younger associates, preferring to avoid controversy. He stayed busy tending to the everyday administrative duties of the parish. He enjoyed a good reputation among the higher-ups in the archdiocese chancery office, and when he asked for something, he usually got it.

ON SUNDAY EVENING, November 30, 1958, Superintendent Mc-Manus drove to Our Lady of the Angels where he had been invited to speak before the school's parent-teacher organization. The meeting was held in the large basement social hall beneath the parish church, where a couple of hundred parents, seated in folding aluminum chairs, had gathered to listen to the superintendent's talk. An articulate man whose speech revealed the hint of an Irish brogue, McManus was dressed in a black suit and white priest's collar. He stood behind a wooden lectern at the back of the room and spoke about the importance of parent-teacher cooperation, and how one had to reinforce the other if a child was to receive an "integrated education" both in school and at home. It was a theme he had been espousing at the time.

The monsignor also related to the parents how he was busy reorganizing the entire archdiocesan elementary school program, attempting to change it from individualized schools to a "harmonious system." Among the items McManus was pushing for included conformity in such matters as the school calendar, textbooks, and pay scales for lay teachers. The changes, McManus explained, would help to bring uniformity into the schools and ensure an equal education for Catholic school students throughout the city and suburbs.

Scanning the audience, McManus was impressed by the turnout, and he could sense that the mothers and fathers obviously cared about their children's education. The reception he received was a welcome change of pace, for during the past several weeks he had been "crabbing a bit" with a number of pastors who had failed to respond to notices issued by the Fire Department for code violations following inspections of their schools.

McManus had been on the job for little more than a year, having succeeded the aging Monsignor Daniel Cunningham as head of the Catholic school board. From the outset he had made it a point to be more active than his predecessor in riding herd on pastors and managing the day-to-day operations of the schools. Cunningham, known as "Diggy" among his confreres, had been noted more for his golf skills than his administrative abilities. He had been in charge of the Catholic school system since the days of Cardinal Mundelein, and his management philosophy was a fairly simple one: leave the pastor alone and let him run his own shop. Hence whenever a violation notice was received from the Fire Department, it was assumed that the pastor of a school being cited would know what to do about it—to respond to the notice or simply let it be. Cunningham would never have thought of calling up a pastor to ask, "What do you intend to do about that fire code violation?" But when McManus did just that—often to men who were very much his senior in the priesthood—the elder prelates would brush him off, treating him as an unwanted nuisance impinging upon their realm. Thus his harping about the urgency of correcting such violations often fell on deaf ears.

Less than twenty-four hours after his Sunday night talk, the superintendent would return to Our Lady of the Angels under much different circumstances. The hope and optimism of the parents gathered inside the church basement that night would be replaced by grief, anger, and disbelief. The north wing of the parish school would be a smoldering wreck, and the name Our Lady of the Angels would forever be linked with death and disaster.

Two

PRELUDE

M ONDAY, DECEMBER 1, 1958, had broken clear and cold in
Chicago.

The temperature outside was a chilly nineteen degrees when
John Raymond awoke in his family's apartment on Hamlin Avenue.
Monday was the first day back to school since classes had ended the
previous Wednesday for Thanksgiving. It was also the first day of
Advent, when Christians, and Catholics in particular, prepare for the
Christmas holy season.

John was eleven years old, a fifth-grader at Our Lady of the Angels School a block away, and one of seven children in his family.
He had recently marked his church confirmation, a rite of passage
for preadolescent Catholics, and to cap the occasion his parents had
scraped together enough money to buy him a new bicycle, a red-
and-white Sonic King purchased from the local Sears, Roebuck
store on Homan Avenue. The bike, with its wide handlebars, shiny
chrome rims, and thick whitewall tires, was the envy of every boy
who passed it on display. For John it was a dream come true. He had
been anxious to break it in, but freezing weekend temperatures and a
light dusting of snow had curtailed his plans for an inaugural spin
through his neighborhood. Instead of whisking down its side streets,
showing off to his friends, he had spent much of his Sunday staring
out the window, dreaming of spring.

On Sunday the city had registered its coldest day of the season.

The mercury at Midway Airport, the world's busiest, had dipped to two degrees above zero. But Monday promised to be warmer, with temperatures forecast to reach into the thirties. John peeked through the curtains. The skies were clear, the streets dry. Maybe after school he could take the bike out for a ride.

With six brothers and sisters, John had never had a bicycle he could call his own. His dad, Jim, a tall, slender forty-three-year-old, was employed as head janitor at Our Lady of the Angels parish, a position that paid little but demanded much. Although the elder Raymond often felt he was lucky enough just to put food on the table for his large brood—let alone buy new bikes for each of the kids—he also knew he had a steady, honest job that allowed him the use of his handiwork skills.

Jim Raymond began working at Our Lady of the Angels in 1945. He was responsible for the upkeep of all parish properties, including the church, school, convent, rectory, and community center. In time he had come to consider the buildings as extensions of himself. His budget might be limited, but he tended the properties with care, maintaining a regular schedule of sweeping and mopping floors, wiping windows, and burning trash. It was a heavy workload, and with the exception of one part-time assistant and an elderly retiree who would occasionally give him a hand, the janitor received little help with his chores. His workday usually began around 5:30 in the morning, and sometimes, aside from dinner with his family, would not end until 9:30 at night. Despite these demands, in the thirteen years he had worked at the parish Raymond had come to develop a deep respect for his boss, Monsignor Cussen. The two men shared a close friendship.

During the winter months Raymond fed the school's coal-burning furnace several times each day, often returning in the early morning hours to stoke it again so that the building would be warm when the children arrived for classes. Many times, when he required help with bigger jobs, he would troop up to the eighth-grade classrooms and enlist a few of the older boys. Raymond's fourteen-year-old, Bob, often was one of the lucky "volunteers" pulled from class to help in such tasks. It would happen that Monday afternoon when Bob and a dozen other boys would be dismissed early from Room 211 to help load old clothes onto a truck as part of the parish's annual clothing drive for needy families.

The parish and its people represented obvious focal points for the Raymond family. The children's mother, Ann, herself a graduate of Our Lady of the Angels, had grown up in the neighborhood. She had met her husband in the late 1930s after he had come to Chicago from his home in Holland, Michigan, in search of work. After their marriage in Our Lady of the Angels Church, the couple set up house in the same yellow-brick two-flat they still called home.

Now, after seven children, the apartment at times seemed to be bursting at its seams. In the mornings the hallway leading to the bathroom often was crowded as the kids took turns washing their faces and brushing their teeth.

The morning of December 1 was no different.

THE 1953 BROWN Chevy coupe sped along the ribbon of concrete linking Chicago's South Side with the Loop. Richard Scheidt was making good time in the rush-hour traffic on South Shore Drive. To the left, the barren trees of Jackson Park whizzed by, exposing the sprawling, grey Museum of Science and Industry, built for the 1893 Columbian Exposition. Off to the right, Lake Michigan glistened, and the morning sun, an orange ball, hung just above the horizon.

Thirty and balding, Scheidt had left his wife and four children in their six-room bungalow on West 97th Street shortly after seven o'clock. Like many Americans of the era, he had become accustomed to the cold war, and during his half-hour ride to the firehouse he paid little attention to the Nike missile installation near 53rd Street, one of sixteen that encircled the Chicago area. Its radar domes, scanning the skies for Russian bombers, frequently caught the eye of passing motorists.

Chicago's downtown skyscrapers loomed on the horizon. Burgeoning traffic forced Scheidt to slow his car near R. R. Donnelley's Lakeside Press, where, inside the huge plant, presses were already at work churning out the day's quota of telephone books, catalogs, and magazines. To the east, at the lakefront, the city's new exposition center, McCormick Place, was under construction.

The brown coupe again picked up speed as the traffic bottleneck cleared. The Grant Park bandshell and the expanse of brown grass surrounding it looked especially lonesome that cold, crisp morning. But beyond the bandshell, to the north, the Prudential Building was a commanding sight. Chicago's tallest building and the city's first skyscraper since the Great Depression soon would be jammed with tourists and proud locals eager to see the city from its observation deck, 614 feet above Randolph Street.

Scheidt was only minutes from the old firehouse at 219 North Dearborn Street, the quarters of Engine Company 13 and Rescue Squad 1. He looked forward to a good cup of coffee with his comrades on the squad.

The city had thirteen rescue squads, several of them busier than Squad 1, but it enjoyed the most prestige because its district encompassed the Loop and the Near North Side. While a squad could be dispatched anywhere in the city in an emergency, Scheidt and his fellow squadmen were chiefly responsible for what fire underwriters called the "high value" district: the La Salle Street financial hub, the fashionable Michigan Avenue shopping area, the high-rises and exclusive mansions along Lake Shore Drive, and City Hall itself.

There was money in the Loop, and the Fire Department traditionally stationed its newest and most elaborate equipment there—equipment that could be seen by the many Chicagoans and tourists who frequented the area. The Dearborn Street firehouse was the closest to Room 105, City Hall, the office of discipline-conscious Fire Commissioner Robert J. Quinn.

Following his two older brothers, Richard Scheidt had joined the Fire Department in 1951 and had chosen squad work. He liked the camaraderie and extra hustle of the men on the "dizzie wagons," a nickname that came from their seemingly constant activity. At fires, squadmen opened roofs, pulled ceilings, conducted search and rescue, and helped engine companies with hose lines. But a special-duty call could mean anything—a heart attack victim, a serious auto accident, a jumper in the nearby Chicago River, a rescue from a building collapse. Squadmen swore that when they arrived at a fire, other firemen on engine and truck companies would begin to work harder. The "regulars" disagreed, calling the whole thing conceit. Any superiority—real or imagined—was not reflected in pay. Scheidt earned no more than any other first-class Chicago firefighter: $5,400 a year.

The silvery Christmas decorations on the light poles along State Street hardly caught Scheidt's eye as he drove west on Randolph Street. The streets were still deserted and the thousands of bulbs on

the large theatre marquees were dark. At 9 a.m., when those marquees came alive, beckoning early theatregoers to *The Geisha Boy, I
Want to Live*, and *Anna Lucasta*, Scheidt would already have been to
his first fire of the day.

Leaving the marquees behind, Scheidt parked his car and entered the three-story red-brick firehouse built in 1872, a year after
the Great Chicago Fire. At 8 a.m. the bells inside the station began
their incessant clanging, a signal that the shifts were changing.
Putting down his cup of coffee, Scheidt walked to the front of the
house and joined the other five members of the squad for roll call.

The new twenty-four-hour shift was beginning.

FIVE MILES AWAY, on Chicago's West Side, the same eight o'clock
signal from the main fire alarm office was ringing bells inside the
quarters of Engine Company 85, where Lieutenant Stanley Wojnicki
and his four-man crew also were coming on duty. The old brick engine house, built in the days of horse-drawn fire apparatus, stood on
the corner of Huron Street and Lawndale Avenue, three blocks south
and two blocks east of Our Lady of the Angels School. Inside, behind narrow red doors that opened at the middle, the company's
1951 Mack pumper, equipped with fifteen hundred feet of hose and
one twenty-four-foot extension ladder, stood at the ready, awaiting
its next alarm.

In 1958 Chicago was protected by a firefighting force of 126
engine companies, 59 hook-and-ladder companies, and 13 rescue squads, all divided into 30 battalions and 6 divisions. These
units, each manned by five to six firefighters, were the city's front-
line defense against fire, and each was responsible for covering its
own "still district." The area covered by Engine Company 85, part
of the 18th Battalion, was typical of a crowded, working-class
neighborhood—modest bungalows, apartment buildings, light industry, and small businesses. The company didn't see many fires,
and despite the bustling nature of its district, compared to other fire
companies in the city it was on the low end of the activity scale—a
"slow outfit" in a well-kept area.

Supplementing the engine and truck companies of the Chicago
Fire Department were nineteen Cadillac ambulances, each manned
by two firefighters with about eight hours of basic Red Cross first-
aid training, and a host of other specialized vehicles and apparatus,

including smoke ejectors, "water towers" (elevating platforms with hoses), high-pressure rigs, and light wagons. Among the new additions to the department's fleet in 1958 was the "snorkel," an elevating platform fitted with a basket and hose nozzle perched atop two hydraulic booms. The snorkel was the brainchild of Fire Commissioner Quinn, who had gotten the idea for the new apparatus after watching city workers in gooseneck cherry pickers trim trees in Lincoln Park.

Sitting on watch at his desk near the front of the firehouse, just beneath the loudspeaker linking Engine 85 with the downtown alarm office, Lieutenant Wojnicki began his paperwork, signing his name in the company logbook to indicate that his platoon had taken over. Across the street, the sidewalks were crowded with children streaming into Ryerson public elementary school. Roll call had ended and the firemen were busy checking their equipment, making sure the pumper's water tank was full, that everything was ready to go.

A short, stocky, muscular figure with jet-black hair and a pleasant demeanor, Wojnicki was dressed in his regulation white shirt and navy blue trousers. Pinned to each lapel of his shirt was a silver bugle denoting his lieutenant's rank. As he completed his morning routine, a small transistor radio on his desk kept him company:

"President Eisenhower has once again warned the Soviet Union the United States will not withdraw from Berlin. . . .

"In France, President Charles de Gaulle's right-wing party has scored a parliamentary victory over the Communists. . . .

"Meanwhile, in this country, the president says he looks forward to 1959 bringing recovery for the American economy, now in its fifth month of recession. . . ."

Chicago sports news was less encouraging:

"Only 13,000 football fans showed up at Comiskey Park Sunday to watch the Cardinals lose to the Los Angeles Rams, 20 to 14. The Bears, in Pittsburgh, were defeated by the Steelers . . ."

The weather report was more cheerful: "Partly cloudy today, not so cold."

That's good, Wojnicki thought. Since joining the Fire Department in 1943, he had been to his share of winter blazes, and he knew that cold weather with its greater use of heating facilities brought more fires. But he felt at ease, for he was in charge of a good group of firefighters, men skilled in their jobs. And on this Monday the company was at full strength: an engineer to drive and work the pump, three firefighters, and himself.

Wojnicki was a good firefighter and a levelheaded officer who knew his district intimately. An orphan, he was forty-three years old and had grown up in this same neighborhood, raised by an older sister. His childhood home was about a mile from the firehouse, and he made his first Holy Communion and confirmation in the old Our Lady of the Angels Church, the building that by 1958 had been converted into the north wing of the parish school.

After his marriage Wojnicki stayed in the neighborhood, buying a two-flat building on North Ridgeway Avenue. He was disappointed when his dream of becoming a police officer was cut short—literally—by the department's height requirement. Wojnicki stood five feet, eight inches tall; incoming police recruits had to be a minimum five feet, nine inches. Instead he took the fireman's test, coming out number twenty-one on the eligible list. When the time came for him to report for duty, he had unaccountably decided to turn down the appointment, but he went ahead and accepted the job, following the advice of his brother-in-law, a police officer, who had threatened to "belt him one" if he didn't take it.

After finishing drill school, Wojnicki's first assignment in the Fire Department had been with Engine Company 85. He later transferred to nearby Engine Company 68, on North Kostner Avenue, but returned to Engine 85 in 1953, after his promotion to lieutenant. The promotion brought with it a bigger paycheck, and in February 1958 Wojnicki, with his wife and three sons, packed up and moved to a larger home on the city's North Side. Until then he had been an active church parishioner, and the oldest of his three children had been a student at Our Lady of the Angels School.

Although he no longer lived there, Wojnicki still enjoyed the old neighborhood. He fit comfortably into the community of friendly, family-oriented people. If matched against the achievements of the movers and shakers of society, his life would seem rather routine, measured by twenty-four-hour shifts at the firehouse followed by forty-eight hours off duty. But if there was a sense of ordinary commonplace to Stanley Wojnicki's life, it would come to an abrupt end later that afternoon.

FOR THE NUNS who taught at Our Lady of the Angels School, the Monday also had begun early. The Sisters of Charity of the Blessed Virgin Mary devoted their lives to prayer and teaching, and began their morning by offering daily devotions inside the wood-paneled chapel of their convent across the street from the parish school.

The BVM order had been founded in 1833 by Sister Mary Frances Clarke, and it began serving the Chicago archdiocese in 1867. The order, dedicated to works of education, was known for its teachers, whose appearance was distinguished from other religious communities by the large square hoods they wore atop their heads. They had another distinction as well: a concern about fire. In 1870 their motherhouse in Dubuque, Iowa, had burned to the ground, and since then—for eighty-eight years—all members of the order offered daily prayers asking that they and their pupils be spared from fire. Monday, December 1, was no different.

After finishing breakfast in the convent dining hall, the sisters walked across Iowa Street to their classrooms in the parish school. They were dressed in their traditional ankle-length black habits offset by stiff hoods and white fluted borders and collars. The women painted a picture of delicate gentleness, and their fair skin glowed in the sunlight. In little more than a half-hour, these graceful visions in black and white would act and appear quite different—as queens before their small, often awestruck charges.

Sisters Mary Davidis Devine and Mary Helaine O'Neill, two of the older, more experienced nuns, climbed the worn wooden stairs to their eighth-grade classrooms on the second floor of the school's north wing. The pair had enjoyed their holiday weekend but were happy to be back to work.

Sister Davidis took up her post at the front of Room 209, a classroom with a high ceiling, varnished hardwood floor, and plenty of wood trim. After wiping clean her spectacles and organizing her desk, she began jotting notes on the chalkboard. The sixty-two pupils assigned to her would be arriving soon, and there was much work to be done.

A teacher for thirty-four of her fifty-two years, Sister Davidis loved her profession, and her students knew it. There was a sense of freedom in her classroom despite the omnipresent atmosphere of

Catholic school discipline. Although a tug on a pupil's ear might occasionally be necessary if that freedom went too far, the years had taught her that equal doses of order and free reign made learning less of a chore.

The contrast in Room 211 next door was sharp. At age fifty-six, Sister Mary "Hurricane" Helaine towered over her sixty-four pupils; the threat of discipline that she represented usually was sufficient to maintain order in her classroom. If not, a gentle reminder, like a jabbing finger, was all that was necessary. From the students' perspective, Sister Helaine was one of the most feared nuns in Our Lady of the Angels, and youngsters in the lower grades knew they had a fifty-fifty chance of meeting this formidable "obstacle" on the way to graduation.

Across the hall, in Room 208, near the back stairway, Sister Mary St. Canice Lyng was busy writing notes in her appointment book. A regal-looking nun with pince-nez glasses, she planned to spend part of the day teaching European history to her forty-seven seventh-graders.

Sister Canice was forty-four years old, a scholarly type who had joined the convent in 1932. When she was growing up her relatives would say, "She's cut out for teaching." Reading was Sister Canice's hobby, and she preferred the classics; Dante was among her favorites. After literature she had a great love of history, especially Irish history, which she had picked up from her late father, a Chicago police captain. Both her parents had been killed two years earlier in a car accident involving a drunken driver. Following this personal tragedy, Sister Canice consoled herself with prayer, and the sisters and children of the parish had become her new family.

Next door, in Room 210, in the middle of the corridor, Sister Mary Seraphica Kelley was also preparing for the school day. Compared with some of the other nuns, her classroom demeanor was considered moderate. She enjoyed teaching the younger children and looked forward to the arrival of her fifty-seven fourth- and fifth-graders.

The lines on Sister Seraphica's face made her look older than her forty-three years. Just two months earlier she had celebrated her silver jubilee as a nun. She had first come to Our Lady of the Angels in 1936, as a young teacher straight from the convent. She was later sent to Hollywood where she taught children of movie stars and entertainers. After several years on the West Coast, she came back to the Midwest to serve as principal of a Catholic grade school in DeKalb, Illinois, eventually returning to Our Lady of the Angels to complete the circle of her teaching life that had begun in Chicago.

Next door, at the west end of the corridor near the front staircase, Sister Mary Clare Therese Champagne was contemplating new Christmas decorations for Room 212. Of all the sisters in the parish, she was considered the artist and enjoyed decorating the school's bulletin boards according to significant world events or seasons of the year. She kept an artist's easel with paper at the front of her classroom and often would have her fifty-five fifth-graders use it rather than the chalkboard to figure their math problems.

Sister Therese had been reared in New Orleans where, before joining the convent, she had once been a Mardi Gras queen. She was pretty, twenty-seven, and spoke with a Southern accent that sometimes made the children giggle. She had an unhurried manner about her and a delightful sense of humor that endeared her to the other nuns and the children. Her good looks had turned the heads of more than a few male parishioners. She was, in the words of one parish priest, "a real knockout."

THE THERMOMETER WAS sitting at twenty degrees when the bell inside the school began ringing at 8:40 a.m. Outside a morning ritual was already under way. Parents and relatives were arriving with children in tow, seeing their youngsters safely to school. The streets and sidewalks around the old school swelled with pedestrians. Patrol boys set up wooden horses on Iowa Street to keep traffic from clogging the building's front entrance, and a couple of priests were standing outside the rectory, next to the flagpole, talking with mothers and fathers. Priests in the parish always made sure one or two of them were on hand in the mornings to stand watch outside, just in case any boys had ideas of starting a fistfight. More times than not, though, the men were in place simply to greet the children, to give them a wink and say hello. And though the priests didn't know all the kids by name, certainly they knew their faces.

The students were toting books and folders, and those living farthest away carried lunch boxes. They marched dutifully through the school's front doors, headed for classrooms they would occupy until the school day ended at three o'clock. Once out of the cold, the children doffed their caps, scarves, and mittens, and hung up their coats and jackets in clothes closets and on coatracks set in the hallways and narrow corridors.

The youngsters were attired according to Catholic school regulations. Boys wore dress shirts, dark pants, and ties. Girls dressed in blue or white sweaters, white blouses and jumpers, and blue plaid skirts. The school sweaters were embroidered with the letters "OLA," an acronym the kids—when safely out of earshot of their nuns and lay teachers—referred to as "Old Ladies Association."

A number of desks in the classrooms were empty that Monday. Colds, flu, and other childhood ailments had taken their usual toll on the school's attendance record. And because it was the first day after a cold holiday weekend, there seemed to be more absences than usual.

One of the empty desks in Room 212 belonged to Linda Malinski, a ten-year-old fifth-grader with long blond hair and hazel green eyes. Linda and her older brother Gerry, a sixth-grader, awoke that morning with colds, and their mother, Mary, decided the children should stay home from school.

The Malinskis' conversion to Roman Catholicism had come a year and a half earlier when the family was visited by a nun canvassing the neighborhood. The process was hastened when a parish priest, Father Alfred Corbo, persuaded the children's father, Nicholas Malinski, to rejoin the church he had left in his youth. Nicholas and Mary were soon remarried in Our Lady of the Angels Church, and all six of their children were baptized in the Catholic faith.

Nicholas Malinski became a devout Catholic, and he and his wife wanted their children to attend parochial schools. In the fall of 1958 Nicholas Jr., the oldest of the Malinski children, was enrolled at St. Benedict's High School, and Gerry and Linda transferred to Our Lady of the Angels. A younger daughter, Barbara, was denied admission because of overcrowding in the first grade. Instead she was enrolled in Ryerson public elementary school, across the street from the family's home on North Lawndale Avenue.

Linda Malinski was a cheerful, happy girl with a bright disposition. She was a joy to her parents and helpful at home. And though she had acquired many of the playful mannerisms of her older brothers, she fell short of being a tomboy.

During the dark, early morning hours of that same Monday,

Mary Malinski awoke in the stillness of the family's home to the sound of someone crying. Outside it was chilly and silent. She listened intently, wondering to herself if she had in fact heard one of her six children cry out.

"Mommy?"

Now certain she had not imagined the muffled sobs, Mary arose and quietly crept past the children's beds. Linda awoke with a start.

"Mommy," Linda cried. "I can't breathe. I can't breathe."

Linda was choking on a nightmare. She dreamed of a fire and imagined that smoke was filling the family's tiny apartment. Mary assured her daughter that everything was all right, that there was no fire. Linda suffered from asthma, and her mother figured the ailment was responsible for the girl's coughs and labored breathing. But what Linda said next would later cause Mary to believe her daughter had had a premonition of the disaster that was to occur later that day.

"Mommy," she cried. "I hear people screaming."

Mary was concerned. She stayed at Linda's bedside and comforted her daughter back to sleep.

Later that morning, after school had already begun, Linda told her mother she felt better and wanted to attend afternoon classes. When Mary took the temperatures of both Linda and Gerry, the readings showed normal, and she told the children they could join their classmates after lunch. The decision would haunt Mary Malinski for years to come.

As Linda prepared for school, she took great pains in fixing her long blond hair, a task usually performed by her mother.

"Mommy," Linda asked, "does my hair look all right?"

Mary looked down at her daughter and smiled. "You look like an angel."

AFTER LUNCHEON RECESS, the schoolchildren returned to their classrooms for the final two hours of study. Up to now the school day had passed uneventfully; the youngsters sat at their desks and endured the normal routines of reading, writing, and figuring.

Inside Room 206, tucked away in the annex on the second floor between the school's north and south wings, lay teacher Pearl Tristano was readying her fifth-graders for their end-of-day chores. Tristano, a dark-haired twenty-four-year-old, was unmarried and lived at home with her parents in suburban Oak Park; she had been teaching at OLA for some time and was one of nine lay teachers on the school's staff.

Sometime after 2:20 p.m., as the school day drew to a close, Tristano assigned two boys in her room to the daily task of carrying wastebaskets down to the basement boiler room. There they dumped the refuse into large metal bins so the janitor could burn it later in an outside incinerator. Their errand completed, the boys returned to the classroom and took their seats. Earlier Tristano had also excused from the room another boy—a bespectacled, blond-haired youth who asked to use the lavatory. This boy also returned a short time later and, with his classmates, sat down to resume his last-minute studies.

There was nothing unusual about these closing minutes of the school day, and nothing would be made of these temporary absences from Tristano's classroom for some time. In fact, there was much movement in the normally deserted hallways of the school that afternoon: boys leaving their rooms to empty wastebaskets in the basement or stepping outside into the courtway to clean erasers; a girl walking to the convent to attend a music lesson; another girl going into a seventh-grade room to pick up a homework assignment for her sick sister; several boys leaving their rooms for neighborhood sidewalk patrol.

Unnoticed, something else was occurring that afternoon in an isolated, seldom-used corner of the school basement.

Located in the north wing, at the bottom of the building's northeast stairwell, beyond a door that was only steps from where students were emptying their wastebaskets in the boiler room, a fire in a cardboard trash drum had been burning for several minutes. And though the exact time of the fire's ignition would never be fixed to the precise minute, the date of its occurrence would soon be etched in the dark ledger of the nation's terrible tragedies.

After consuming refuse in the container, the fire smoldered from a lack of oxygen, elevating temperatures in the confined stairwell. Suddenly, when a window in the basement broke from the heat, a fresh supply of air rushed in, and the deserted stairwell turned into a blazing chimney. Without a sprinkler system in place to check their advance, flames, smoke, and heat roared upward, feeding on the old wooden staircase and bannisters, melting asphalt tile covering the stairs.

On the first floor a closed fire door blocked the fire's path. But no door was in place on the second floor. Consequently heavy black smoke and superheated air began pouring into the second-floor corridor. Lurking behind the smoke, flames crept along, feeding off combustible ceiling tile, painted walls, and varnished hardwood flooring.

At the same time hot gases from the fire entered an open pipe shaft in the basement stairwell and flowed upward into the cockloft between the roof and ceiling of the school. Flames erupted as well in this hidden area directly above the six north-wing classrooms packed with 329 students and six nuns. The out-of-control blaze was now raging undetected through the school, devouring everything in its path, cutting off escape for the unsuspecting occupants.

Despite the intensity of the fire, several minutes passed before anyone realized the school was ablaze. Two teachers wondered why the building seemed excessively warm, but they mistakenly assumed the janitor had overstoked the furnace. Finally a chain of events occurred alerting the entire school to the danger at hand.

THE FIRE IN THE SCHOOL was discovered in close sequence by several people, though no one at the time realized that this discovery would turn into a race against death.

School janitor Jim Raymond was one of the first to notice that something was wrong. Sometime before 2:30 p.m., Raymond was walking west on Iowa Street, returning to the school from a job in a nearby parish property on Hamlin Avenue. As was his habit, when he reached the rectory he turned right and walked north through the narrow gangway separating the priests' house and the rear of the school. He was headed for the school's boiler room, and as he approached the building's northeast corner, he noticed a faint wisp of smoke.

Puzzled at what could be burning, Raymond quickened his pace. When he moved toward the corner of the building, he was startled to see a red glow coming from the frosted window pane near the back stairwell. He retreated into the gangway and ran through a door leading down into the boiler room. Once inside, Raymond peered between the two cylindrical boilers and saw that the interior door leading to the stairwell was slightly ajar, and that a fire was raging upward on the other side. The fire appeared to be out of control. It was too big for Raymond to fight himself.

Fifth-graders Ronald Eddington and James Brocato were in the boiler room, emptying waste paper baskets from Room 205, when the janitor appeared. The noisy boilers had masked the sound of the fire in the stairwell, and the boys apparently did not realize that a blaze was burning only a few feet away. They were startled to see Mr. Raymond so excited.

"Go call the Fire Department!" he yelled to them.

The boys looked at each other, puzzled. Then they caught a glimpse of the fire.

"Let's get out of here!" Ronnie shouted.

The janitor left too. He raced back outside to the rectory next door. When he stormed into the residence, Nora Maloney, the silver-haired, thick-brogued housekeeper was standing in the kitchen, preparing a sauce for the evening meal. She jumped when the back door slammed.

"Call the Fire Department! The school's on fire!" Raymond shouted to her.

Nora Maloney was unaware of the situation beginning to unfold only a few yards from where she stood. She set her ladle down on the stove and walked over to a small window above the sink that faced the back of the school. She looked out and saw smoke. When she turned around to respond, Raymond was gone. He had already run back into the burning school; inside were four of his own children.

ELMER BARKHAUS, an amiable, sixty-one-year-old part owner of a glue company, turned his black Buick off Augusta Boulevard and drove south on Avers Avenue that afternoon. He spent most of his working hours traveling, selling his wares to local floor-covering contractors, and he had a few more stops to make before starting the long drive to his home on the city's South Side.

As Barkhaus neared Iowa Street, something caught his eye. He slowed his car to a crawl and peered into the alley just north of the maroon-brick building of Our Lady of the Angels School. Smoke was pouring out the rear stairwell door.

Barkhaus thought a second. Stay calm. Don't get excited. He had to be careful. The ulcers in his stomach were fragile. He pulled over to the curb, then looked for a fire alarm box on the corner.

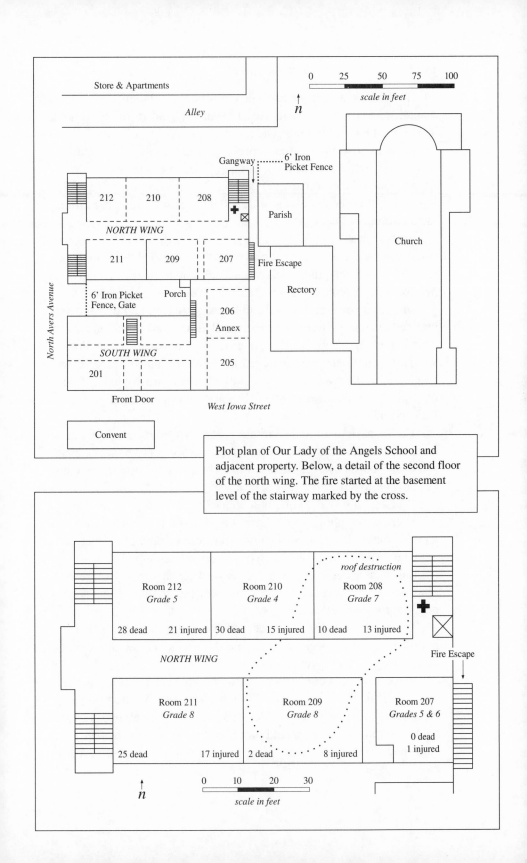

Store & Apartments

Alley

0   25   50   75   100
scale in feet

n

Gangway ········· 6' Iron Picket Fence

212   210   208

NORTH WING

Parish

Church

211   209   207

Fire Escape

6' Iron Picket Fence, Gate   Porch

Rectory

206 Annex

205

SOUTH WING

201

Front Door

West Iowa Street

North Avers Avenue

Convent

Plot plan of Our Lady of the Angels School and adjacent property. Below, a detail of the second floor of the north wing. The fire started at the basement level of the stairway marked by the cross.

roof destruction

Room 212
Grade 5

Room 210
Grade 4

Room 208
Grade 7

28 dead   21 injured | 30 dead   15 injured | 10 dead   13 injured

NORTH WING

Fire Escape

Room 211
Grade 8

Room 209
Grade 8

Room 207
Grades 5 & 6

0 dead
1 injured

25 dead   17 injured | 2 dead ······· 8 injured

n

0   10   20   30
scale in feet

He didn't see one; not all Chicago schools had them. He spotted a small candy store next to the alley directly north of the school. There must be a telephone inside.

Barbara Glowacki, the store's plump, twenty-nine-year-old owner, was sitting in the back kitchen, next to the living room, riffling through the newspaper. Duke, her German shepherd, was barking as Joseph, her three-year-old, pedaled his little blue car around the apartment.

Barbara was waiting for school next door to let out in another twenty minutes, when her store would be invaded by youngsters stopping in to spend their nickels and dimes on the array of candy she had for sale. Helena, her seven-year-old, would be among the kids.

Only two years earlier she and husband Joseph had become naturalized citizens of what she fondly called her "promised land." The couple had met and married in postwar Germany. Being Polish, Joseph had not been well received in Germany, and Barbara, a German, had been unwelcome in Poland. After shifting around, the couple followed thousands of other displaced Europeans, emigrating to Chicago in 1950.

The front door rattled. Barbara looked up from her TV listings, her view blocked partially by a refrigerator. She saw it was a man, someone she had never seen before. He looked worried, nervous. Perhaps he was ill. She went to see.

"Ma'am," he said, "you got a phone?"

There was a phone in the back, but Barbara thought it unwise to let the stranger use it, not when she was home alone. She was leery.

"No," she replied, "I don't have a public telephone."

Barkhaus wheeled around and headed for the door. Before running out he turned back to the woman at the counter. "The school next door is on fire!"

The salesman darted outside and across the street to a two-flat building where he began ringing the doorbells of both apartments, hoping to find a telephone.

Barbara was skeptical. Why would he say such a thing? He must be mad. Still, she was curious. Shoving her hands in the pockets of her sweater, she walked outside, shivering as she stepped into the cold. She took a few steps and turned left into the alley between her store and the school. Everything seemed normal. She took a few more steps. Then she saw it.

A tongue of bright orange flame was curling up over the transom above the back stairwell door. "Oh my God!" she yelled.

Barbara clutched herself, then pictured Helena, whose classroom was on the first floor. She turned around, hoping to see someone, anyone. She looked for the stranger. He was gone. She turned back to the stairwell. Smoke and flames pouring out the doorway were all that met her frantic glances.

For the moment Barbara was alone in the cold, quiet alley. She looked up at the school windows. The building was filled with children, but she heard no fire alarm. Suddenly her fears were realized.

They don't know!

Barbara couldn't move fast enough. She ran back to her building and crashed through the front door, knocking down a candy display in front of the store. Her mind was scattered. Everything was a blur except the black telephone sitting on the kitchen table.

When Barbara reached the kitchen, she picked up the phone. Her hands were shaking and she was out of breath. She thought "Fire Department" but drew a blank; she couldn't remember the seven-digit number. Instead she dialed the operator.

"Give me the firemen, quick!"

After she was connected, a man on the other end responded: "Chicago Fire Department."

"Our Lady of the Angels School is on fire. Hurry!"

"Somebody called in already. Help is on the way."

The fire alarm operator's voice was cool and reassuring. For the moment it had a calming effect on Barbara.

FRANKIE GRIMALDI raised his hand.

"Yes?" Miss Tristano asked.

"May I go to the washroom?"

"You may."

Frankie got up from his seat in Room 206 and walked out of the classroom. Something strange caught his attention. There was smoke in the hallway. When he turned, Miss Tristano was right behind him. She too had caught a whiff of the smoke.

"Get back in the room," she ordered the boy.

Following Frankie back inside, Tristano looked to her students. "Stay here," she said. "I'm going next door."

When Tristano returned to the hallway, the smoke had grown

darker and hotter. She walked next door to Room 205 to alert Dorothy Coughlan, the lay teacher there.

"What should we do?" Tristano asked, aware of the strict rule that permitted only the mother superior, the school's principal, to ring the fire alarm.

"I'll go to the office," Coughlan said. "You stay here."

When Coughlan reached the principal's second-floor office in the middle of the south wing, she found that the superior, Sister Mary St. Florence Casey, was substituting for a sick teacher in a first-floor classroom. By the time Coughlan returned to her own classroom, the smoke entering the tiny annex corridor had worsened. She and Tristano decided not to wait for an alarm and instead to evacuate their classes.

Tristano reentered her room. "Everybody get up," she announced to her students. "We're leaving the building."

The two teachers lined up their pupils in fire-drill formation, then marched them into the corridor and down a set of stairs in the south wing that led to the first floor. Once downstairs, the two groups filed through doors leading to the Iowa Street sidewalk. When Tristano reached the first floor behind the children, she flipped the switch on the wall-mounted fire alarm located at the bottom of the stairway. Nothing happened. She darted outside. Coughlan was yelling. "Take them to the church. I'm going to the convent. I'm calling the Fire Department."

Obeying her older colleague, Tristano hurried the two classes into the parish church next door. Then she returned to the school and the fire alarm. The alarm on the wall resembled a light switch and was almost six feet off the floor. When Tristano flipped it the second time, the audible buzzer started sounding in the school. But the alarm was merely a local one—it rang only inside the school; it did not transmit a signal to the Fire Department.

It was now 2:42 p.m. Nearly eight minutes had elapsed since Tristano first noticed the smoke.

A MILE SOUTH of Our Lady of the Angels School, the merchants along Madison Street were looking forward to the holiday shopping season, optimistic that sales would improve over the recession-ridden Christmas of 1957. They were already dressing up their storefronts and the streetlights along the avenue with decorations in green, red, silver, and gold.

Mary Stachura picked up a packet of invoices and looked around the crowded back office of Madigan's department store. She was happy to have this, her first Christmas job, now that both her sons were in school. And the fashionable ladies' store, located in the midst of the area's main shopping hub—Crawford Avenue and Madison Street—was just minutes from home.

Mary loved the family atmosphere in the neighborhood. She and her husband, Max, could reach out and almost touch the bricks of Our Lady of the Angels Church from their two-flat on Hamlin Avenue. They never had an excuse for being late for Sunday Mass.

Max's parents lived upstairs and last year began teaching Polish to Mark Allen and John, both students at Our Lady of the Angels. Proud of their European heritage, the elder Stachuras, like many Chicago Poles, hoped that heritage would be treasured by their grandsons.

Mark was tolerant of his language lessons, but one aspect of his ancestry bothered him: his blond hair. "Why can't I have black hair like all the other kids?" he would grumble.

His schoolmates were mostly dark-haired Italians, and Mark hadn't seen them in a week; he'd been home ill. In his eagerness to get to school that morning, he'd almost forgotten to kiss Mary goodbye.

"Bye, Mom," he had said, planting a kiss on her cheek. Running down the short flight of stairs, the fourth-grader had been singing. His glee may have been due in part to being over his recent minor illness, but for some reason Mary had a feeling of apprehension.

It was going on 3 p.m. when she looked up at the clock and thought of Max. He'd soon be picking up their children, and at five o'clock they would meet her and go to dinner. Later they would take the boys to see Santa Claus.

Mary was fingering through invoices when a dissonant sound began to mingle with the generic, piped-in Christmas music. At first she didn't notice it. But soon the wailing sirens grew closer, louder, demanding to be heard.

"There must be a big fire somewhere," Mary thought.

Instinctively she clutched the gold crucifix around her neck.

IT HAD BEEN only seconds since the calming voice of the fire alarm operator had assured Barbara Glowacki that help was on the way. But when she ran back outside, the scene in the alley had changed dramatically. The single flame she had first seen in the school doorway had grown into a raging inferno. The windows of the second-floor classrooms had been thrown open and were filling with dozens of terrified, familiar faces. Some were screaming, gasping for air. Black smoke was billowing over their heads. The little faces in the windows seemed to be piled on top of one another.

Barbara trembled. "Lord have mercy!"

The kids were screaming to her. "Get me out of here! Catch me!"

Some of them knew her name. "Barb! Help us! Help me!"

Sister Mary Seraphica was leaning out the middle windows of Room 210, hacking and coughing. She spotted Barbara. "Please help, help!" she screamed. "Call the Fire Department!"

Barbara yelled back. "Why don't you get out?"

"We can't. We're trapped."

"Hold on, sister! Help is on the way! The Fire Department is on the way!"

The nun kept on screaming and Barbara wondered why she and the children didn't leave their rooms and run down the stairs. She didn't know the fire and smoke had completely engulfed the upstairs corridor, making escape through the hallway seem impossible. She ran over to the side door near the front of the school to see if it was jammed shut. When she pulled on it, the door opened an inch or two, but black smoke inside pushed out and drove her back. The smoke was too much; it was burning her lungs.

Suddenly Barbara was overwhelmed by fear. She remembered her daughter Helena, whose second-grade classroom was on the first floor.

"My child! Where's my child!" she screamed.

She scurried around the corner and ran through the school's front door on Avers. A nun was leading a group of frightened students out of the building. They were filing out fast, one after the other.

"Oh sister," Barbara cried. "They can't get out. They can't get out."

The nun was calm; she didn't realize what was happening upstairs. "We all got out. We all got out."

Barbara ran back into the alley. All of the windows were open and children were hanging from the sills. They were throwing books and shoes and screaming for rescue. She ran back and forth, yelling up to them. "Help is coming! Help is coming!"

Then . . . children began jumping from the windows, landing on the pavement twenty-five feet below.

Still no firemen. The alley was filling with people. A woman ran up to Barbara.

"Why don't the firemen come?" they asked each other simultaneously.

It had been only a minute since Barbara called the Fire Department, but it seemed like an eternity had passed.

Youngsters were landing all around. Some of them had been burned. Others were bleeding. A few got up and hobbled away. Still more lay motionless and silent. They looked broken up. Barbara began dragging kids out of the way, setting them against the wall of her adjacent store.

Some youngsters clearly had broken bones—arms and legs—and Barbara kept thinking, "Isn't it wrong to move injured people?" But she had no choice; she had to make room or the injured would be struck by other falling bodies. She grabbed one boy whose leg was dangling over the other. He was big and heavy, almost too much for her. Still, she found the strength. She grabbed under his armpits and yanked, dragging him out of the way.

Barbara placed six youngsters against the side of her building. Their faces were blistering and swelling up. On some, their clothing was smoldering. Barbara ran into her store and filled a pot with water. Returning to the alley, she began pouring water over the children.

She walked some of the youngsters into her store, out of the cold, shielding them from the awful sights outside. She put them in the kitchen and bedroom, setting them in chairs and laying them in her bed. She grabbed her rosary and handed it to a girl. "Pray for the children," Barbara told her.

Then, once again, thoughts of her daughter flashed through her mind: "Where is my Helena! She hasn't come out."

Barbara rushed back outside, her eyes searching. She brushed past a nun carrying an injured child. She saw Monsignor Cussen, his face contorted in horror, running through the alley, crying. Finally, she spotted Helena's nun in the street.

"Where is my child? She didn't get out."

"She did get out," the nun screamed. "Someone grabbed her and took her to one of the houses."

STEVE LASKER saw the plume of smoke in the distance as he drove along Grand Avenue. He was trying to warm up. The twenty-eight-year-old newspaper photographer had just completed an assignment outdoors at a fire extinguisher company. The firm had conducted a test, dropping an extinguisher from its roof to prove that its product wouldn't explode upon impact. The test was in response to a charge that one of its units had done just that.

The smoke in the sky to the south was growing thicker and blacker.

Looks like a good fire, Lasker thought. He grabbed the microphone on his two-way radio and called the *Chicago American* city desk. "Do you have a fire working somewhere on the West Side?"

The day city editor came back. "Don't know anything about it."

Just then the police radio in Lasker's car started blaring. "Send all the help you can! They're jumping out all over!" It was the excited voice of a lone patrolman, the first to arrive at the school.

"Attention, cars in the 28th District," responded the police operator. "Assistance is needed at Our Lady of the Angels, Avers and Iowa."

Lasker stepped on the gas and headed toward the smoke.

MARIO CAMERINI, a friendly twenty-year-old who had grown up in the neighborhood, emerged from the back door of the church basement carrying a case of empty Pepsi bottles. In his part-time job as assistant janitor, he helped out in the church, and on Mondays he always returned the empties from the week before.

Mario was walking into the alley, on the way to Barbara Glowacki's store, when he heard the commotion. He looked up to the windows of Room 208, next to the back stairwell, and saw dozens of seventh-graders jamming the open spaces. Smoke was pouring from the windows. Only a few years ago Mario had been a student in that same classroom. He recognized some of the faces of the youngsters who were screaming down to him for help. He set the bottles down and ran to the garage behind the rectory. There were ladders stored inside.

MAX STACHURA was napping on the front-room couch facing the television set when he looked at his watch and saw that it was almost time to pick up the boys at school. As a driver for United Parcel Service, Max worked odd hours. He was catching up on his sleep.

Max arose and stepped into the kitchen, putting water on for coffee. Smoke wafted past the back window. When it cleared for a moment, he was startled to see that it was coming from the school. Like many parents, the Stachuras had been concerned about fire in the old building. Only a few weeks before, a small blaze had erupted in the school's basement, just papers and rags. The family consoled Mark, who had come home that day worried.

"Always listen to your nun, and the Fire Department will help you," Max had told him. And to Mary: "We live so close, if there's any big trouble we'll get them out."

Following his own advice, Max grabbed his jacket and ran out the back porch, down the stairs, and into the alley where he saw Mario struggling with a ladder in the garage.

"C'mon," Max yelled. "I'll help you."

The two men picked up the extension ladder used to put up screens and hurried to the burning school. They heaved it up against the wall, raising it to an open window of Room 208. As soon as the ladder touched the sill, seventh-graders began crowding and pushing in a rush to get on it. They started climbing down.

Max felt a momentary sense of relief. But when he glanced over to the smoke-filled windows of the classroom next door, his heart sank.

"That's Mark's room!" he screamed.

Sickening black smoke was pouring over the little faces of students who fought for every inch of space in the small, dark openings. The fourth-graders' heads barely cleared the sills. Mark's face had to be among them. Kids were climbing over one another. The windows were filling with teetering children. Then the pushing and jumping started.

Max fretted. "Where's Mark?"

Finally he spotted his son's little blond head bobbing up and down in the crowd.

"Daddy!" the youngster shrieked. "Help me!"

"Stay there!" Max yelled. "Don't jump!"

Max looked around. He was surrounded by chaos. The fire alarm was ringing over the shouts and screams. Bodies were dropping and landing all over, hitting the pavement and crushed rock with sickening thuds. One man caught a girl whose hair was on fire. He used his coat to smother the flames. Another man standing nearby was being battered to the ground by more falling bodies. Men and women were dragging limp children away from the burning building. Some were badly injured, screaming. Others were deathly still.

"This is crazy! They're killing themselves," Max thought.

He looked back up. Mark was getting ready to jump too.

"No, son! Wait! I'll get you down!"

He ran to his garage in the adjoining alley. Fumbling for his keys, he unlocked the overhead door, grabbed a paint-spattered ladder, and ran back to his son's window at Room 210. The cloud of black smoke pouring from the school was turning darker and denser by the second. The whole place looked like it was ready to explode.

Mark was still struggling at the windowsill when Max returned with the ladder.

"Hold on son! I'm coming!"

The father's heart was pounding wildly. He was nearly out of breath when he flung the ladder against the wall. His momentary elation turned sour. The ladder was too short.

In fact the north side of the building was now dotted with home ladders perched against the school's outer brick wall. All the ladders were too short; children hanging from the windows couldn't reach them. The screams from above forced Max to refocus his attention on Mark's position in the window.

His son called for him. "Daddy!"

The large man's shoulders slumped, and tears began to fill his eyes. The ladder had been his only chance. What else could he do?

"Mark!" he yelled. "Jump! I'll catch you!"

Mark's eyes never left his father. The little fourth-grader tried one last time to pull himself over the windowsill. But just as his elbows touched the ledge, a whoosh of flames crawled up and pulled him back down into the room. Max watched in horror as his son disappeared in the smoke. He was standing in the alley, arms outstretched, helpless. It was the last time he would see Mark alive. The crushing grief dropped him to his knees. He was too late. Despite the nearness of his home, it wasn't close enough.

Three

STRUGGLE

I RENE MORDARSKI was seated patiently at her desk in the back of Room 208, listening to Sister Canice's history lesson, watching an electric wall clock above the blackboard tick away the final half-hour of school.

Like many of her classmates, Irene's parents had been born in Europe and survived World War II. Her father had served in the Polish army, had been taken prisoner by the Germans, and had later escaped from a concentration camp. Still, Irene had little liking of history, even though she herself was a naturalized citizen of the United States. "It's my least favorite subject," she would often remind her girlfriends.

Sister Canice had already told her pupils there would be a history quiz later in the week, and Irene knew she would have to study. She was hoping something would happen so they wouldn't have to take the test. Her wishful thinking was suddenly interrupted when the room's two wooden doors started rattling.

"Must be ghosts," whispered one boy, and some of the girls giggled. Another boy sitting near Irene stood up from his desk, curious to see what was causing the strange sound. He walked over to the back door.

"There's smoke in the hallway!" he exclaimed.

Sister Canice walked to the front door and opened it. A cloud of black smoke swirled into the room. She slammed the door shut, but almost immediately more smoke began seeping in through the partially opened glass transoms and cracks around the two doors. Irene and her forty-six classmates stopped giggling. As more smoke poured into the room, they started rising from their seats, looking nervously at their nun.

"Just sit tight," said Sister Canice. "The janitor's probably done something with the furnace."

The nun's speculation, of course, was in error—the coal-burning furnace in the basement was working just fine. The truth of the situation at that moment was much more fearsome. The janitor was running into the rectory, yelling to the housekeeper to call the Fire Department, as flames and smoke roared unchecked up the back stairway adjacent to Room 208.

Within seconds the scene inside the classroom began to change rapidly. Smoke passing through the transoms was turning thicker. The children began coughing, confused by the sudden turn of events.

For the moment everyone was silent. Sister Canice could feel her heart starting to pound as her mind raced for answers. A fire was burning somewhere in the building. But how? The fire alarm had not sounded, even though at that moment it no longer mattered. The hallway outside was already impassable. The only way out now was through the windows. Stay calm. Maintain order. Don't lose control. The Fire Department will come. Everything will be all right.

The room was quickly turning warmer and darker. The children were getting nervous. Sister Canice clutched the silver crucifix hanging from her neck. "We mustn't panic," she said. "Get down on your knees. Say a prayer. The firemen will come."

The nun meant well. It was a natural reaction for her, at first, to have her pupils seek divine help. But as conditions inside the room quickly worsened, prayers were discarded, replaced by the instinct for survival. One boy jumped up from his desk. "I'm not staying here any longer." Impulsively, he and the others rushed to the four windows overlooking the alley. Sister Canice followed. So did Irene. But the girl's approach to the last window on the west end of the room was blocked by a crowd of classmates who had jammed themselves in front of the sill. Those nearest the windows threw up the sashes and leaned out into the fresh, clean air. They began screaming. "The school's on fire! The school's on fire!"

The room was growing hotter with each passing second. The old paint covering its worn, wooden walls was changing color—from white to tan to brown. Irene was gasping for air. She yanked a handkerchief from the breast pocket of her navy blue uniform and pressed it against her face, trying desperately to breathe through it. That day was the first time she had ever worn nylon stockings to school, and in the morning, she had slipped on a pair of bobby socks over the stockings to keep out the cold. Heat in the classroom was becoming unbearable, and she could feel the nylons melting to her legs.

Suddenly the big round globe lights that hung from the ceiling began popping from the intense heat, sending shards of glass crashing to the floor. The students dropped to their knees, terrified. Irene now became aware of the crescendo of screams coming not only from her room but from the other classrooms in the stricken school. The screams were loud, chilling. Irene would remember them for the rest of her life.

Then it happened—a bright orange flash followed by a loud, thunderous boom. The fire exploded into the room. It crashed in the doors and burst through the walls. Flames swarmed unhindered across the flammable ceiling tile, spilling like a molten waterfall down to the floor, devouring everything in their path. They ate away at the old wooden flooring and swallowed up desks, tables, and wall hangings. The fire started grabbing the scrambling figures trying to outrun it.

Irene fell to her hands and knees. She could feel her skin burning. She had only seconds to get out of the room. Thoughts of her parents flashed through her mind. Stanley and Amalia Mordarski, Polish and Austrian by birth, had brought her to the United States in 1952, when she was just six years old. She thought of her little sister, Monica, a first-grader downstairs.

I've got to get out for them, Irene reasoned with youthful logic. If I die, what will they do?

With a sudden surge of energy, the girl sprang up and pushed her way through the pile of children bunched in front of her, stepping over those who had passed out or were already dead. Crawling over desks and chairs, she made her way to the window. Then she felt a tug on her shoulder. It was Sister Canice.

"Quick," the nun beckoned. "Get up here!"

A high radiator sat next to the windowsill, and with the help of her nun Irene managed to climb up and gain access to the ledge. Dense smoke was obscuring her vision. She couldn't see her classmates descending the ladder placed at the room's east window by Mario Camerini and Max Stachura. At least one boy had already jumped from another window near the front of the room, breaking a leg as he landed on the sloping roof of a basement window enclosure that shortened his fall.

Irene looked down at the hard gravel and asphalt surface twenty-five feet below. The drop was daunting. A neighbor had propped another ladder directly beneath the windowsill. But it was a few feet short. That's okay, she thought. I'll use it anyhow. She stood up on the ledge and pivoted her body around. Then, dangling from the sill, she reached down with her toes, attempting to get a foothold on the ladder's top rung. Just then the hot fire gases building inside the room ignited and blew out through the windows. The blast caught Irene square in the face, knocking her unconscious. She dropped off the sill, falling straight down, scraping her face all the way against the building's rough brick wall. She hit the pavement with a crash, shattering her pelvis.

When Irene awoke she was in a daze. She found herself sitting against the north wall of the blazing school, inexplicably clutching a string of white rosary beads. The beads had been in her uniform pocket when she plummeted to the ground; she had no idea how they came to be in her burned hands. Nor did she know how long she'd been lying on the ground—seconds or minutes. She couldn't remember if she had fallen from the window or was pushed out by Sister Canice.

Irene looked down at her feet. Both of her black suede shoes were missing.

"Oh, my new shoes," she murmured. "They're gone."

Her entire body was numb and hot. The fresh, cold air felt good against her skin. She was drifting euphorically into shock and began to feel an overwhelming sense of relief in having escaped the inferno above. Still, she didn't feel right; she knew something was wrong.

Her face was cut and bleeding from rubbing against the wall. Her pelvis was fractured in two places. Both her legs were covered with second- and third-degree burns—from her knees to a point just above her ankles, where her bobby socks had provided some protection against the searing flames. Her face, arms, and hands were burned.

She looked up dazedly at several of her stunned classmates who were gathering around her.

"Somebody, please help me," she cried.

IN ROOM 209, Gerry Andreoli was sitting in the second row of desks, near windows overlooking the U-shaped courtway separating the school's north and south wings. Sister Davidis was teaching a math lesson, charting figures on the blackboard. At full capacity Room 209 held sixty-three students—"wall-to-wall kids," Sister Davidis would say with resigned good humor. But because of absences there were only fifty-five pupils in place that Monday, thirty-four boys and twenty-one girls.

The first sign of trouble came when Danny Patano rose to begin his daily chore of collecting waste paper from his classmates. When he walked over to pick up the metal basket near the back of the room, the basket for some reason felt hot. At the same time Richard Sacco, another student sitting near the back door, raised his hand.

"Yes?" inquired Sister Davidis.

"Sister, I think I smell something burning."

Gerry Andreoli and the other eighth-graders turned to see what was happening. Sister Davidis was standing at the front, or west end, of the room and had not detected the odor herself.

"Let's check it out," she said.

It was a little before 2:30.

Sister Davidis moved toward the front door, Richard Sacco the back door. The boy was closer, and when he grabbed the knob and opened the door, a mass of heavy smoke looking like large bales of black cotton rolled into the room. When the nun reached the front door, she touched the metal knob but withdrew immediately. It felt red-hot. She and the children were becoming aware of the fire tornado gathering force in the ten-foot-wide hallway separating the upper classrooms in the north wing.

Sister Davidis quickly sized up the predicament she and her students were facing. She knew the odds were against trying to escape through the hallway. If she started her kids out that way, chances were they'd get lost in the smoke, maybe even pass out and be trampled to death. She couldn't chance it. Her street-smarts took over. She moved into action.

"All right," she announced. "You boys start gathering up books and start blocking up the cracks at the bottom of the doors. The rest of you stay put."

The boys responded, grabbing books off the desks and stacking them around the doors to keep out the smoke. When the job was finished, Sister Davidis directed her students to the south windows overlooking the twenty-foot-wide cement courtway.

Gerry Andreoli felt the room growing warmer as he and his classmates crowded near the four windows. In his haste to reach the window on the west end of the room, he had climbed over his nun's desk, knocking a stack of papers to the floor. He managed to stake out a small space for himself, and it was only then he realized that the occupants in the classrooms across the courtway, in the south wing, were still unaware of the unfolding situation.

"Call to them!" Sister Davidis said.

The eighth-graders began yelling as loud as they could. "The school's on fire! The school's on fire!"

Kathy Meisinger was one of those in the opposite classroom. She was staring out her second-floor window, trying to pay attention to a music lesson, when she noticed students across the courtway in the north wing jumping up and down on their desks, looking like they were having a party. It was then she and her classmates heard the screams. They began evacuating their room just as smoke started drifting into the south wing. The fire alarm had not yet sounded, and the occupants in the room directly below Kathy's remained oblivious to the excited shouts. Sister Davidis told her students to start throwing pencils at the lower windows. When the teacher there heard them bouncing off the glass, she knew something was wrong. Sister Davidis's students were not in the habit of hanging out windows, throwing pencils.

At that moment Sister Davidis heard a loud crack. She turned to see that the glass transoms above the doors were shattering from the intense heat. A wave of flames came pouring into the room, spreading across the acoustical wheat-fiber ceiling tile. A small canopy was located a few feet below the room's back window. Eddie Maggerise turned to his nun. "Sister, it's not far. Can I go?"

Sister Davidis yelled back. "If you can make it, jump."

He could and did. After dropping himself to the canopy, the boy jumped down to the ground. He looked up to his nun in the smoke-filled window. She leaned out to shout him an order. "Go get help!"

Eddie ran to the front of the courtway. He climbed over the high iron picket fence and took off running.

Sister Davidis stayed with her students at the windows. The smoke was getting worse, obscuring her vision. The heat was intensifying. The flames were flowing across the ceiling. The room was growing dark. She feared one of her charges might stray from her sight. She felt herself losing consciousness. She forced her head out the window, gasping for air.

"Smoke's coming through the floor!" yelled one of the boys, more astonished than frightened as he pointed to an opening around a radiator pipe.

"Just keep your heads out," the nun said.

Gerry Andreoli had spent all his grammar school years at Our Lady of the Angels. But behind his shy demeanor was a sense of fierce determination, one that would carry him through his ordeal. He would be one of the last pupils to escape the inferno inside Room 209, and one of the most critically burned students to survive the catastrophe. With time slipping away and flames bearing down, he glanced at the forbidding cement courtway two and a half stories below. It looked awfully far.

SAM TORTORICE had just returned home to his two-flat on Hamlin Avenue, directly across the street from Our Lady of the Angels Church. He had spent the day shopping, and he was reaching inside his car to collect his grocery bags when he noticed the pungent odor of burning wood. Tortorice, forty-two, was short, dark haired, and wore glasses. He looked up in the direction of the smell. It was strong. He took only a few steps before he saw a cloud of black smoke rolling from the top of the parish school. Inside were his two daughters, thirteen-year-old Rose and eleven-year-old Judy.

Tortorice took off running for the burning building. When he reached the front of the school on Avers, he looked up to the smoke-filled windows overlooking the courtway. There was Rose among the frightened faces crowding the far window of Room 209.

"Rose," he screamed, "wait! I'm coming!"

Tortorice ran around to the Iowa Street doors, where he entered the school and, dodging children making their way down, ran up the stairs to the second floor. There he made his way into the annex corridor, then crawled to a set of windows overlooking the courtway and directly adjacent to the windows in Room 209. Tortorice threw up the sash, then swung his left leg over the ledge. Straddling the windowsill, he reached over with his arms and began swinging the panicky eighth-graders into the annex.

"Rose," he yelled, "come closer!"

Try as she might, Rose could not reach the rescuing hands of her father. She was stuck behind the others lined up at the window. With smoke pouring over her head, she pleaded for help. "Daddy!" she cried, "come quick!"

Tortorice knew he had to reposition himself. He swung his legs over the window ledge, lowering himself down onto a small canopy roof set over a doorway directly beneath him. Another neighbor had tossed a ladder over the fence into the blocked courtway. Tortorice dropped down to the pavement and grabbed the ladder, using it to climb back up onto the canopy. "Hold on," he shouted to the kids above.

At about the same time Father Joseph Ognibene was driving east on Iowa Street, returning to the rectory after lunch with friends in a neighboring parish. As he neared Avers Avenue, the south wing of the school came into view, and Father Ognibene could see smoke pouring from the building and children being led outside onto the sidewalk.

Tall, dark-skinned, and athletic, "Father Joe" was thirty-two, the senior curate assigned to the parish. He was popular with the students and active in the school's physical education programs. During spring and summer months he could often be found on neighborhood ball diamonds, wearing a T-shirt and old slacks, shagging fly balls with boys from the parish. The older children were especially fond of him; they enjoyed it when he came out to play ball with them, and they were impressed to find that he was pretty good at it too. The girls in the parish liked him as well. They thought he was "cute."

Immediately Father Ognibene screeched his car to a halt, curbing it in front of the convent, then darted across the street and entered the school through the front doors on Iowa Street. It was approximately 2:40 p.m. The first call to the Fire Department had yet to be made.

Bounding up the stairs to the second-floor landing, Father Ognibene was met by a scene of crowded confusion. Some of the students gathering in the hallway were frightened by the thickening smoke. Father Joe didn't fully realize what was happening, but he knew he had to hurry them down.

"Let's get going," he shouted. The priest began shoving the students one by one toward the stairs. One of the children having difficulty was a sixth-grade girl. She had polio, and the heavy metal braces strapped to her legs were causing her to struggle. Father Ognibene scooped the girl into his arms and carried her down the stairs. He didn't care that her braces tumbled off when he did so. After handing the girl off to a nun, he raced back up the stairs to the second floor. It was then Father Ognibene realized that something more terrible than he imagined was unfolding.

Unable to stand up because of the worsening smoke, he dropped to his hands and knees and began crawling through the dark abyss of smoke filling the tiny annex corridor, headed for the doomed classrooms of the north wing. He was able to go as far as the end of the corridor, but that was all. Beyond him in the smoke were raging flames, which cut off further access. On his left were the two corner windows facing the courtway. Father Ognibene looked out and saw Tortorice standing on the ladder, trying to lift children out of Room 209. "Here," the priest yelled, "swing them to me."

Quickly Father Ognibene doffed his black suit coat and clerical vest. Thus unencumbered, he hoisted himself up to the ledge of the corner window adjacent to Room 209. Straddling the window frame, he leaned out, placing himself in a position to help Tortorice by reaching for students hanging from the adjacent window. Together the two men proceeded with their daring joint rescue: Tortorice yanking the children from the burning classroom, Ognibene reaching out and swinging them into the annex.

Gerry Andreoli watched as the two men pulled his classmates from the corner window. Smoke inside the room was getting worse. Unable to breathe, Gerry dropped to the floor and curled up in a ball. He was losing track of time. He noticed his girlfriend, Beverly

Burda, lying next to him. Her white sweater was turning color. "I'm getting out of here," he yelled to her.

Gerry got back up and grabbed onto the windowsill, stepping up to the ledge. As he mounted the sill he was being enveloped by flames and smoke shooting around the window frames. Suddenly a whoosh of flames crashed down through the ceiling. Fire was now shooting from the sides of the windows, burning Gerry on the head, arms, and shoulders. His vision became clouded, but he could still see well enough to spot—for the first time—a ladder resting just below the windowsill, short by about two feet.

Gerry wavered on the ledge, feeling dizzy, like he might fall back into the flames or straight down to the concrete below. He somehow managed to maintain his balance, long enough to lower his feet onto the ladder. The flesh on his hands had been peeled back, resembling bloodied pieces of raw meat, and his elbows were burned to the bone. Yet he was able to slide his feet down far enough to reach the top rung. Then, in an awkward, forward fashion, he descended the ladder, hooking his feet around the rungs and working his way down, one step at a time.

Once on the ground he could see only a few feet ahead of him. He felt he was about to collapse but managed to stagger the few feet to the iron fence. Firefighters who had managed to break down its gate were running into the courtway carrying ladders and life nets. Children bunched up at the windows were jumping like crazy, bouncing off the pavement. Firemen were trying to catch them or break their falls.

Gerry thought of walking to his father's clothing store on Chicago Avenue when his endurance finally gave out. He looked—for the first time—at his hands and began to realize the seriousness of his injuries. His face had swelled up and his body felt sunburned. His white shirt was tattered, disintegrated by flames; only the dangling cuffs remained intact.

He stumbled to the front of the courtway.

"Get me some help," he pleaded to a fireman, who directed him to an ambulance parked on Avers Avenue.

SISTER SERAPHICA could feel her heart skip as the rock came crashing through the middle window in Room 210. She was busy handing out a homework assignment to her fourth-graders and walked to the window to look outside. Standing below in the alley was a handful of adults, each pointing and shouting, trying to get her attention.

"Sister! Sister! The school's on fire!"

The nun looked to her right. "Oh, my God!" she shrieked, raising her hand to her mouth.

Smoke and flames were licking out the back stairwell enclosure. More smoke was billowing out the open windows of Room 208 next door, and children inside were climbing out onto the ledges. By the time the startled Sister Seraphica returned to her desk at the front of the classroom, smoke was already seeping through cracks around the doors. She tried to catch up with the scene. Why isn't the fire alarm ringing? There had been no warning. She looked at her little fourth-graders, then made a decision.

"Listen, everyone," she said, feigning a smile, trying to look calm. "There's a little fire in the stairway. Everyone say a 'Hail Mary,' and when the firemen come we can leave."

Vito Muilli didn't understand. The twelve-year-old had arrived in the United States from his native Italy the previous June, and because he spoke little English, had been placed in the fourth grade. He turned to a girl sitting next to him who spoke Italian.

Cosa dice, lei? "What is she saying?" he asked.

La scuola è in fuoco. Bisognamo di pregare. "The school's on fire. We have to pray."

Vito laughed. Why, he asked himself, does she want us to pray if there's a fire?

He didn't wait for an answer.

Sister Seraphica was a petite woman whose diminutive size in no way hampered her authoritarian reign in the classroom. But as noxious smoke continued to fill the room, her hold on the students began slipping. Struggling to maintain control, she ordered them to gather in a semicircle around her desk. They began reciting the Rosary, one of the longest prayers in the Catholic church. Vito and another boy got up and lunged for the back door. When they swung it open, a hot blast of smoke crashed through like a hammer, knocking them back.

Unable to enter the hallway and reach the front stairs that led to Avers Avenue, the boys scrambled to the open windows, joining their classmates at the sills. The gasping fourth-graders were several deep. They were stacked on top of each other, fighting for space. Pandemonium reigned as an ocean of smoke, followed by raging flames, poured inside the room through the open door.

Conditions in Room 210 deteriorated rapidly as flames swarmed across the ceiling, engulfing the entire room. Children at the windows were hysterical, pulling and clawing each other in a mad fit to reach safety. With temperatures climbing to furnace-hot levels and flames bearing down, the children began jumping to the ground. But not all of the little fourth-graders could reach over the high windowsills that stood more than three feet off the floor. Those too short—or too weak—to pull themselves up onto the ledges fell to the floor, where they were trampled and left to die.

Diane Traynor had been sitting in the row of desks next to the windows at the back of the room. The nine-year-old would not recall hearing the fire alarm until Room 210 was entirely filled with pitch black smoke. Diane was just over four feet tall, and after running to the window she found the high ledge difficult to reach over.

Suddenly flames burst through the ceiling in the front of the room, and Diane knew she had to get out. She turned and saw one little redheaded girl sitting at her desk, frozen in fear. I'm not going to die like that, Diane thought to herself. I'm getting out. Maybe not yet. But I'm going.

She didn't wait long. Diane was struggling to reach over the windowsill when she saw one of her classmates, a boy, climb up onto the ledge next to hers and jump off. He struck the pavement hard, breaking both of his ankles. Then another little girl leaped into the air, fracturing her spine and hip when she hit the ground.

Diane's patent-leather shoes started smoking. She kicked them off. Her white socks caught fire and her hair started burning. Flames swarmed down from the ceiling and began devouring her back and shoulders. If she didn't jump immediately, she'd burn to death.

"Oh God. Please help us," she screamed.

Using her final ounce of strength, Diane pulled herself up onto the window ledge. Then, with smoke blocking her view, she somersaulted out the window.

Fortunately for Diane Traynor, her fall was broken when she glanced off the shoulders of a man standing below in the alley. She tumbled to the pavement, landing on her back. Somehow, amid the chaos in the alley, she managed to get to her feet and walk to the candy store next door. She went into the back room and telephoned her mother.

"Ma," she said, "the school's on fire, but I'm all right."

Diane left the store and sat on a wooden bench just outside the front door next to the sidewalk. She was going into shock. She got up from the bench and started to walk away.

"Grab that girl!" a woman yelled.

Someone threw a blanket over Diane and carried her to a waiting police car parked in the street. Diane felt like she was burning up inside. Her entire body ached. She was placed in the back seat of the squad car along with two other children. A policeman jumped in and took off to the hospital.

Meanwhile, for the rest of Diane's classmates still trapped inside Room 210, time had just about run out. The scorching heat was nearing its flash point and smoke had reduced visibility to less than a foot. From his spot at the window, Vito Muilli glanced one last time into the room. He couldn't see his nun or the other children at the adjacent windows. Like Diane, Vito knew he had to jump. Flames were dancing around the window frames but had not yet engulfed the center. The boy reached for the sill and pulled himself up. Suddenly he felt something hit his hand and the room exploded in flames.

Someone had placed a ladder at the window, but it was about three feet short of the ledge. Vito swung himself around and hung himself out backward. He was trying to set his feet on the top rung, but when he let go of the ledge, he missed the ladder and slid down along its beams, striking his side on the pavement.

Vito felt his body go numb. He was covered in soot and his ears felt like someone had stuck him with a thousand prickly needles. A clump of his bushy black hair was missing, burned off by flames, exposing his scorched scalp. His arms were burned and bleeding. When he looked around him he saw other children on the concrete. Some were screaming. Others lay still, motionless. At the windows above, scores of other youngsters were jumping off ledges, tumbling to the ground. Thump. Thump. Thump, they landed.

For a second Vito shut his eyes. This can't be happening, he thought. It's too unbelievable.

A policeman was dragging kids out of the way, setting them

against the wall of Barbara Glowacki's store when he spotted Vito lying on his back. "Hang on, kid," he shouted. "I'm coming."

But the frightened youngster didn't understand what the big man had said. He didn't want to. He was scared of police. He was scared of everything. He wanted his mother. Just then he regained some feeling in his legs and jumped up. He took off running, headed for his home and his bed two blocks north.

FROM BEHIND HIS DESK in the back of Room 212, John Raymond looked over to the windows, making sure the sun was still out, that clouds had not invaded the deep blue sky. He shifted his eyes to the clock on the wall next to the flag. It was 2:30. He knew it wouldn't be long before he could run home and ride his new bike, leaving all to hear the clackity-clack of the playing cards he had pinned to its spokes.

His nun, Sister Therese, was busy teaching a last-minute geography lesson to the fifty-five fifth-graders. Even though she was strict, the students adored her. Among all the sisters she displayed a delicious sense of humor. On the day before, the young nun had decorated the school's bulletin boards for Christmas. Afterward, when she returned to the convent, she crayoned a message to Sister Andrienne, her roommate, on a medicine chest mirror.

"Today is Recollection Sunday," it read. "We can't celebrate, but tomorrow we'll make whoopie."

It was a whimsical, lighthearted thought that was never fulfilled.

John was still daydreaming when another boy jumped up.

"Sister," he said, pointing to the door. "There's smoke!"

At the edges of the transoms, over the doors, black smoke curled into the classroom, fanning out along the twelve-foot-high ceiling.

That's odd, thought the nun. Maybe the chimney's backed up.

She walked to the front door and handled the doorknob. It felt unusually hot. Another boy rose from his seat and opened the back door, allowing a wave of smoke to pour inside.

"Close it," yelled the nun. "Everybody be quiet."

For a moment, Sister Therese was dumbfounded. The smoke was too dense for a backed-up chimney. It must be a fire.

They couldn't leave the room, certainly not until the fire alarm went off. That was the rule: "Never leave the building until the fire

alarm rings." She remembered it from earlier fire drills and knew
that it took about three minutes to evacuate the entire building—lining up the students and walking them down the stairs. What she
didn't know at that moment was that the primary means of escape
used during those orderly, efficient fire drills was being cut off by
roaring flames and smoke in the corridor outside.

Sister Therese returned to her desk. The students looked at her,
seeking direction.

"We can't go until we're told," she said. "Let's pray."

Sister Therese crossed herself. "In the name of the Father, and of
the Son, and of the Holy Ghost. . . ."

Precious seconds were ticking by. The nun looked to the doors.
Smoke passing through the transoms was growing denser, the smell
of burning more acrid. The children were starting to cough. It was
getting darker, hotter.

" . . . pray for us sinners, now and at the hour of our death.
Amen."

More seconds ticked by. Still no fire alarm. Suddenly the heat in
the corridor shattered the large glass transom over the front door,
sending a thick current of black smoke billowing into the room.

"Get to the windows!" Sister Therese screamed. "Now!"

The children obeyed, jumping up from their desks and scrambling to the four windows overlooking the alley below. They threw
up the sashes, gasping for air. Smoke rolled out over their heads.
There was no turning back.

"Get out on the ledges!" commanded the nun. Then, seeing no
other way out, she started pushing them out. "Go! Go! Save your-
selves!"

John Raymond didn't know what to do. He couldn't believe
what was happening. Just a few moments before he was daydreaming about his bike. Now he found himself in the midst of a deadly
panic, a bit player in a tragic production. Somehow he ended up
on the floor. He started to crawl. It was like being in a tunnel. There
was air near the floor and it was easier to breathe. He was crawling
around desks, snaking his way toward the front of the room. He
didn't know where he was going or why he was doing it, he just
did it.

Where's the light? he wondered. It's getting dark in here. When
he reached the front of the room, all he could see were figures. Kids

were screaming for their mothers. Others were calling for the nun. She was embracing them. She was surrounded by kids, just draped with them. They were hanging from her.

"Sister," they shrieked. "Help us. Where are you?"

John looked up at the big globe lights. They probably had five-hundred-watt bulbs, but he could hardly see them. The smoke was that thick. He looked toward the windows. Outside it was bright and sunny, but he could hardly see daylight. He turned toward the front door and could feel heat at his face. It felt like being under a sun-lamp.

At that point John took in a lungful of smoke. He was losing control, unable to breathe. He started to panic. "Please, God, help me," he said. He kept saying it and saying it and saying it. He was ready to pass out. "Please, God, help me. Please, God, help me."

Then he jumped up and sprang for the window. He pulled kids out of the way. Pushed them away. Dragged them away. Then he dove out. He had to. He was going to die.

Floating through the air, John felt a strange sense of relief. He knew he was falling, that he might be hurt, yet it was the greatest feeling in the world because it was air and he could breathe. He landed hard on the pavement, on his right side, and a sharp pain shot through his body. But whatever damage the fall had caused didn't matter. He was just glad to be out.

The scene in the alley where he had landed was one of utter chaos. Blood from the broken bodies of other children marked the pavement. Frantic neighbors and parents were running in all directions. They were screaming to students hanging from the window-sills, pleading with them not to jump, to wait for firefighters' ladders and nets.

John crawled the few feet to Barbara Glowacki's candy store, meeting another boy from his class. The youngster had also jumped, breaking both his ankles. He was crying; his face was turning grey.

"Jimmy," John asked. "What's wrong? Are you okay?"

When the boy didn't answer, John figured he was in shock. He just stared into space, his mouth hanging open.

Barbara Glowacki appeared with a blanket. She threw it over the two boys. "Stay here," she cried. "The ambulance will come."

John sat with his back against the bricks. His side was hurting and his throat felt like he'd swallowed a jar of tacks. He looked up at his burning school. The sights and sounds jolted his senses.

There was screaming. Women screaming. Children screaming. Kids were hanging from the sills and dropping to the ground. They landed with dull, hollow thuds, sounding like sacks of potatoes smashing on concrete. He saw a girl on fire coming down to the ground. She just stood up on the windowsill and jumped. She landed head first, cracking her skull. He saw one man break the fall of a boy, and then saw him go down after he was hit by the next falling child. He didn't get up.

When the smoke cleared for a second, John could see Sister Therese in the window. A handful of girls clutched her sleeves. Just then smoke puffed back out and they disappeared behind its oily black curtain.

John felt light-headed, like he wanted to faint. He was sick from smoke, drifting into shock, losing touch of his whereabouts. One of his aunts lived across the street on Avers. He looked over and saw people carrying injured children through the front of the building. John stood up, deciding to go there. Staggering like a drunkard, he teetered out of the alley, oblivious to the crowd of frightened faces and the terror they conveyed. Instead all he saw were mental images of his father, his two brothers, and his younger sister. Had they made it out?

EARLIER THAT AFTERNOON Sister Helaine had told her class that the pastor needed about ten boys to help load donated clothes onto a truck parked outside the church. Thirteen boys in Room 211 raised their hands to volunteer their services. "All right," the nun said, "all of you can go."

About an hour later, as the class was working on its English lesson, a girl who temporarily had been out of the room rushed in the back door and went to the nun's desk. She was coughing loudly. "Sister," she said, "there's a lot of smoke in the hallway!"

Some smoke had already entered the room when the girl opened and closed the back door. Sister Helaine got up from her desk and told the students to stand and walk calmly to the front door. When the nun opened the front door, she and the eighth-graders were driven back by black smoke.

"Try the back door," Sister Helaine ordered. The rear door was opened with the same result: hot smoke poured into the room.

With both doors closed and with Sister Helaine unwilling to risk sending her pupils into the hallway in an effort to escape down the front stairs only a few feet away, the same pattern of behavior occurred in Room 211 as in other rooms in the north wing. The nun ordered her students to the windows, then started saying Hail Marys. The children joined her in prayer, but not for long.

FATHER CHARLES HUND was feeling ill.

The twenty-seven-year-old priest had celebrated Mass that morning in the parish church, and after lunch had decided to retire to his second-floor room in the rectory. It was his day to be on duty, and the effects of the flu had left him tired and sluggish. He laid himself across his bed and went to sleep.

Inside the house it was empty and quiet; his fellow religious were out. Father Alfred Corbo and Father Joseph McDonnell were away visiting patients at nearby Walther Memorial Hospital, and Father Joseph Ognibene was having lunch with friends at a neighboring parish. Monsignor Cussen, the pastor, was roaming outside on church grounds, overseeing the parish clothing drive, while the two other monsignors who shared the house, Joseph Fitzgerald and John Egan, were downtown on church business.

It didn't take long for Father Hund to nod off. He'd been napping for more than an hour when the first screams came filtering through the wall.

"Help! Please help us!"

The priest stirred and sat up, damp with sweat. He rubbed his eyes and looked at the clock. Two-thirty. Some dream, he thought. He lay back down and closed his eyes.

He heard it again.

"Help! The school's on fire!"

That, he knew, was not a dream. It was real, and it sounded close. He bolted upright in his bed. What the hell's going on?

The sole window in Father Hund's dimly lit quarters was next to his bed and faced the back of the school. He leaned over to peer through the curtains. What he saw sent him reeling. Crowding the windows directly across the narrow gangway were a dozen or so terrified faces of students, smoke pouring over their heads. The children were banging on the window frame, shouting, "Father! Save us!"

The children, he knew, were in Room 207, the "Cheese Box," so called because of its small dimensions. The classroom had once housed the school's library. It was located near the southeast corner of the north wing, next to the building's only fire escape. But Father Hund could see that the fire escape door was closed, that no one was coming down. He sprang from the bed, threw on a leather jacket over his T-shirt, and ran down the stairs. As he passed through the kitchen and headed out the back door, he could hear Mrs. Maloney on the phone, wrestling with her brogue, trying to describe the fire's location.

Father Hund ran into the gangway and looked up. Smoke was pouring out of the school. "Hang on," he shouted. "I'm coming." He slipped through the back door of the school's annex and bounded up a flight of stairs to the second floor. When he reached the landing he found the smoke so thick that he couldn't see more than a foot ahead. He remembered what he had been told as a child: If you're ever in a fire, stay near the floor. That's where the air is.

Instinctively he dropped to his knees and began crawling through the dark, narrow corridor, inching his way forward, trying to get into the north wing. But even here, near the floor, he couldn't escape the choking effect of the smoke. Heat from the fire was pressing against his face, making his eyes water. Black mucus started dripping from his nostrils. The smoke was pushing into his lungs, making him gag and cough. It felt like someone was shoving a hot rag down his throat. He thought he might vomit. He started to panic, and for a second he felt he would pass out. He knew he had to get out. To go any farther would be crazy. He'd never make it.

The young priest backed out of the corridor and retreated down the stairs, all the way to the basement. He was arguing with himself. He had to get back up to the second floor. But how?

He dashed through the chapel at the bottom of the north wing, then through a door in the boiler room that opened into the small area at the foot of the northeast stairwell where the fire had originated. Curiously, the flames here had subsided a little, though the area was super hot, with fire licking through the stairs themselves. Father Hund decided to try them anyway. He rolled up the bottom of his baggy black trousers, then started up. But he didn't go far; the inferno engulfing the upper part of the stairway stopped him short. Any farther and he'd light up like a torch. He was turning to leave when flames suddenly flared up underneath him, catching his shoes on fire. It was so hot in the stairway that he thought it would explode at any second. He had to get out, fast.

He ran back into the basement, cut off but still determined somehow to make the second floor. He returned to the annex and raced back up the same staircase he had tried the first time. His second attempt was successful, and when he reached the landing he was surprised to see the smoke had cleared a bit, though the ceiling above was now burning pretty well.

Father Hund was ducking burning embers and falling debris when a harried face appeared in the darkness. It belonged to the janitor, Jim Raymond, and he looked horrible. Raymond too had worked his way up to the smoky second floor, managing to open one window, using his flashlight to break out another. But in breaking the window he had caught his arm on a piece of jagged glass, slicing open his left wrist. He was bent over, squeezing it with his right hand, trying to stop the flow of blood.

Father Hund grabbed his arm. "What the hell's going on?"

"I don't know," Raymond replied, confused from blood loss.

The priest motioned to Room 207. "Why can't they get out?"

"They can't. The fire's too bad."

"What about the back door? By the fire escape?"

"It's locked."

"You got a key?"

"Yeah, I think so."

"Then open the damn thing."

MATT PLOVANICH was lying on his back, watching smoke fill up the Cheese Box.

The fifth-grader was slowly losing consciousness, contemplating the oddity of dying at ten, trying hard to remember what his nuns had always preached. "You never know when God is going to come calling on you. Always be ready for Him."

It's not that Matt wasn't ready. He was. It's just that it seemed unfair. He and his classmates hadn't done anything wrong. They were good kids, tried to do good deeds. They obeyed their nuns, listened to their parents, did their homework on time, never skipped school. They said their prayers and went to Mass, asking for God's forgiveness when they sinned. And now they were burning up in their classroom.

It was strange, but Matt felt dying wouldn't be so bad after all, just something that happens to everyone, a natural occurrence in the cycle of life. Still, he was feeling sorry for his parents. His father, Rudy, was a policeman, and his mom, Irene, a housewife. If he died, he knew they'd be sad. He hoped God would watch over them. He thought of his three brothers. Jimmy was four years old. Mike was a seventh-grader in the south wing. Danny was downstairs in the first grade.

The smoke was getting worse. It was thick and toxic, filling up the ceiling, making it harder to breathe. Matt could feel himself drifting away, like being on a life raft, floating alone in the middle of the ocean. The panic that had gripped him only moments before had dissipated, replaced by a comforting sense of serenity. Some of his classmates were still kicking and scratching each other, crying for their mothers, trying to escape the room. To Matt it seemed futile.

What good does that do? he thought. We're trapped. We can't get out.

His teacher, Sister Mary Geraldita Ennis, was somewhere inside the room, lost in the darkness amid her forty fifth- and sixth-graders. When smoke first invaded the classroom around the door cracks, she rose to investigate. The front door faced the burning stairway, and when she opened it, a wall of flame was blocking the exit.

Sister Geraldita was just five feet tall. She was strict but fair, with a good sense of humor. After closing the front door, she started quickly for the room's back door. The back exit opened into the narrow, coat-lined hallway separating Rooms 207 and 206, and led to the building's only fire escape.

But when Sister Geraldita grabbed the door knob, it didn't turn. It was locked. She reached into her pocket, feeling for her key. It was empty. She closed her eyes, remembering now that she had been running late that morning and had left her keys behind in the convent.

Matt was sitting at his desk next to the back door. When he looked up at his nun, he saw the look of absolute terror cross her face. He knew what it meant: he and his classmates were trapped, their means of escape cut off.

"Come here," waved Sister Geraldita, gathering the students in a semicircle near the back of the room. "We're in trouble. We must pray for help."

She began leading the class in the Rosary, but as the room turned pitch black, all control was lost. Soon the children, especially the girls, started screaming in terror. They were huddled in the back corner of the room, Matt among them, pressing their faces against the smooth wooden floor, trying to breathe. A few broke ranks and rushed to the windows overlooking the small gangway behind the school. They flung up the sashes and cried out.

"Help! Help! Save us! Save us!"

One boy picked up a planter and hurled it out the window, against the wall of the adjacent rectory. Another boy leaped out the window, landing on the fire escape below. The rest of the class stayed down on the floor, waiting uncertainly.

Smoke was banking down to the floor. Matt couldn't see. It was like nighttime. Orange flames were burning through wooden panels on the front door. It wouldn't be long now.

Just then Matt heard a tearing noise, like someone ripping apart an old T-shirt. There in the smoke stood the janitor, Mr. Raymond. Father Hund was behind him. "C'mon!" they yelled. "This way! It's clear!"

When the pair had reached the classroom, Raymond used his key to unlock the door. But he still had to push it open, for the opposite side was blocked by cardboard posters taped across the inside of the doorjamb.

For little Matt Plovanich, it was like the cavalry coming; the men might have been wearing blue hats. It was that dramatic, that close. They were on their last breaths. Time had just about run out.

Smoke rushed out the open back door as Matt and his classmates climbed to their feet. They were sluggish, unsteady, slow-moving. "Let's go!" yelled Father Hund. "Faster! Faster!" The men started grabbing the children by their collars, pulling them up off the floor, shoving them out the door.

Raymond followed them out. He was shaking, sweating, holding his bloody wrist. Squeezing his way between the children, he moved to the front of the line, then shoved open the door leading to the weighted steel fire escape ladder that dropped down into the gangway behind the school. But the youngsters, frightened and hesitant, balked. Intense heat inside their room was blowing out the windows above them, and the sound of shattering glass was scary.

"Keep going!" shouted Father Hund.

The line started moving. Soon they were down. Sister Geraldita was the last person to leave the classroom. As soon as she exited, it burst into flames. When she reached the top of the fire escape, she too hesitated. Her face was reddened and she was coughing on smoke. She turned to Father Hund, making a move to return to the room. "I can't go! They're not all out!" she screamed.

Father Hund was not entirely sure himself that all the students had made it out safely. But it no longer mattered. It was too late. The room was awash in flames. There was no turning back.

"No!" he barked. "Keep going!"

He grabbed the frightened nun by the arm and together they fled down the ladder, praying—but not yet knowing—that all the students had indeed escaped, that Room 207 would be the only second-floor classroom in the north wing not to record a fatality.

TEACHERS AND STUDENTS in the school's south wing were the farthest from the fire and the last to learn of the calamity occurring in the other side of the building. Although no deaths or serious injuries would occur in the south wing, escape from second-floor classrooms was nonetheless made difficult by waves of thick smoke drifting through the hallways.

Seventh-graders in Room 201, located in the southwest corner of the wing, were busy reading about the life of St. Joan of Arc when the tragedy struck. In her prologue, Sister Mary Andrienne Carolan described the torment of the French heroine, telling how Joan had been condemned to death and burned at the stake. The youngsters were stirred by the story. The drawings in their texts showed the Maid of Orleans perishing impressively in the flames.

Sister Andrienne had a knack for storytelling. She liked to use anecdotes to paint word pictures for her students. She was thirty-five, Irish, and proud of her heritage. "The name used to be O'Carolan," she'd smile. "Same as the last of the Irish bards."

She was in her eleventh year at Our Lady of the Angels, had charge of the altar boys, and helped supervise children who remained at school during luncheon recess. And though she was small—she weighed only 105 pounds—she still had a way of dealing with "disciplinary problems," a fact evidenced by the number of troublesome boys who were shunted to her care. But if she was strict, she was also compassionate. She had a soft spot for the children of troubled West Side families, often lending a sympathetic ear to one in need.

One girl she was particularly fond of was Mary Ellen Moretti, whose father, Michael, a former Chicago police officer, was serving a life sentence for murder at Stateville Penitentiary in nearby Joliet, Illinois.

The Moretti case had been a sordid affair, widely publicized in the press. One night in August 1951, after getting his fill in a tour of several South Side taverns, Michael Moretti had gone on a rampage, firing his gun into a parked car, killing two youths and wounding a third. Moretti, then a city patrolman assigned to the state's attorney's office, said the shootings were in the line of duty. But evidence corroborated by the survivor led to Moretti's indictment and conviction. "*È brutto*,"—It's ugly, he mumbled in Italian when the judge in the case sentenced him to life. After his conviction, three of Moretti's brothers were found guilty of attempting to bribe and intimidate the major witness against Michael. Six years later the family was shaken by more tragedy when another brother, Salvatore Moretti, fell victim to an unrelated gangland murder.

In the fall of 1958, at the urging of Sister Andrienne, Mary Ellen Moretti had enrolled as a transfer student at Our Lady of the Angels. The two had met during a summer religion course that the nun taught to Catholic students from local public schools. Sister Andrienne was sympathetic to Mary Ellen's plight, and their friendship blossomed. "You can't blame the children for the sins of their fathers," she'd say.

In time the two developed a pleasant rapport, and when the term began, Sister Andrienne had wanted Mary Ellen in her classroom so she could provide the emotional support she knew the girl needed. But when September arrived and Mary Ellen was assigned to Sister Canice's room in the north wing, Sister Andrienne was disappointed. Her lingering regret would turn to grief later that afternoon when the body of Mary Ellen Moretti, blond, blue-eyed, and only twelve years old, was pulled by firefighters from the charred ruins of Room 208.

But for now Sister Andrienne was finishing her talk on Joan of

Arc: "On May 30, 1431, she was led into the marketplace at Rouen to be burned at the stake. She was not quite twenty years old. Her ashes were tossed into the Seine. She is the patron saint of France and of French soldiers. She is portrayed in art as a bareheaded girl in armor, holding a sword and wearing a banner with the words 'Jesus: Maria' on it."

A few boys in the room scheduled for afternoon patrol duty were getting up from their desks, putting on their bright orange patrol belts, when the fire alarm started to ring. They and Sister Andrienne looked out the windows. Nothing unusual, just a few bare tree branches reaching over the neighboring rooftops. The nun looked at the clock. It was too close to dismissal time for a fire drill. Besides, they rarely had them in such cold weather. Maybe a prankster was up to no good.

The patrol boys rushed to the door on the east end of the room. They tried pushing it open. Strangely, it wouldn't budge.

"What's the matter?" the nun asked.

"It's stuck."

Sister Andrienne looked at them, puzzled. "I'll get it for you."

The nun stepped between the boys and began pushing on the door herself. It seemed to weigh a ton. She didn't know that the door was being held shut by the tremendous draft flowing through the hallway—the fire was sucking all the fresh air from the south wing.

"C'mon, give me a hand," she said to her boys. Together they pushed against the door with all their might. It let go, sending them tumbling into the hallway, right through a cloud of thick black smoke. They realized immediately the alarm was no prank.

"Hurry, go tell the others," said Sister Andrienne, motioning the boys to neighboring classrooms. She reentered her own room. "Let's go. Everybody up."

When the students saw smoke swirling in the hallway, they became frightened. Sister Andrienne lined them up, and one by one they headed out the door for the nearby staircase. Visibility diminished rapidly. It was getting dark. They had to feel their way along. "Get on your knees," said the nun. "Start crawling!"

Heat from the fire was now at their backs, and the youngsters were coughing and gasping for breath. Some were hiding their eyes. When they reached the landing, they panicked. They were becoming disoriented and, like a bunch of frightened horses, refused to budge.

In the haste of the moment, Sister Andrienne began shoving them down the smoke-filled stairway. "Don't be afraid," she urged. "Nothing will harm you."

The group started moving, and when all had reached bottom, Sister Andrienne followed. But, unknown to her, during the ensuing panic one of her girls had stayed behind in the classroom, slamming the door shut. The other fourteen students still inside the room reacted by scrambling to the windows.

Outside on the Iowa Street sidewalk, Sister Andrienne sensed that things didn't seem right. There were seventy children in her class, but the group seemed thin. Suddenly she realized that not all had gotten out. When she looked up to the windows, her fears were confirmed.

"Stay there!" she shouted to the students at the windows. "Don't move!"

The nun darted back into the building, running up the stairs to the second floor. The smoke in the hallway had turned decidedly worse. She dropped to her knees, feeling her way along the wall. When she reached the room she started calling for the students to follow her voice. "Hang on to each other," she said. On hands and knees they began snaking their way through the dark classroom, out into the smoky hallway. When the procession reached the stairway, Sister Andrienne stood to the side, making way for the youngsters. "Go!" she ordered. The first girl balked and the nun nudged her down. She began rolling the remaining children down the stairs like logs. One by one they bounced to the bottom. Neighbors rushing inside scooped up the youngsters and carried them outside.

When the last of the children had made it to safety, Sister Andrienne limped down the stairs herself. Smoke had penetrated her lungs, making her hack and gag. She had strained her back, and her left leg throbbed from where the children had clutched her.

Outside, above a crescendo of shouts and screams, the fire alarm was still ringing, and a siren grew near. A single fire truck, its red lights flashing, was turning the corner onto Iowa Street, trying to pass through the crowd of people in the streets. At last the firemen had arrived. But, unknown to them, they had been given the wrong location. In the confusion of the moment they were told that a blaze was burning in the rectory on Iowa Street, not in the school around the corner on Avers Avenue.

Four

FIREFIGHT

A T CHICAGO'S MAIN fire alarm office, Monday had been unusually quiet. Located in City Hall in the heart of Chicago, the office was responsible for dispatching all city fire equipment stationed
north of 39th Street. Inside the big, airy room, a huge electric wall
map pinpointed the location of every fire station in the city. Most of
its lights were on, indicating fire companies were in service, in quarters. For most of the day the keys on the master telegraph had been
silent, with only a few fires being logged since the shift had begun at
eight o'clock that morning.

At 2:42 p.m. a loud buzzer signaled an incoming emergency
call. Senior fire alarm operator Bill Bingham was sitting at the
switchboard. He picked up the phone. "Chicago Fire Department,"
he answered. His tone was calm, businesslike. A woman's voice was
on the line. She was excited, heavily accented, almost unintelligible.
It was Nora Maloney.

"There's a fire in our building," she cried. "Send help!"

Experience had taught Bingham how to pry out the location.
"Where are you, ma'am? Where exactly is the fire?"

Maloney was confused, her mind racing. "Our Lady of the Angels. On Iowa. 3808 Iowa."

The location she gave was that of the rectory. Unknown to Bingham, the burning school was around the corner and half a block
away, at 909 North Avers. As soon as he had an address, Bingham

set down the phone and pulled the run card showing the nearest fire companies. Engine 85, Hook and Ladder 35, Rescue Squad 6, and the 18th Battalion chief were due to respond. Fire Patrol 7, a salvage unit operated by insurance underwriters, also was assigned. Another operator at the alarm board started flipping switches, cracking the intercom to transmit the "still alarm" (Fire Department jargon for an alarm received by phone) to the companies housed five miles away on the city's West Side.

Almost immediately other calls began pouring into the office. Bingham answered one call from a woman who "sounded like she was describing the Hindenburg disaster."

The mood in the alarm office was growing tense. "Sounds like we've got something," said chief fire alarm operator Joseph Hedderman. He looked up the nearest fire alarm box—number 5182—located one block east and one block south of the school, at Chicago and Hamlin avenues. Following standard procedure, he began tapping it out on the telegraph, transmitting the box alarm to every firehouse in the city. In more than a hundred fire stations, blue-shirted firemen stopped what they were doing to count the toll of the bell as 5-1-8-2 rang in four times over the ticker, punching red dots on a sheet of paper tape, turning on lights and setting off alarm bells for the companies that were due to respond. Three more engines, two more hook and ladders, another battalion chief, and the 2nd Division marshal were now pulling out.

FIVE BLOCKS AWAY from the burning school, inside the quarters of Engine 85, Lieutenant Wojnicki was sitting on watch at the front of the firehouse. Since he had come on duty the company had answered two alarms to extinguish small rubbish fires, one in the morning and one around noon. Now, as the brisk December day moved to mid-afternoon, there was little noise or movement in the station save for a mild debate in the kitchen over the merits of the evening dinner menu. The repartee was suddenly interrupted when an operator's voice crackled over the loudspeaker:

"ENGINE 85, STILL ALARM FIRE, 3808 WEST IOWA."

Wojnicki scribbled the address on a small chalkboard, then picked up the watch desk's "joker" phone, which brought him into contact with the downtown office. "Eight-five," he repeated, "3808 West Iowa. Fire."

His response was departmental procedure ensuring verification of the alarm's address: 3808 West Iowa Street, a run that would take two minutes.

The lieutenant rang the house bells, then took up his position in the front cab. Engineer Henry Holden was already behind the wheel of the red-and-black pumper, revving the motor, waiting for the company's three remaining firemen to pull on their boots and coats and jump onto the rig's backstep. Thirty seconds later the engine pushed out into the wintry street.

AT THEIR downtown firehouse, Richard Scheidt and his fellow firefighters were standing in front of the apparatus bay, peering out a window of the overhead door as groups of pedestrians walked along Dearborn Street. The firemen were too far away to hear the sirens. But they knew something was happening.

Whenever a fire was reported, the main fire alarm office alerted all eighty-seven North Side firehouses, letting them know equipment was being sent out. The alert came into each firehouse over the "sounder," a Teletype instrument using a numerical code.

At 2:42 the sounder began its familiar clacking. The firemen stopped to listen:

"5-5-5-8-5"

"5-5-5-3-4-5"

Engine 85 and Truck 35 were being "stilled-out" to a fire.

One of the officers on watch was curious about the location. He picked up the "joker" to listen: "Thirty-eight-o-eight West Iowa. A fire."

He repeated the address to Scheidt and the others standing around the desk.

"Must be the church," said one fireman who lived in the same West Side neighborhood. No one took particular notice. It was just another still alarm, one of dozens that Chicago firemen responded to each day. And the address was well out of Squad 1's district—too far west. They wouldn't even go on a 5-11. Besides, five-alarm fires were rare for such good residential neighborhoods.

The men returned to their thoughts, hands in pockets, awaiting their next alarm.

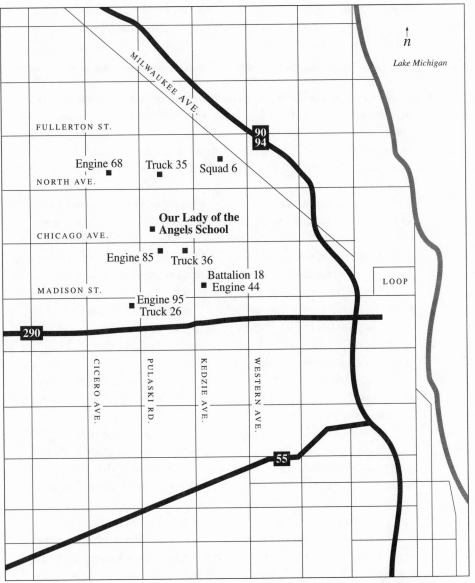

Chicago, showing the locations of Our Lady of the Angels and neighboring fire companies.

ENGINEER HENRY HOLDEN followed a direct route through the neighborhood toward Iowa Street. As Engine 85 crossed the intersection of Chicago Avenue a block away, the firemen could see smoke rising in the sky.

"We got a fire," said Holden.

Wojnicki nodded. "Probably a garage."

Based on the address given by the main office, Wojnicki figured the garage behind Our Lady of the Angels Church was ablaze. The smoke was black, like that given off by burning tar paper. But as the engine approached Iowa Street and as Holden swung left, past the church, the firemen knew immediately they had been given the wrong address.

Swarming in the streets and sidewalk outside the church and south wing of the parish school were hundreds of students, nuns, and lay teachers. Neighbors and parents were carrying injured and frightened children from the school. Other youngsters were leaning out the open second-floor windows overlooking Iowa Street.

After maneuvering his rig through the swelling crowd, Holden pulled to a stop in front of the school. Wojnicki could see he had an emergency on his hands, that more help was needed. He grabbed the microphone on the engine's two-way radio. "Eighty-five to Main!" he yelled. "Give me a box!"

"You've already got a box, Eighty-five," responded the operator in the alarm office, where telephone calls reporting the fire were now clogging the switchboard.

When Wojnicki ran around to the Avers side of the building, he saw plenty of smoke coming from the school, but no flames. Where is it? he thought. He had to find the source of the fire first, then get a line out and start water. He looked up. Children were throwing books and shoes out the windows, pleading for rescue.

"Goddammit," he shouted, "stay up there! Help is coming!"

Holden was spotting the pumper at a fire hydrant on the corner when Wojnicki brushed past a harried clergyman pleading with the firemen to hurry. "Don't worry, we'll handle it," he told Monsignor Cussen. The pastor had rushed over from the church hall on Hamlin Avenue, where he'd been helping the group of eighth-grade boys load clothes onto a truck destined for the Catholic Salvage Bureau.

Wojnicki ran a few more steps, stopping at the iron fence

fronting the courtway between the school's two wings. Smoke was pouring out the upper windows, and frightened students were crowding the open window spaces. They were screaming, getting ready to jump.

Suddenly Wojnicki heard someone shout, "They're jumping," and he ran a few more steps, turning into the alley north of the school. There he came face to face with the true horror of the moment. It was a sight that would haunt him for the rest of his life.

Black smoke was billowing from every open space on the building's upper story. Horrified parents were running back and forth, screaming as children at the windows were throwing out objects, hanging off the sills, dropping or hurtling themselves to the ground. Scores of inert bodies—children who had already jumped or had been pushed out the windows by classmates—covered the pavement. Wojnicki recognized a few of the kids at the windows. The youngsters' faces were turning color. Some had clothing on fire. He had never imagined anything like it in his life. He was witnessing a nightmare.

"Jesus Christ!" he sputtered.

The fire had been burning for nearly a half-hour, and heat inside the classrooms had grown so intolerable that children were now plummeting out the windows two and three at a time. Old painting ladders had been thrown against the building, but most were too short. Students trying to reach them were dangling from the sills, hanging by their fingertips, dropping to the ground. The scene in the alley was now complete chaos, and only then did Wojnicki begin to comprehend the full extent of the disaster at hand.

As officer of the first engine company on the scene, he knew his priority was to get water on the fire as quickly as possible. He spotted flames shooting out the back stairwell door and figured it had to be the source of the fire. Pushing aside distraught mothers begging him to save their children, he decided to stretch a hose line to the burning stairway, hoping to cut off the flames there, then try and fight his way into the burning building.

When the lieutenant returned to the street, the engine's soft-suction line had already been connected to the hydrant. Holden and another fireman, Ralph Clark, were pulling off the company's twenty-four-foot extension ladder. "Over here! Over here!" Wojnicki yelled, motioning them to the alley.

On the upper floor of the north wing, three classrooms over-looked the alley. Room 208, with its forty-six seventh-graders, was in the back, next to the burning stairwell. Room 210 was in the middle and included fifty-seven fourth-graders. Room 212 was in the front, nearest the street, and held fifty-five fifth-graders.

As soon as Holden and Clark rounded the corner of the building, they caught sight of a boy hanging from the window ledge of Room 212. The men threw their ladder up against the wall. It was short by a few feet. Charles Robinson, another fireman from Engine 85, nonetheless managed to run up and pluck the youngster from the ledge, the first of several children he would bring down from the room.

Just then two firemen from Truck 35 appeared in the alley with a life net. Almost immediately youngsters began dropping into it. But the laddermen hardly had time to dump the big, round, metal-rimmed canvas before more bodies came plummeting down, some missing the net entirely.

Meanwhile Wojnicki and Holden had run back to the engine, and with the help of several civilians, the lieutenant and fireman Thomas Moore started leading out a two-and-a-half-inch hose line from the back bed of the pumper. The men dragged the heavy hose across the street, into the alley, stretching it all the way to the back stairwell. Once the hookup and hose layout were completed, Holden opened a discharge valve at the pumper, sending water to the other end of the line. Moore opened the nozzle and started attacking the flames, directing a heavy stream into the stairwell, trying to clear a path so the firemen could get inside.

The men were squatting behind the nozzle, throwing water on the flames, trying to inch their way forward. But the inferno in the stairwell continued to roar unimpeded. It was loud, crackling, out of control. The fire had gained too much headway. Passage up the stairs, at least for now, was out of the question. Moore redirected the stream down into the basement, hoping to cut off the chimney effect being created by the fire's fierce upward draft.

It was then that Wojnicki began to piece it all together. Experience told him the fire had too great of a head start, that the firemen had been called too late. "Sonovabitch," he cursed. Up above, flames were bursting out of the middle room. A grey-faced little fourth-grader, his clothing ablaze, stood on the ledge. Wojnicki caught a glimpse of him. He and Moore quickly swung their line around, spraying water all around the youngster, hoping it would force the boy to leap from the ledge, into the net.

"Jump, kid! Jump!" Wojnicki screamed.

FIRE COMMISSIONER Robert Quinn was in his City Hall office looking over a stack of blueprints spread across his desk when the telegraph register outside his door started its familiar pinging. He glanced up, counting the toll of the bell as Box 5-1-8-2 began ringing over the system.

He looked at his watch. It was 2:44.

"A still and box alarm fire at 3808 West Iowa Street," a dispatcher was announcing over the Fire Department's radio system. Something was brewing. The West Siders were getting some business. No need to worry, thought Quinn. Engine 85's district was not an area where the department expected severe fires. Probably just a storefront. Maybe a two-flat.

He returned to his papers.

HOOK AND LADDER 35 was racing south from its Springfield Avenue firehouse one mile north of the school. Lieutenant Charles Kamin and his truck men were making good time. There were four traffic lights between the firehouse and the school, and each was green. Not once did his driver, fireman Walter Romanczak, have to let up on the accelerator.

When the still alarm was transmitted by the main office, the same urgent directive came across the speaker in the truck's house: "TRUCK 35, TAKE IT IN, 3808 WEST IOWA." The school was in the southernmost portion of Truck 35's district, which extended south to Chicago Avenue. The company numbered five men, and its truck carried a full complement of ladders that reached twenty, twenty-six, thirty-six, and fifty feet in length. Its aerial, or main, ladder stretched eighty-five feet.

Three minutes later, as the long hook and ladder neared Iowa Street, Kamin could see a dark haze floating through the neighborhood. It was smoke, no doubt about it. He knew they had a "job."

When Romanczak swung right onto Iowa Street, the truck men were met by the same chaotic scene that had greeted Engine 85's crew a minute earlier. Kids were bunched at the upper windows overlooking the street, and hundreds of other frightened youngsters were streaming from the school's ground-floor exits. Frantic parents and adults were running into the crowd, scooping up children, carrying them into the church and rectory next door. Based on the address given by the alarm office, coupled with the smoke pouring from the windows, Kamin assumed he was in the right spot. He leaped from the cab barking orders. "Start a ladder run-up!"

The firemen responded, pulling a twenty-six-foot extension ladder from the back of the truck, raising it to a window on the Iowa Street side of the building. Kamin started for the front door when something caught his eye. A man dressed in a plaid jacket was standing on the corner, jumping up and down hysterically. He was pointing and shouting. "This way! Over here. The fire's over here!"

Kamin followed the man around to Avers and saw the calamity unfolding in the north wing.

Shit, he cursed. They were in the wrong spot. They would have to reposition. He ran back to the corner to summon his gang. "Pull the truck around!" he yelled to Romanczak. "It's on Avers!"

Kamin ran back to the courtway separating the two wings. Immediately he saw panicky students crowding the smoke-filled windows. Scores of injured and dying children who had already jumped were lying on the pavement.

Time was running out quickly. The red-brick school, with its wooden interior and asphalt roof, was belching out smoke like a boiler. Kamin's job was search and rescue. He knew he had to get inside the U to start laddering the windows. But still another delay was slowing his progress—the iron picket fence that blocked access into the courtway. The formidable seven-foot-high obstacle impeded the path of rescuers. Men from the neighborhood—grandfathers, fathers—were trying to break it down. Some were dressed in suits, others in overalls and work clothes. They were ordinary citizens showing tremendous strength. They were going crazy trying to push the fence in, to somehow get over it. One had located a sledgehammer and was swinging it feverishly at the locked gate. But it was no match for the fence. The dull, clanging raps bounced off with little effect. The gate wouldn't budge. Kamin was getting agitated. He felt inept. "Goddammit!" he shouted.

Just then the hook and ladder came wheeling around, stopping in front of the north wing. Romanczak set the transmission in neutral, then pulled on the parking brake. When he looked up at the school, he could hardly believe his eyes. A boy leaped from a window and bounced off the pavement.

"Strip the truck! Strip the truck!" Kamin yelled.

The firemen pulled off a thirty-six-foot extension ladder and threw it over the iron fence into the courtway. Then they grabbed a second, twenty-six-foot ladder, and with the help of civilians began battering it against the gate like a ram, trying desperately to break it down. Finally, after five or six blows, the lock gave way. Once inside the courtway the firemen lifted their thirty-six-foot ladder and heaved it against the front window of Room 211, an eighth-grade classroom in the north wing. They placed the twenty-six-footer at Room 209 in the back corner of the U. Children began climbing down from Room 209, but those in Room 211 were having difficulty getting onto their ladder.

Kamin next split his crew. Two of his men, aided by civilians, took the company's fifty-foot ladder into the alley north of the school. Romanczak and fireman Jess Martens followed with their seldom-used life net.

Seconds later Squad 6 pulled up, and its five firefighters, under the command of Lieutenant Jack McCone, joined the laddermen in the courtway. The firemen were stepping over bodies, unfolding a second life net, trying to get in position next to the wall. No sooner did they open the device and lift it waist high than the first eighth-grader came hurtling down from the back window of Room 211. The boy was large, and he landed on his back. The firemen dumped him out, quickly raising the net back into position, ready for the next child. Another student came flying down into the net. The men repeated the process, dumping him out and standing back up.

Then came another child. And another. And another. Soon the youngsters were plummeting into the net three and four at a time. It was only seconds before the number of kids dropping from the windows became too much for the net to handle. "Hold on!" shouted the firemen. But the kids could wait no longer. The classroom was too hot. Their shirts and sweaters were starting to burn. The firemen had no time to clear the net for other children to land. It wasn't going to work. In desperation the rescuers dropped the net at their feet and starting reaching out with open arms, trying to catch the leaping students or otherwise break their falls before they hit the concrete.

The youngsters were jumping one right after the other. Some of them were caught by adults and firemen crowding the courtway. Others landed flat on the concrete, their falls uninhibited. Lieutenant McCone of Squad 6 tried catching one youngster, but the large boy fell through his outstretched arms, cracking his skull on the pavement.

The pace of rescue now quickened. Firemen were climbing ladders and grabbing children off the sills, bringing them down one at a time or dropping them to the ground. They were moving injured students out of the way, dragging them to the sidewalk to keep them from being hit by other falling children. Some youngsters jumped out as firemen were coming up the ladders to grab them. The kids were pretty heavy—eighty-five to a hundred pounds. The wooden ladders bounced under the strain.

Kamin turned and noticed that an elderly man had started up the ladder leading to Room 211. The man was standing on a lower rung, waving his arms, pleading for the children to come down. But the kids were stuck, unable to reach the ladder on their own. They had jammed themselves so tightly in the window space that those up front were literally pinned against the ledge, unable to move.

"Look out," Kamin yelled. He grabbed the old man by the legs and pulled him off before climbing to the window himself.

Thirty-six and built like an ox, Charlie Kamin had been a fireman for nine years. Most of his career had been spent on ladder companies, whose members usually possessed the upper-body strength needed for forcing entry into buildings, pulling ceilings, and carrying bodies over their shoulders. Kamin fit the mold of a truck man well. He was large, strong, and imposing, standing six feet, two inches and weighing 220 pounds. The muscles in his arms and back were hard, and he had grown accustomed to the sights and sounds of peril.

But nothing in his worst nightmares could have prepared him for the scene he was about to encounter at the top of the ladder. When he reached the window he came face to face with the most terrifying sight in his life. Bunched before him in the smoke was a pile of eighth-graders stacked in more layers than he could count. Dozens of hysterical kids were crowding the opening, all screaming and pulling at each other in a mad fit to reach safety. Burning debris was falling from the ceiling, and those nearest the ledge were fighting to grab hold of the ladder. They were gasping on smoke, trying desperately to breathe fresh air. "Hold on!" Kamin shouted. "Don't jump!"

Kamin could feel the heat inside the classroom. It was unbelievable. The animal was hot. It was on the loose. The heat was pressing against Kamin's face, burning the skin on his forehead beneath the brim of his leather fire helmet. Experience told him the room was ready to light up, that he was dealing in seconds. The children crowding the open window space were yelling, yet he could hardly hear them. All he could think was "Get them out! Get them out!" He shoved a few kids back, away from the sill, so he could reach in and start plucking the tangled children one at a time.

Michelle Barale was one of those reaching for help. The fourteen-year-old was fighting her way to the window after being blocked by the throng of classmates who stormed in front of her. Only moments before she had been sitting at her desk in fear. She heard herself scream when the round light fixtures above exploded from the intense heat. The shattered white glass rained down upon the children. Michelle had thrown her arms over her head to shield herself from the flying glass, then jumped up from her seat, determined to escape. Moving toward the window, she could hear Sister Mary Helaine shouting something to her—Michelle couldn't make it out. The normally austere nun had lost control of her charges. She looked pathetic as hot embers fell from the ceiling, burning holes in the big, square hood she wore on her head.

Michelle was growing furious as her path to the window was blocked by the growing pile of bodies on the floor and the tangled mess of classmates before her. A boy next to her was putting his hands around another girl's neck, pulling her out of the way. Michelle looked down to the floor and spotted one of her girlfriends, Frances Guzaldo, lying on her side. Michelle kicked the girl, trying to rouse her. "C'mon, Fran! We have to get out!"

When Frances failed to respond, Michelle moved on, stepping over her friend and the other bodies that lay in the way, ducking burning chunks of lathe and plaster falling from the ceiling. The room was growing darker and she was now a few feet shy of the window. Her path was blocked by a couple of students stacked on the floor beneath her. A fireman appeared at the window. He was reaching in, pushing and shoving students out of the way. Michelle climbed over her downed classmates, then, using their bodies as a springboard, launched herself forward, reaching and crawling over the shoulder of other students blocking her way.

Standing atop the ladder, Kamin could see the girl coming at him. With one hand on the ladder, he reached in and grasped Michelle around the waist, pulling her out through the narrow opening. He swung her around the right side of his body until he felt her feet settle on the rungs of the ladder. He knew he didn't have time to take her all the way down. He leaned over, setting her feet first on the ladder, leaving her to climb down by herself.

Kamin turned back to the window and, from that point on, worked like a robot, reaching inside the room and grabbing students—all boys because he could pluck them by their belts. He was lifting them up, pulling them out, swinging them around his back, and dropping them on the ladder behind him, hoping they would catch hold of the rungs. If they grabbed the ladder, fine. If not, he had to let go. He didn't have time to worry about the ones he dropped. If they were to live he had to get them out. A broken bone was better than death.

The room was growing hotter and hotter and Kamin knew instinctively that time was running out. Smoke was pouring in through an open door, following a path straight to the windows. It was rolling into the room with so much force that, for a second, he thought it might blow him off the ladder. It was getting blacker and blacker, obscuring his vision, filling his lungs, making him hack and cough.

The children were screaming, but still he could hardly hear them. The heat was getting worse and the kids were changing color. Each time he turned to grab another child, Kamin could see their shirts turning from white to tan, darker and darker. He had been at the ladder for about a minute and a half and could sense that his time was just about up. When he looked in again he saw a flame. The room had finally reached its flash point. The air was igniting.

And then it blew. It just burst. One thunderous "poof." The blast caught Kamin square in the face, searing off his eyebrows, burning his ears. He ducked his head and reached in one last time, managing to grab hold of a boy whose clothes were on fire, pulling him out.

He then saw the rest of the children in the window just wilt and turn dead, like a bunch of burning papers. It was the oddest thing.

They didn't tumble or fall over. Instead their knees simply buckled, dropping them straight to the floor like a house of cards.

Kamin limped down the ladder carrying the boy, one arm supporting himself, the other wrapped around the child's waist. Flames from the youth's burning clothes were shooting up inside Kamin's worn black fire coat, scorching the skin on his right hand and forearm. "Goddammit," he cursed. The pain was incredible, shooting up his arm like a bolt. It was the hardest thing not to let go. But he held on for a few more seconds, long enough to feel his left boot hit the bottom rung. When he reached the concrete he handed the eighth-grader off to another fireman, who began slapping out the flames with his mitt. He slung the boy over his shoulder and ran for an ambulance.

Kamin dropped his helmet and leaned against the building. He bent over, placing his hands on his knees. He was rubbing his arm, catching his breath, trying to contemplate the deadly scene he had just witnessed. Only a few short minutes had elapsed since Truck 35 pulled up to the school. Yet for Kamin it seemed like hours. He glanced around the courtway, trying to catch up with the unfolding disaster.

What he saw inside the narrow U resembled a war zone. Injured and dying children were lying everywhere. Those still conscious were moaning in pain. Police and neighbors were running into the areaway, scooping the kids up, carrying them away. Kamin looked back up at the window. A boy's body was hanging off the sill, his arms dangling. He was dead. One of the squadmen rushed up with a pike pole. He reached up with the tool and tried to pull the boy out, but the body slipped back inside the room. Another fireman in the courtway bent over and started vomiting. Even for the professionals, the sight was too much.

FIREMAN FIRST-CLASS Salvatore Imburgia was behind the wheel of Hook and Ladder 36, steering the long apparatus around a backup of mid-afternoon traffic, past the stores and shops lining Chicago Avenue. The truck men were due on the box alarm and were moving pretty well, knowing they were in for rescue work.

Imburgia was feeling tense and had a sense of foreboding. A small bull of a man who took pride in his physical strength, he wasn't worried about himself, for he was fearless at fires. Rather he

was concerned about his two young sons. Both boys attended cate-
chism classes on Wednesdays at Our Lady of the Angels School. Imburgia was having trouble recalling what day it was. He was racking
his brain, trying to remember.

"What's today? Monday or Wednesday? It's Monday. Okay."

That mystery solved, he still felt uneasy. He lived in the neighborhood; Our Lady of the Angels was his parish. He'd been married
there, attended Sunday Mass there. Most of his buddies' kids attended school there. His fears started mounting when the frantic
voice of Henry Holden came crackling over the radio: "Engine 85 to
Main! Give us a two-eleven and send all available ambulances.
We've got a school on fire. Kids are trapped on the second floor.
They're jumping from windows!"

Imburgia felt his stomach tighten as he floored the accelerator.

FIRE COMMISSIONER QUINN also heard the urgency in Holden's
voice as the engineer called for the second alarm—a request usually
reserved for battalion chiefs and above. The telegraph was going
crazy, spewing out tape, ringing incessantly. Nine more fire companies, including the snorkel, were now en route to the school.

Quinn grabbed his hat and overcoat and hurried out his office
door.

"Let's go!" he shouted to his driver.

It was 2:47 p.m.

Five minutes had now elapsed since the Fire Department first
learned of the fire.

CHIEF MILES DEVINE of the 18th Battalion pulled up in his sedan at
Our Lady of the Angels within three minutes of the first alarm. The
18th took in a big chunk of the West Side, and no matter what type
of emergency he was called to, the fifty-eight-year-old Devine had
learned how to keep his composure intact. The firemen in his battalion trusted his judgment. But after taking one look at the burning
school, the normally cool Irishman started coming apart.

The scene greeting him was one of bedlam. Firemen were climbing ladders, plucking students from windows, slinging them over
their shoulders or simply dropping them to the ground. Police, firemen, and civilians were standing beneath windows, catching students in life nets or with outstretched arms. They were picking up

the injured off the pavement, carrying them to police cars and private autos or into neighboring homes.

The chief grabbed his radio. "Battalion 18 to Main! Send me eight more ambulances and tell the police to start squadrols! We've got lots of injured here! Some are DOA!"

Seeing the enormity of the situation, Chief Devine went right to work, deploying his box-alarm companies. Hook and Ladders 26 and 36 were ordered into the alley to start laddering windows there. Truck 35's aerial ladder was raised to the roof of the north wing, and more truck men were sent up to swing axes and chop holes in the roof to vent the deadly heat and smoke mushrooming through the cockloft and second floor. Incoming engine companies were directed to lay hose lines for an interior attack on the flames.

In an attempt to make the main second-floor corridor usable for rescue, Engine 95, the second pumper to reach the scene, led out with two hose lines up the front stairway in the north wing. Working without air masks (they didn't have them in 1958), the firefighters dragged their hose lines through the hot, blinding smoke, crawling up the stairs on their hands and knees, inching their way toward the flames. Engine 44 stretched two more handlines up the rear fire escape while Engine 68 took another line into the south wing off Iowa Street.

To ensure that an ample supply of water was being delivered to the fireground, second-alarm engine companies were ordered to drop additional supply lines through neighborhood alleys and side streets. Lines were laid up and down Iowa and Avers. Firemen were dragging hose lines over curbs and sidewalks, through the swelling crowd of frantic parents assembling outside the school.

By now the fire had been burning for more than a half-hour, eating its way through most of the second floor in the north wing. But the flames had not yet burned through the roof. They couldn't. Through the years as many as five hot-tar roof coverings had been poured over the building, creating an impermeable seal that now prevented the fire from burning through on its own. Consequently flames, heat, and smoke were being held inside the classrooms and cockloft, sandwiching the victims inside. Had the old tar been stripped after each new application, the fire could easily have burned through the roof and vented itself, making conditions inside the building much more tenable. Instead the results were disastrous.

Suddenly and without warning, as firefighters were inching their hose lines up the front stairs, a resounding crack resonated through the neighborhood. A large portion of the roof near the burning back stairway had been weakening for some time. Finally it collapsed, sending the roof and second-floor ceiling crashing down into the burning classrooms. The rush of smoke and superheated air accompanying the collapse sent a shock wave throughout the structure, snuffing out the last traces of life from most of those still trapped inside. The blast knocked firemen down two flights of stairs. Rescuers atop ladders were chased to the ground.

WHEN THE CONCUSSION from the collapsing roof blew through the upper windows, it seared the eyelashes right off firefighter Salvator Imburgia's face.

The fireman was teetering atop a ladder, reaching through a window of Room 208, trying to pull out a seventh-grader when debris from the falling roof came crashing down before him. The tiny space where the boy's feet were wedged between the inside wall and a radiator was now filling with burning timbers and ceiling plaster. In an instant the blond-haired youth disappeared in a massive cloud of smoke and dust. All that remained were pieces of his flesh that had rubbed off his body onto Imburgia's gloves.

Imburgia was knocked off balance. When he regained his footing and looked back inside the room, it was like a twilight zone. The children were lit up, burning like human sparklers. Everything inside the room was blazing.

Imburgia couldn't believe what he was seeing. He had boxed his way through the navy and had seen combat in the South Pacific, but he had never dreamed of anything this awful. He knew the room was filled with children, how many he couldn't estimate. At that point no one knew. He had managed to rescue six youngsters, pulling them through the window and tossing them to the ground. But when he reached in for the last badly burned boy, he couldn't free him. Imburgia called on every ounce of his strength, reaching in with both arms, vainly trying to yank the lad free. The child was now buried under heavy debris. Imburgia ducked his head and tried one last time to reach back over the sill, to try and feel his way to the floor, hoping to grab hold of the boy's arm. But he couldn't find it.

Below in the alley, Imburgia's captain was yelling for him to retreat. "For chrissakes!" the officer shouted, "get down here. Don't be stupid!"

CHIEF DEVINE keyed his walkie-talkie. "Battalion 18 to Main!" he shouted. "We've got a roof collapse. Occupants are trapped. Gimme a five-eleven!"

The chief was jumping straight to a fifth-alarm—the most serious—skipping the normal routine of first calling for a 3-11 and 4-11. He knew he was breaking protocol, but he didn't care. The situation called for it.

In the main fire alarm office, however, the operators weren't so sure. "Battalion 18," one of them replied, "say again?"

The chief barked back: "I said five-eleven! And don't knock it down. Gimme a five-eleven for Box Five-One-Eight-Two!"

"Okay Battalion 18, we'll give you a five-eleven."

In firehouses and newsrooms across the city, fire tickers started pinging out the "five-bagger." The alert crackled over the fire radio to notify companies that were out of quarters: "A five-eleven alarm fire, 3808 West Iowa Street, on the orders of Battalion 18."

A huge cloud of thick black smoke was now rising into the afternoon sky. It could be seen for miles, like a homing beacon for the army of emergency vehicles headed for the school. Sixty fire companies, including ten ambulances, were now on the scene or responding. Seventy stretcher-bearing police squadrols also were en route.

It was 2:57 p.m.

Fifteen minutes had passed since Nora Maloney called the Fire Department.

Five

DISASTER

M ONSIGNOR WILLIAM MCMANUS, the archdiocesan school superintendent, was sitting quietly in his downtown office on Wacker Drive, signing his name to letters he had dictated earlier that morning. Outside, directly across the Chicago River, the huge Merchandise Mart maintained its commanding presence on Chicago's skyline. Soon the giant grey edifice would be emptying of workers, each making their way to buses or trains for the daily rush home.

McManus looked up from his papers as his secretary peeked her head through the door. "Monsignor," she said. "The *Sun-Times* is on the phone. They want to know how many students are enrolled at Our Lady of the Angels School."

McManus raised his brow. "Why is that?" he replied.

"They say there's a fire out there."

McManus stirred. A fire? How could that be? He had just been there the night before. "How bad is it?" he asked.

"They didn't say, just that the school is on fire."

McManus knew he should go to the school. That way he could see for himself how serious these fire problems plaguing the archdiocesan schools really were. Maybe then he could pressure those pastors who were slow to correct the violations being noted by the Fire Department.

The monsignor reached for his hat and coat, then headed for the door. "Go ahead and release the figures," he told his secretary. "I'm going out there."

After riding the elevator down to street level, McManus walked out onto Wacker Drive to hail a cab. "900 North Avers," he told the driver. In the western sky the sun was beginning to set, and soon McManus could see smoke billowing up in the distance. He felt suddenly uneasy. He sensed it was a serious fire.

With fire engines screaming past, his fears began to mount. The cab made its way further west in traffic that started to slow, then ground almost to a standstill. It was a very cold day, and McManus was startled by the harrowing sight of schoolchildren running along sidewalks without coats and hats. Some were soaking wet. Equally alarming was the sight of panic-stricken adults running in the opposite direction—parents, he gathered—racing to the school in search of their children.

The cabbie inched his way through the bottleneck before being stopped by police, who began blocking the street, trying to make way for the caravans of fire engines and ambulances squeezing their way into the neighborhood's tiny side streets. Already McManus could see there was plenty of fire equipment parked along the avenue. Quickly he reached over the seat to pay his fare, then jumped from the car, running the remaining few blocks to the school.

IT WAS JUST before three o'clock when Steve Lasker parked his car next to a fire engine on Iowa Street. The news photographer reached into the back seat, grabbing his large four-by-five lens camera and tote bag filled with fresh film and flashbulbs.

Lasker jumped from the car and ran the few steps to the front of the school. He looked up. A huge cloud of smoke was pouring from the building. Big fire. Plenty of action. He heard shouting and ran north, stopping at the courtway dividing the two wings. Firemen had battered down the fence leading into the narrow area, and children standing at the windows inside were screaming for help. Still more children, scores it seemed, were down on the pavement, moaning in pain.

For a brief, fleeting moment, Steve Lasker was bewildered. He'd been to his share of fires, and he knew the sight of death. But the scene before him was unlike anything he had ever witnessed.

Suddenly a voice in his mind jarred him back to reality. "Shoot! Shoot!"

He reached in his tote bag and took out some film.

WORD OF THE FIRE spread rapidly through the community. Residents and merchants had heard the continual wail of sirens, and soon telephones were ringing in homes, apartments, and shops all over the neighborhood. Bulletins on radio and TV reinforced these word-of-mouth reports and communicated the first official news of the disaster to the general public.

Emma Jacobellis was at home folding clothes in the living room of her brick two-flat on North Monticello Avenue, waiting for Victor, her nine-year-old, to arrive home from school. Nick, her husband, was at his job as a liquor store manager. Grace Ann, the couple's four-year-old, was watching television with Emma's father, who also shared the home.

Finished with the laundry, Emma looked at the clock. It was almost time to start supper. She was moving toward the kitchen when the telephone rang. She picked up the receiver. "Hello."

"Emma!" the caller shouted. Emma recognized the excited voice of her cousin in the next block. "Where's Victor?"

"He's not here yet. Why?"

"Emma, the school's on fire! It's on the radio. You better get over there. Some of the kids can't get out. They're jumping out windows!"

Emma hung up the phone and grabbed her coat, sliding her short arms through its worn woolen sleeves. "Pa," she said, heading out the door, "watch Grace Ann. I'm going to the school. There's some kind of fire."

Two miles south, Nick Jacobellis was going over his inventory sheets, checking his shelf stock at the Armanetti's store he managed at Crawford and Fifth avenues. The holidays always meant more business, and he was readying the store for the increased traffic the coming weeks were sure to bring.

A transistor radio was filling the store with Christmas music when an announcer's voice interrupted the regular programming: "A 5-11 alarm fire is raging at Our Lady of the Angels School in the 900 block of North Avers on the city's West Side. Initial reports say as many as twenty students have been injured in the blaze. Children are reportedly trapped on the building's second floor, and some have jumped from windows. Police are asking that you avoid the area if at all possible. Stay tuned for further details as they become available."

Nick couldn't believe it. Just last week he had been talking about the school, when he and Victor had walked through the building during an open house. "If there's ever a fire," Nick mentioned to his son, "those stairs will burn like kindling."

Victor was a student in Sister Seraphica's second-floor classroom in the middle of the north wing. He had developed an early sense of things mechanical and had a flair for electronics. He was a whiz at building erector sets. He didn't seem concerned with his father's observation. "Don't worry, Daddy," he said. "If there's ever a fire, I'll jump out the window."

Nick set down his papers and reached for his overcoat. "Sam," he yelled to the young clerk behind the cash register, "watch the store. I'm going up to the school."

Nick didn't have a car, and he figured it was too far to walk. He ran to the street corner, looking for a bus. Instead he saw a police car, its red light flashing, trying to squeeze its way north through the traffic on Crawford Avenue. Nick figured the officer was headed for the fire. He started waving his arms, hoping to flag down the squad. It worked. The patrol car pulled over. Nick ran up and opened the passenger door. "I need a ride to the school," he shouted to the lone police officer behind the steering wheel. "My kid goes there."

The officer wanted to help. He couldn't have civilians riding in the squad. But this was an emergency. Protocol could be broken. "Get in," he said.

The officer stepped on the gas and hit the siren. Nick was jerked backward. He looked up. Black smoke was brushing across the sky ahead.

ALFRED AND MARY ANDREOLI were priding themselves on the fact that they had already decorated their men's store on Chicago Avenue for the Christmas season. The small shop was located a block south of the school, where the couple's children attended classes. Gerry and a younger son, Randy, were in the main school; Barbara was enrolled in the first grade in a building around the corner on Hamlin Avenue.

The Andreolis were passing the afternoon when a young man came into the store and began looking through a rack of trousers. "I'd like to buy a pair of slacks," he said to Mr. Andreoli, standing behind the counter.

As the two men talked about size and style, they could hear the sound of fire sirens piercing the air. Andreoli looked up. "I wonder what that's all about."

"Oh, the school's on fire," the customer answered rather casually.

"What school?"

"The one over here on the corner," the customer pointed. "The Catholic school."

Mary Andreoli slipped on a coat. "I'm going over there," she said to her husband, hurrying out the door.

As he heard more sirens, Mr. Andreoli began growing uneasy. He was trying to hurry the transaction with his lone customer, without being too abrupt, when the telephone rang. It was his wife's sister. "Al," she gasped, "the school's on fire! Kids are jumping out the windows!"

The excitement in his sister-in-law's voice was frightening. "Mary just went over there," Andreoli said. "Can you come and watch the store?"

"I'll be right there."

As soon as he set down the phone, Andreoli saw his two younger children enter the store. They were hatless and coatless. Randy's chin was smudged with soot.

"Where's Gerry?" their father asked.

"I don't know," Randy answered. "I didn't see him."

FOUR MILES AWAY, at the Radio Steel plant on Grand Avenue, Mario Maffiola was busy operating his punch press. The short, handsome Italian immigrant took pride in his work, and he consistently outperformed his coworkers, turning out more steel hinges each hour than any of his peers. His weekly paychecks were always a little larger, part of the pay-for-performance program the company had implemented the year before.

Mario's foreman, a large muscular man with friendly brown eyes and a worn baseball cap atop his head, walked up and placed his hand on Mario's shoulder. "Mario," the foreman shouted over the banging machinery. "Doesn't your boy go to Our Lady of the Angels?"

"Yes," Mario answered. Joseph, his ten-year-old, was a fifth-grader in Sister Therese's room.

The foreman placed his face next to Mario's ear. "There's some kind of fire at the school. Maybe you should go over there."

Mario looked puzzled. A fire? "How bad is it?" he asked.

"I don't know," the foreman answered. "It's on the radio."

Mario looked at the clock. It was a little after three. Della, his wife, was still at her assembly-line job at a nearby Motorola factory. The couple's three-year-old, Linda, was in day care at a local preschool. Mario decided to pick them up. That way, he figured, they could drive to the school together. He switched off his machine and fumbled for his keys.

MONSIGNOR ED PELLICORE, a big, friendly extrovert of a man, was sitting in his office inside the rectory of Our Lady of Perpetual Help Church, three miles away from the fire scene, when he received a call from a friend whose son was in the seventh grade at Our Lady of the Angels.

Pellicore had served as an associate pastor at Our Lady of the Angels before the north wing had been converted to classroom use. He was familiar with the composition of the building. He also knew many of the Italian families in the parish.

"Monsignor," Mary Sansone said. "They've got a big fire at OLA, and Jimmy hasn't come home yet. I'm worried."

"I'll get over there right away," the monsignor answered. He called to an associate, Father Tony Spina, to accompany him. Spina had attended Our Lady of the Angels School as a boy. As the two priests drove north, Pellicore could see the column of smoke in the sky.

"Oh, boy, Tony," he said. "This is bad. That place is like a matchbox. Those stairs are dry as a bone!"

MATT PLOVANICH was sitting restlessly with his classmates inside Our Lady of the Angels Church. The smell of smoke permeated the interior of the long building, and lines of children evacuated from the burning school next door continued to stream into its pews. Matt watched as nervous teachers busied themselves by taking head counts. He didn't hear anyone praying, just a lot of talking. "The school's on fire. Did you see it? The school's on fire. Oh my God!"

Matt decided he didn't want to stay any longer. He wanted to go home. Hatless and coatless, he stood up on his own and walked to the side door, then slipped out into the cold. When he reached the alley, he looked up at the school. The scene was still one of sheer panic. Firemen were running up ladders, and kids were tumbling out windows. The alley was littered with bodies. Firemen on the ground were running from window to window, trying to catch kids in life nets. It was futile; there were too many windows to be serviced.

In one of the windows Matt could see the outline of a figure struggling to get up over the ledge, its hands grabbing on to the windowsill, just trying to hold on. The little grey face was silhouetted by smoke, and for a second or two, it bobbed up and down. Then it slipped back into the flames. At the next window was a small girl, her long brown hair on fire. She started falling. Matt watched as she hit the ground. He couldn't tell if she had jumped or was pushed out. It didn't matter, for Matt knew he was seeing horror. There was horror coming from every window. It left him stunned. He knew he and his classmates had been in a bad situation, but he couldn't imagine anything like this. Standing in the alley, he was frozen both in fear and in awe. This was his school. These were his friends. He couldn't believe what was happening.

Terrified, Matt took off running for his family's apartment building on West Division Street. He didn't know yet that his father, off duty from the Police Department, had arrived at the school only a few minutes earlier. Rudy Plovanich had made a date to drive some of the nuns downtown for shopping. Instead, at that moment he was making his way through the south wing, looking for his sons, helping to evacuate other stricken children.

When Matt reached his apartment building a few minutes later, he went around to the back porch and ran up three flights of stairs. He turned to look back toward the school. To the east, smoke was rising in the sky. It was black and thick, like an atomic bomb. Matt was pounding on the back door when his mother opened it and let him in.

"Where's your coat?" Irene Plovanich yelled. She grabbed Matt by the arm and pulled him inside the doorway. "Who've you been fighting with?"

"Mom," Matt answered, "the school's on fire!"

"Yeah, right. C'mon, get in here."

"No, Mom, really. It's on fire. It's bad."

It wasn't until they were inside the tiny kitchen that Matt's mother noticed the black mucus running from her son's nostrils. Then she caught an odor of smoke coming from his disheveled clothing.

"Matty," she said, "are you serious?"

"Mom," he repeated, "it's bad."

Just then the front doorbell rang. It was Mr. Gordon, the elderly man who lived across the hall. He looked worried. "Reenie," he asked, "do you have all the kids?"

"No. Matty just came home."

"Reenie. The school's on fire. It's really bad."

Matt's mother turned to look back at her son. "Oh Matty," she cried, pulling him close. "What happened?"

MICHELLE BARALE picked herself up and started walking along Avers Avenue. She felt dizzy, like she might faint. Her throat was burning and her stomach felt sick from smoke. She wanted to vomit. Instead she coughed. From the sidewalk she wandered across the street. An old Italian couple, their faces streaming with tears, took her by the hand and led her into their home.

Michelle was coughing when she sat down on a big overstuffed chair in the living room. Outside, smoke and screams filled the air. The girl's face was smudged from soot, and her blue skirt was ripped. Her white blouse was wrinkled and wet, and both her shoes and one of her socks were missing.

The old couple tried talking to her, but they spoke little English. They were rubbing her shoeless feet, trying to get her to drink from a glass of anisetta, an Italian liqueur, to help soothe her throat.

The old woman handed Michelle the telephone. "Call mother," she said in her broken English.

Michelle dialed a number. Her mother was at work. Her grandmother answered.

"Grandma," she cried. "Come get me."

ON THE NEAR WEST SIDE, the bums and down-and-outs of Skid Row were fighting the cold, scrounging for change and half-smoked cigarettes in the gutters along Madison Street.

Around the corner, inside the Aberdeen Street firehouse, Hal Bruno was spending his day off riding with Squad 2. A reporter for the *Chicago American*, Bruno was thirty years old and had literally grown up in the Fire Department. He began hanging around fire-houses in Rogers Park when he was eight. At fifteen he started rid-ing the rigs, and in his early twenties he began performing the same duties as a firefighter, complete with his own set of black turnout gear and fire helmet.

Squad 2 shared the narrow brick firehouse with Engine 34, and the two companies were among the busiest in the city. So far, how-ever, Monday had been quiet. Bruno was passing time in the firehouse kitchen, sipping coffee and thumbing the pages of a magazine. He was waiting for five o'clock, when he would leave to teach a skiing class downtown at the Merchandise Mart.

At around a quarter to three, Bruno's ears tuned in to the fire radio at the front of the station. He could hear urgent voices coming over the air. Leroy Dean, the captain, was sitting on watch when a 2-11 alarm was struck for Chicago and Hamlin. He reached over his desk and turned up the radio.

"Send us all available ambulances," a voice cried. "We've got a school. Kids are injured!"

"Get ready," Dean warned. The men were jumpy. Squad 2 would be due if it went to a 3-11.

Bruno and the other firemen gathered around the desk. Hearing the commotion on the radio, they stepped over to the rig, donned their fire coats and helmets, and slipped into their boots. Just then the joker started its incessant clacking, and a voice blared over the radio: "Battalion Eighteen to Main! Give us a 5-11."

Dean hit the house bells. "Let's go!" he shouted.

The men didn't wait for the speaker. They jumped on the rig and pushed out the door.

AFTER THE COLLAPSE of the roof, firefighters had regained their footing and began to battle their way back into the blazing school. Smoke poured furiously from the upper windows, and flames licked angrily from the large, gaping hole in the remaining roof. Two fire companies operating in front of the school picked up their hose lines and, on hands and knees, climbed back up the front stairway, trying desperately to push back the fire blocking access into the main corridor and classrooms. Without breathing apparatus, the men were hit hard by the intense heat and smoke. But they refused to retreat, fighting for every inch of space. Outside, other firefighters straddling ladders were trying to climb through windows and enter the second-floor classrooms where, still unknown to them, scores of children and nuns lay dead.

When Squad 2 pulled up at Hamlin and Iowa, in front of the Our Lady of the Angels Church, Hal Bruno and his partners grabbed their pike poles and axes and started running to the school. Smoke blanketing the neighborhood was thick, the smell of burning strong. Ambulances and police squadrols were pulling away with injured children.

The sidewalks in front of the church and south wing were crammed with adults searching for their children. As he ran through the crowd, Bruno saw a woman in hair curlers and a scarf, her face in absolute anguish. "Where's my baby!" she yelled. "Where's my baby!"

When the squadmen reached the front of the south wing, they climbed up an aerial ladder to the roof, where they were ordered to cut holes to ventilate the smoke. Once up top, Bruno looked across to the north wing where fire was leaping up through the collapsed hole in the roof. The firemen started swinging their axes, ripping apart the roofing material, pulling it back with their pike poles. Next to them an engine company was throwing a heavy stream of water across the courtway.

Standing on the edge, Bruno peered down into the courtway. Through a window he could see another company stretching a line into the annex. Never before had he seen a group of firemen look so determined. The smoke was incredible. They were taking a terrible beating. Bruno wondered: What's going on? Why are they trying to get in there like that?

Bruno watched as another fireman climbed up a wooden ladder to one of the windows inside the courtway. When he reached the top, the man ducked his head inside the window and nearly fell off the ladder, dropping his pike pole. "Oh my God!" he screamed. The shrill of his voice was terrifying. Bruno felt the hairs standing up on his neck. "These classrooms are filled with children!"

For Bruno, the fireman's discovery was the first indication of what lay inside the smoldering ruins. They had plenty of firemen on the scene, but as far as he knew, he was the only reporter. He turned to Dean. "Cap," he yelled. "I gotta go to work as a reporter!"

"Go!" Dean said.

Bruno descended the ladder and sprinted around to the Avers side of the building. Almost immediately he bumped into a priest. "There's gotta be seventy-five kids in there!" the cleric shouted to him. Bruno pulled out a pen and notebook and started scribbling notes. He ran around the corner into the alley. The sight was incredible. Unbelievable. He had to find a telephone. Running north on Avers, he began picking up eyewitness accounts along the way. "I'm Bruno with the *American*. What did you see?"

After taking more notes, Bruno ran up to a woman standing outside her home across the street. "Lady," he shouted. "I'm with the *American*. You got a phone?"

The woman led Bruno into her kitchen. "There," she pointed.

Bruno picked up the telephone and quickly dialed his paper. He looked at his watch. They still had time to get a bulletin out for the afternoon edition. After a couple of rings, the harsh voice of an editor came on the line. "City desk."

"This is Bruno. I'm at this school fire. Stop the press!"

The editor connected Bruno to a rewrite man, and the reporter began to relay his story.

LIEUTENANT JOHN "RED" WINDLE, in charge of the Fire Department's new snorkel unit, was standing inside the department's repair shops at 31st Street and Sacramento Avenue when the box alarm was struck for the school. The snorkel was due, and as the company began its long trek to the scene, Windle was worried. There's going to be a mob of people around there, he thought to himself. We might have a tough time getting in.

The lieutenant's fears gradually diminished as the snorkel cleared the clogged streets and was quickly maneuvered into position in the alley north of the school. Windle climbed into the snorkel basket and took himself high into the air, steadying the basket just above roof level. Once he had water, he cracked the turret pipe and began directing a powerful stream into the gaping hole in the roof and through the windows of the second floor. He looked down into the rooms and could see one or two children slumped at their desks. He had to be careful not to come down too low with the pipe, fearful that he might wash the kids right out of their seats.

Flames were shooting out the two roof ventilators like blow torches. Windle raked his stream back and forth through the windows on Rooms 208 and 210, washing the plaster off the walls and ceilings, directing the stream into the cockloft where the fire had been burning unchecked for some time. The water from the turret had a tremendous cooling effect, and the flames soon began to subside. Firemen started climbing into the darkened classrooms. Although the men wore no breathing apparatus, they were now able to gain a footing inside the smoke-filled classrooms. They began to pass lifeless forms through the windows, descending the ladders with limp, blackened figures of children slumped precariously over their shoulders.

Windle could see that the second-floor classrooms had been badly ravaged by fire. He knew it was unlikely anyone inside had survived.

AT 3:09 P.M. the first of two special alarms was sounded for additional manpower, and the loudspeaker inside the downtown firehouse of Squad Company 1 came to life:

"SQUAD 1, TAKE IN THE FIVE-ELEVEN, AVERS AND IOWA."

Richard Scheidt and his mates on the squad dropped what they were doing and ran to the rig. Thirty seconds later the squad pushed out the door, headed north and west through the mid-afternoon traffic.

Standing on the back step, Scheidt winced as the cold wind brushed against his face. On the horizon, a column of black smoke was climbing into the sky. He turned up the collar on his fire coat and pulled his boots up over his knees. A few minutes later, when the rig was stopped by traffic, Scheidt and the four other men assigned to the squad jumped off and fell in line behind their captain, Harry Whedon, who took off running for the school two blocks away.

By this time all squad companies on the scene had been ordered to the front of the school building. Whedon reported directly to Fire

Commissioner Quinn who, flanked by two other chiefs, was standing outside the north wing, directing fire crews already engaged in
firefighting. Quinn looked stunned. Never before had he seen smoke
this black or this thick pour from a building under such pressure. It
was the worst he had ever seen or ever would see. "Harry," he
shouted to Whedon from under his battered white fire helmet, "take
your gang upstairs and start making those rooms."

Without hesitation the firefighters bounded up the crowded front
stairway. At the top of the landing, conditions were barely tenable,
the heat incredible. The main corridor was still impassable. Firemen
from several engine companies were crouched on their knees,
wrestling charged hose lines, trying to push back the smoke and
flames. Scheidt and his mates began swinging their axes and sledge-
hammers, trying desperately to breach the walls so they could access
the classrooms and search for signs of life.

AT 3:30 P.M. Monsignor William Gorman, the Fire Department
chaplain, crawled out of the building to inform newsmen that ten to
fifteen children were dead. Fifteen minutes later a fearful Gorman
raised the figure to twenty-five. As firemen advanced their hose
lines deeper into the smoky school, the loss of life became more evident. Gorman's figures to the press grew steadily higher.

As word of the blaze spread, the narrow side streets around the
school soon were clogged with spectators, fire vehicles, ambulances, and police squadrols. Broadcast warnings to stay away from
the area only drew more people. Parents left work and rushed to the
scene. Firemen with children attending the school left their fire-
houses in other parts of the city to join in the rescue efforts. All
drove as close to the school as possible before parking their autos in
the streets and running to the fire.

Disbelieving parents grew more agitated with each passing
minute. This could not be happening, they thought. Not here. Not
now. Not to us. Some tried several times to break through police
lines. Women spilled into the streets, chasing ambulances and
squadrols, trying to open the back doors to get a look at the feet of
victims being transported to local hospitals, hoping to identify the
children by their shoes. Some parents, after learning their youngsters had left school without coats and jackets, stood outside clutching the small coats they had brought with them.

As more fire companies arrived, firefighters laddered all windows on the school's north wing, and hose lines were spread through the streets like loose spaghetti. The narrow streets became so clogged with emergency vehicles and spectators that firemen were ordered to cut down trees and shrubs so that ambulances and police squadrols could drive along the curbs and reach the front of the school.

With sufficient manpower and fire equipment at the scene, the fire was gradually brought under control. At 3:45 p.m. all companies not engaged in actual firefighting operations were ordered to the front of the building on Avers to assist in the search for the dead. Although some victims had already been removed, fire officials were waiting to take out the remaining bodies, fearing a stampede of frantic parents.

At the top of the second-floor landing, through the grimy smoke, firefighters were swinging their axes, pike poles, and hammers, pulling away splintered pieces of wall. After a few minutes, an opening had been breached large enough to allow entry into the burned-out classrooms. Guided by lanterns and flashlights, the men groped their way forward through the smoke, searching for life. What they found instead was a gruesome scene of death that would forever be etched in their memories. The devil himself could not have created a more horrible picture.

Strewn about the smoky, blackened classrooms, amid the charred woodwork and caved-in ceilings, were piles of small bodies. Overturned desks and charred books and papers bore witness to the swift unexpectedness of the blaze. Water-drenched plaster and wood lathing hung down from what were once the walls. Chalkboards had either fallen or had been burned off the walls, and broken glass from shattered transoms and light fixtures littered the floors. Scorched religious statues lay toppled beneath pieces of burned timber from the collapsed roof. In one room a porcelain figure of the Virgin Mary stood on a bookcase. It had been a planter, but the leaves were now ashes. Outside in the hallway, a blackened statue of Christ looked down over the scene.

With tears streaming down their faces, the firemen crawled into the rooms, hacking at the debris to reach the bodies. The children had been burnt to varying degrees, and some were virtually cremated. The men wept as they carried the bodies to the windows, handing them off to other firefighters perched outside on the ladders.

The stench of death permeated the darkened corridor. Still, the firemen pressed on with their work. They began separating the charred remains, carefully placing the little ones into canvas body bags or wrapping them in blankets and tarps. They scoured the rooms with their flashlights, overturning desks and furniture, searching the floors and debris for signs of life. There were none to be found. They had been called too late.

Inside Room 212 firefighters found twenty-seven dead children. Lying on the desk tops were waterlogged books and papers that would never be graded. Sister Therese was dead. Her desk had been hurled forward as she struggled to reach her charges and avoid the flames.

In Room 210 a stack of dead fourth-graders was found beneath the windowsills, the tiny victims unable to reach over the high ledges. Underneath another pile of students lay Sister Seraphica. She had stayed until the end and was among the room's thirty fatalities.

In Room 208 the badly burned body of Sister Mary Canice was found draped over another pile of dead pupils, evidence of her futile attempt to shield the children from the flames. Ten of the room's occupants were dead. Lying on the floor was an electric wall clock. It had stopped at 2:47 p.m.

Across the corridor, in Room 211, Lieutenant Charles Kamin and his crew from Truck 35 slogged through water that in some places was ankle-deep. They entered the room carrying blankets, salvage tarps, and hose covers—whatever they could use to wrap the fragile remains. The sight was appalling. Several blackened shapes resembling small human forms were stacked by the windows. In the back of the room, against the east wall, more bodies lay piled atop one another. Kamin counted fifteen of the pathetic figures. Just a mound of dead bodies. Looking closer, he could see that some of the children had the skin burned off their bodies. Others were tangled or fused together by the intense heat. A few had bones sticking out where fire had consumed flesh. One child's skull was plainly visible.

Kamin could feel a sickness rising in his stomach. It was the same room from which he had earlier rescued students while atop the ladder. Tears were rolling down his cheeks. He felt helpless. All he could do now was untangle these kids and cover them and take them away.

When firefighters entered Room 209 they could locate only one body. Beverly Ann Burda, the thirteen-year-old who had dreamed of becoming a nun, was found lying near the window, felled by smoke.

Across the hallway, inside Room 208, Captain James Neville of Engine 43 could see that the men were having trouble removing the remaining bodies from the classroom, where the children had been exposed to the worst of the fire's fury. The bodies were fragile, and as the firemen tried picking them up, some broke apart. "Hold it," Neville yelled. "Find all the blankets and hose covers you can and start making packages."

This is what they did.

During one of his many trips outside the school, Neville was stopped by Captain Tony Pilas of the Fire Prevention Bureau.

"Jimmy!" Pilas asked, "are all the kids out?"

"I don't know," Neville answered. "But I'll find out."

Pilas's twelve-year-old daughter, Nancy, was one of the packages.

NUMBED BY FATIGUE, firefighter Richard Scheidt was slowly making his way down the front stairs, part of a procession of somber, black-faced firemen removing dead children from the school. The men were headed for a side door on the north wing that opened onto the alley, where other rescue workers waited with stretchers. In Scheidt's arms was the limp, water-dampened body of a young boy. Using his flashlight as a guide, Scheidt had located the youngster lying on the floor below a window inside Room 212. The boy's hair was tousled and his face and clothing had been smudged by smoke. Both of his shoes were missing. He weighed about ninety pounds, and Scheidt guessed he must have been about ten years old.

Standing on the back step of a fire truck parked just inside the alley, Steve Lasker raised his camera as he saw the firemen coming down the stairs carrying the bodies. He noticed Scheidt. As soon as the figure came through the doorway, the shutter on Lasker's camera snapped. Scheidt didn't notice the cameraman standing before him. He bent down to set the boy on a waiting stretcher, then went back upstairs.

The image of Scheidt and the boy captured by Lasker's camera at that moment would become famous the world over, describing better than words the tragedy of the school fire.

INSIDE THE SCHOOL, amidst the destruction of the north-wing class-rooms, Salvatore Imburgia leaned out a window and peered down at the crowd of parents on the sidewalk below. He was grimy from soot, and beneath his heavy, black fire coat his body was soaked with perspiration. The adults were standing in silent disbelief, watching as firemen carried stretcher after stretcher through the front doors. To Imburgia, the spectators bore familiar faces; he recognized many. This was his parish, his neighborhood. They were his people.

Imburgia was shaken, wrestling with his emotions. His kids were this age. What if his kids had burned up like this? What would he do? How would he react? How would he tell his wife?

The number of bodies was overwhelming. When he first entered the classrooms he couldn't believe how many were dead. He expected to find ten, maybe twelve kids. But then it was fifty, sixty, seventy, eighty. What the hell is this? What the hell happened?

Imburgia shelved his questions. The time to think would come later. Right now he was a fireman, a professional. He had a job to do. Go for the bodies. Find the bodies. Be careful. Don't get emotional.

He and three other firemen bent over to pick up the body of an eight-year-old boy slumped over a desk. The men laid the boy on a stretcher, covering the little figure with a blanket. As they carried him downstairs, Imburgia thought of his wife's aunt. She had a child enrolled in the school. He didn't know at the time that the boy had stayed home sick that day. How many kids in the family were here?

In the foyer just inside the front door, priests with purple stoles around their necks were bending over, administering the final rites of the church to victims being carried from the building. Imburgia and his partners stopped momentarily. A priest pulled back the blanket covering their stretcher. He began anointing the forehead of the child who lay underneath. Imburgia looked down. The boy's eyes were closed, as if he were sleeping. When the rite was completed, the firemen carried the boy into the street to a waiting police squadrol. Imburgia looked at the crowd. He saw a few of his friends. They ran up, grabbing him by the arm.

"Sal," one cried, "did you see my kid? I can't find him!"

Imburgia didn't answer. He couldn't. Right now he was a fireman. He had to be strong. He couldn't break down in front of civilians. Besides, he wasn't sure if he recognized any of the kids he had pulled out. To him they all looked the same. Young. Innocent. Helpless.

AT 4:19 P.M. Fire Commissioner Quinn radioed the main fire alarm office, ordering that the 5-11 alarm be "struck out" on his authority. Although almost thirty minutes had passed since firefighters first brought the flames under control, the commissioner had decided to wait before officially declaring so, hoping that perhaps some signs of life could be discovered.

Soon after, Mayor Daley and Archbishop Albert Meyer arrived at the scene. Quinn, his face begrimed by smoke and soot, accompanied the two men inside the school for an inspection of the ruins. The mayor was dressed in an overcoat and galoshes. He sloshed through the darkened interior, touring the grim scene in stunned silence. The father of seven children, Daley was not a cold, unfeeling man as some of his political foes portrayed him. Now, standing outside Our Lady of the Angels School, he appeared bewildered, as though wondering why God had allowed innocent children to perish. Few if any people outside his immediate family knew the mayor's innermost thoughts, but clearly he took the tragedy personally and considered it an irreparable stain on his beloved city and church.

By the same token Daley was pragmatic and had to be thinking about the legal ramifications of the disaster. Was there negligence involved in the fire? Would the city or Fire Department be held accountable? And what about the liability of the Catholic archdiocese?

After viewing the classrooms on the fire-ravaged second floor, Meyer was so overcome by grief he had to be led away to the convent across the street, where the school's principal, Sister St. Florence, was being sedated by doctors.

Outside, an endless parade of gaunt-eyed firemen continued to emerge from the school carrying sheet-covered stretchers, all trying their best to shield the bodies from the spectators' view. They placed the inert little forms into waiting ambulances and police squadrols staged in a long line running north on Avers past the school's front doors. Once loaded with their dreadful cargoes, the vehicles crept slowly northward to Augusta Boulevard and headed for the Cook County Morgue four miles away.

For the hundreds of students who had escaped the hell on the school's second floor, the world suddenly took on a new, ugly face. No longer was it a safe, friendly place. Here and there adults would pluck youngsters from the crowd and wrap them in a blanket or overcoat. "You're safe now," the children were told. "It's okay." But things were not okay. Nor would they ever be. Some unclaimed children wandering in the crowds were taken into nearby homes. Others were stopped by adults who begged them for information regarding the whereabouts of their own missing sons and daughters. One woman located her daughter after ninety minutes of frantic searching. Other parents would not be so lucky.

On Iowa Street, sheet-covered bodies were laid on the lawn outside the parish rectory, and a temporary morgue was located inside a private home across the street on Avers. Parents and relatives of missing schoolchildren let out crazed shrieks as the line of bodies outside the rectory grew longer and longer. Some parents who watched bit trembling hands and pulled at their hair. One grandfather standing in the crowd suffered a heart attack. The sight was too much.

A temporary Red Cross station was set up inside the rectory, and workers began compiling names of the known dead and injured, listing the hospitals to which they had been transported. The information, however, was sketchy, and nothing could be confirmed. With hundreds of emotionally distraught adults roaming outside in the streets, the little office soon became overwhelmed. "Go home," the parents were told. "Wait for a phone call."

Instead the adults continued plodding through the neighborhood, ringing doorbells at houses and apartment buildings. Many youngsters had been taken into homes by neighbors and passersby, and scores of children were found lying on floors, on furniture, in kitchens, and in bedrooms. The houses smelled like smoke, and the cries of injured and frightened children filled every room. Still more injured children had been carried away by strangers to parked cars and driven through almost impassable streets to local hospitals. Police began advising parents unable to account for their children to start searching the seven area hospitals where the injured had been taken. As hope began to dwindle, adults began their bitter rounds.

A mile and a half away, at the Austin District police station on Chicago Avenue, a missing-persons bureau was established, and detectives in the squad room began reading names off hastily prepared lists to the parents who showed up there. Those whose children were on the injured lists ran from the police station and drove to local hospitals. Others unable to get answers stood in line at a single pay phone, placing calls home to see if their little ones had showed up. Still others heard the two dreaded words: "County morgue."

Darkness soon arrived, and a cold wind swept the neighborhood. Streetlights began to glow, and two Fire Department light wagons were called in to illuminate the burned-out building. By seven o'clock firefighters had recovered the last of the victims from the charred classrooms. For the firemen, there was little more to do, just the "routine work" of salvage and overhaul, checking for hot spots, picking up hose lines. Fire and police officials turned their attention to finding the cause of the blaze. But for those parents who had failed to locate their children, a long and in some cases heartbreaking search was under way.

Six

SEARCH

A T 2:52 P.M. that Monday afternoon, nurses in the emergency room of St. Anne's Hospital were preparing for the three-o'clock shift change when they heard someone screaming and banging on the doors leading to the ambulance bay outside. "Open up!" cried a man's voice. "I've got lots of kids here. They're all burned!"

When the nurses pushed open the doors and kicked down the door stops that would hold them in place for the next five hours, they found the pleading samaritan standing in the cold, holding a nine-year-old girl in his arms. The girl's reddened face was swollen from burns and the hair on her head was singed from their roots. The globe of her scalp, white and waxy, glistened with water.

The man motioned to his car parked in the ambulance bay. "In there!" he yelled.

Inside the vehicle were five more burned and injured children, each moaning and screaming in pain. The youngsters' blue uniforms and white shirts smelled of smoke, and their faces, arms, and hands were bloodied and black. As the nurses carried them into the emergency room, the man shouted a warning: "There's more coming!"

There were more indeed. Many more. Almost immediately the 322-bed hospital operated by a small band of nuns known as the Poor Handmaids of Jesus Christ was besieged by a steady stream of vehicles, from ambulances and police squadrols to milk trucks and newspaper vans, arriving en masse with injured and dying children from the burning school sixteen blocks away.

In the next hour eighty children would arrive—children on stretchers, in policemen's arms, supported by firemen; children shivering from cold, dazed by shock, whimpering in fear; children with cuts and bruises and broken limbs; children overcome by smoke and poisonous gases; children with the ugly odor of burned flesh, skin blackened or angry red with swelling blisters; children who were already dead.

Sister Mary Almunda Klaus, the hospital's administrator, was immediately alerted. "Sister!" a nursing supervisor shouted excitedly over the telephone. "There's a big fire at Our Lady of the Angels School. We're receiving lots of injured."

For twenty years Sister Almunda had supervised the emergency department at St. Anne's, and she was experienced in dealing with emergencies. She had been on duty one day in 1947 when twenty-four horribly burned men, their lungs seared by live steam, died after being brought to the hospital following an explosion that ripped through a nearby factory.

As Sister Almunda moved toward the emergency room, she glanced at the hospital's busy switchboard. Every line was lit up with incoming calls. She knew something dreadful had happened. She reached for a telephone and placed calls to Dr. James Callahan, the hospital's chief of staff, and Dr. James Seagraves, chairman of the disaster plan committee. "Get down to the ER, quick!" she said, her voice ringing with authority. "Something major is developing."

St. Anne's 647 employees, its medical staff of 104, and its 120 student nurses moved into action with quiet precision. Ten minutes after he was called, Dr. Seagraves stepped into the emergency room and assembled a triage team to begin screening the victims according to the degree of their injuries. Hospital gurneys were brought into the emergency room, and intravenous racks were rolled into the auditorium of the hospital's nursing school, designated as a temporary receiving area. Student nurses cleared away auditorium chairs and set up long tables for bandages, needles, plastic tubing, drugs, and syringes. Housekeeping sent down blankets and sterile sheets. Pharmacy workers checked their supplies.

Children were placed on gurneys, some unconscious, others rubbing at burned arms and hands, and wheeled from the emergency room to other areas for treatment. Those with life-threatening injuries were immediately taken upstairs to the hospital's sixth-floor surgical area. The next level of injured were treated inside the emergency room. Children with the least serious injuries were wheeled or walked into the auditorium, where student nurses began tending the wounds.

"It was a long wait," recalled Vito Muilli, who, after running home from the school, was driven to the hospital by his older brother. Vito was treated in the emergency room before being admitted that evening for a two-week hospital stay. Both his hands were chewed up like sausages, bloodied and black, with peeled skin. "All the kids there were lined up. They were all screaming. Many of them were burned worse than me."

As the magnitude of the situation became apparent, the hospital's emergency disaster plan was put into effect, bringing in stores of drugs, plasma, and other medical supplies. Other calls went outside the hospital, and a team of fifty doctors was mobilized, many summoned from private practices. Fortunately, because the fire occurred just as the hospital was beginning its three-o'clock shift change, twice the number of medical staff was present, and beefed-up physician-nurse teams were placed in action. Other physicians, nursing departments, interns, residents, and floor supervisors were also alerted.

Soon the community at large became aware of the grim struggle to save lives being waged inside the hospital, and before long the streets surrounding it became clogged with traffic. An ordinary community hospital, St. Anne's was facing the greatest challenge in its history, stretching its resources to the limit.

Within the first hour, thirty-seven children and three nuns—Sisters Helaine, Davidis, and Geraldita—were admitted to the hospital. Ten other students, along with Sister Therese, were dead on arrival, their bodies taken to the basement and placed on the floor of an x-ray room. Two more students died before being admitted.

Of the students who arrived first, six had been burned over 60 percent of their bodies. Thirteen more had burns of 40 percent. Twelve had broken bones, including one broken neck, two fractured skulls, a crushed chest, and a shattered hip—thirty-six fractures in all. Included among the injured was a seventy-four-year-old man who had suffered a stroke while attempting to catch children jumping from the school windows. Four injured firefighters also were received.

AT THREE O'CLOCK that afternoon, Michelle McBride was wheeled into St. Anne's emergency room, the first "bad one" to arrive. She was thirteen, an eighth-grader, one of a group of six girls who played and studied together. Of her clique, she would be the only survivor. Inside Room 209 Michelle shrank back from jumping while frightened classmates pushed and clawed their way to the windows. By the time she reached a ladder, the fire had swept its way through the room. A few rungs down the ladder, she fell.

Michelle's head was cut and almost two-thirds of her body was burned. Thick bobby socks protected her ankles, but the rest of her legs had been seared, the left one to the knee, the right one up to her thigh. Skin was also burned off her back and both hands, and burns seared her forehead and left cheek down to her earlobe.

Michelle's heart was affected, its output diminished. Kidney action faltered and wastes were retained. Her blood pressure dropped. Her pulse rate rose. The rate of red blood cell destruction was increasing. She was sick and getting sicker. Within eight hours she would be in danger of death from shock. Her body, it seemed, was a big open wound.

"Wheel her in here," someone shouted, pointing to an examining room. "She's a bad one."

Other "bad ones" were close behind.

GERRY ANDREOLI sat in the Fire Department ambulance parked on Avers Avenue for what seemed like a long time. At one moment he felt like he might lose consciousness. A classmate lying behind him was moaning in pain, and firemen were crowding other students into the vehicle. Gerry felt extremely hot, as if he were next to a campfire. He rested his head against a side window. Finally the driver hopped inside and took off for the hospital. Gerry looked out the window. Shocked faces stared back at him as the ambulance moved down the street.

Eight minutes later, when the ambulance pulled into the emergency entrance at St. Anne's, Gerry was able to walk into the hospital by himself.

"In there," somebody said, pointing Gerry into a small examining room off to his right. Inside another injured boy lay on a cot, his face and body swollen from burns.

A nurse stepped in. "What's your name?" she asked.

"Gerry Andreoli."

"How old are you?"

"Thirteen."

Quickly and methodically, the nurse looked Gerry over. He had burns over 36 percent of his body, more than half of which were third degree. His head was swollen and encrusted, and parts of his ears had been burned away. The nurse pointed to a chair, then barked a command. "Wait right here," she said.

Gerry obeyed, sitting down. It was the hardest thing to sit and wait. There was no place to lie down. People were running back and forth, hollering and shouting orders. He started to fall over when someone walked inside the room and helped him to a gurney in the hallway.

Gerry lay down on his back. Then he passed out.

IRENE MORDARSKI was lifted out of another ambulance, then carried inside the emergency room where she was placed on a gurney set just inside in the hallway. Inside the scene was one of hectic confusion. Nurses were running back and forth all around her. Someone kept saying, "What happened? What happened?"

"There was a fire at Queen of Angels," someone else answered.

Irene tried to correct them. "It's Our Lady of the Angels," she said, but apparently no one could hear her. Then a nurse ran up and asked Irene her name.

"Irene Mordarski," she answered.

"What?" said the nurse, unable to understand.

"Irene Mordarski," the girl repeated.

"Spell it."

"M-O-R-D-A-R-S-K-I."

Irene thought for a moment. She was speaking clearly. Why couldn't the nurse understand what she said? Had she looked in the mirror, she would have known why: her burned lips were swelled to five times their normal size.

The nurse was in a hurry. More kids were coming in. Quickly she scribbled something on paper, but what she wrote was incorrect.

Consequently Irene's name was misspelled on the hospital's admitting sheet. The error would cause anguish for Irene's parents, who had already begun searching for their two daughters. Little Monica was safe. But Stanley and Amalia Mordarski would end up traveling to three other hospitals and the county morgue before finally locating Irene at ten o'clock that night.

When Irene was wheeled into an examining room, her uniform was cut off and she was found to have third-degree burns on her legs, arms, and parts of her hands. First- and second-degree burns covered other parts of her body. She was sedated and her left hip was x-rayed. After being administered antibiotics and plasma, she was wheeled into surgery.

Irene looked up from the operating table. Someone was placing a cup over her face. She started feeling drowsy. She looked up again at the masked doctors bending over her on the operating table. She felt a jab from the metal pin being inserted into her left ankle. Then everything went dark. Anesthesia swam through her body. She was unconscious.

AS DOCTORS scrubbed down for the surgeries that would keep them busy through the evening, the hospital's tiny corridors soon became crowded. Nurses and nuns ran from room to room carrying blankets, sterile sheets, and medications. Still more congestion developed. The three slow hospital elevators, each able to hold only two gurneys at a time, delayed movement of the sickest children to the sixth-floor operating rooms. Incoming calls jammed the telephone lines, and new lines had to be hastily installed.

Then came the parents, arriving in droves, parking their cars in the street or in nearby parking lots. Others riding city buses jumped off at the nearest bus stops and ran the rest of the way to the emergency room. More than a hundred parents jammed the hospital's narrow corridors. They had rushed in from homes, shops, offices, and factories. The men wore work clothes, the women were pale and shaken. "Where are the lists? Where's my baby?" They peered at each passing gurney, hoping—yet fearing—that a burned face would be familiar.

Nine-year-old Linda Friedeck was brought to St. Anne's by her aunt after the woman located the girl in a home next to the school. Linda, a fourth-grader assigned to a first-floor classroom, escaped with her classmates relatively unscathed by the fire. But she was still frightened and darkened by smoke, and her aunt decided to take her to the hospital. After squeezing their way through the crowd of people outside the school, the pair walked south to Chicago Avenue, where they flagged down a milk truck whose driver picked them up and took them to St. Anne's. When they arrived at the hospital around six o'clock, the scene inside the emergency room was still chaotic.

Linda remembered walking inside the emergency room where parents literally attacked her. "I was grabbed from everywhere," she later recalled. "My aunt kept trying to cover me. The mothers, my God, they were screaming. 'Did you see my Mary? Did you see my Johnny? Did you see my Paul?' They were just hoping, just grabbing at something. They were asking my name and what grade I was in."

One nurse recalled: "A lot of these children were Italian, so it wasn't just the parents coming in but the whole family. It was hard to control. We had statues at the end of each corridor. They were kneeling at the statues and praying out loud, and some of them were hysterical. Of course they wanted to be with the children. They were very emotional. We had to refuse admittance to some of them, and they weren't happy about that. They went from being very sweet people to very mean, bitter, cantankerous."

Soon the parents began impeding the hospital's medical care, and a decision was made to huddle them into a large lounge located inside the hospital's nursing school. There sandwiches, hot coffee, and bulletins on the children awaited.

Sister Stephen Brugeman, a strict but compassionate nun who was director of the nursing school, had been supervising a group of student nurses who were about to walk through the hospital and sing Christmas carols when word of the disaster first reached her office. After running to the emergency room, she was directed to the nurses' lounge where the corralled parents waited nervously for word of their children. Finally someone brought Sister Stephen a clipboard with the names of the injured children who had been received at the hospital. "Please listen," she said, stepping onto a chair so that her voice could be heard above the anxious crowd.

Slowly and methodically the nun began reading names, confirming that those on the list had been received at the hospital. But the list did not provide condition reports, which served only to heighten the parents' tension and uncertainty. As more of them arrived, the noisy room grew substantially noisier. No longer could Sister Stephen be heard. She pointed to a man standing beside her. "Will you read these?" she asked.

The man stepped forward. He grabbed the list and started hollering out names. After the ninth name he stopped suddenly. "That's my daughter!" he cried. Another father took over the reading.

From time to time Sister Stephen was joined by other attendants who would come from the emergency room with more names. The amended lists contained additional information, including condition reports. The news was either good or bad: fair, serious, critical, dead.

One woman slid to the floor when the word came of her daughter's death. After another name, an anguished husband yelled at his wife: "Why didn't you keep her home today?"

As the hours passed, scores of worried parents continued to arrive at St. Anne's, and the streets outside stayed crowded with vehicles. Some parents showed up after searching other local hospitals and police stations. All screamed, sobbed, or otherwise whispered the same question: "Is my child here?"

Some were told yes, others were left to continue their search elsewhere. In the midst of the confusion, errors were made. One nun in the emergency room identified the body of a girl only to have the girl's mother telephone the hospital later in the evening to say that her daughter had arrived home safely. One family's joy turned to grief for another.

ALFRED AND MARY ANDREOLI arrived at St. Anne's after searching for their son along the crowded sidewalks outside the burning school. While still at the fire scene, the couple had spotted a parish priest standing outside the rectory. They asked if he had seen Gerry.

"Yes," the cleric answered. "Gerry's in the hospital, at St. Anne's. They weren't all hurt but they took them just the same."

Alfred Andreoli could sense that the priest was being only half honest, that he didn't wish to alarm them further by admitting that Gerry was badly injured. If Gerry was okay, they'd have found him outside the school looking for his brother and sister. He was that kind of kid.

As soon as they entered the hospital's main doors off Thomas Street, the Andreolis saw one of Gerry's classmates sitting in a wheelchair. The boy's clothes were smirched by smoke, his face smeared with grease. He looked in a daze. Alfred figured Gerry had to be there too, but in what condition he couldn't imagine. He took his wife's hand and walked to the reception desk in the lobby.

"Has Gerry Andreoli been brought in?" he asked.

"We don't know yet," the receptionist replied. "We don't have the lists yet. Why don't you sit down in the waiting room. Somebody will bring you some coffee."

Alfred thought it odd that they be asked to wait and then be served coffee on top of it. He could see other parents arriving. They must be expecting a siege. He still didn't know ambulances were streaming into the opposite end of the building, dropping children off in the emergency room.

More than an hour would pass before the Andreolis learned that Gerry was in the hospital, that he had been admitted in serious condition. Each time a nurse entered the room, Alfred would ask when they could see Gerry. "Just be patient," came the reply, "you can't see him yet." Finally, at nine o'clock that night, a nurse came to collect the couple and take them upstairs. "Mr. and Mrs. Andreoli, you can come up now."

Alfred and Mary followed the nurse to an elevator which transported them to the fourth-floor surgical recovery room, where twenty badly burned and injured children had been assigned. At the end of the corridor the nurse stopped and turned. "He's in here," she said, opening the door and showing the parents into their son's room.

When Alfred and Mary passed through the door and looked down at the stricken figure lying in the bed, they were shocked. Gerry looked like a monster. His head, face, and arms looked like one large scab. His blackened face was grotesquely swollen and parts of his ears were burned away. His eyes were almost swollen shut; his eyelids resembled two tiny slits cut into a piece of burlap.

Gerry was sedated, and his parents fought to control their emotions as they laid eyes on him for the first time. Alfred broke the silence. "How do you feel?" he asked his son.

Gerry answered wearily, trying to smile. "Okay, I guess. How's Randy and Barb?"

"They're all right," Mary said. Her two other children, thank God, had arrived home safely.

"Is Beverly okay?" Gerry asked.

"We don't know," Alfred hedged, not wanting to upset his son, "we're not sure what happened to her." Alfred knew his son was fond of the Burda girl, that they had gone dancing together at a school party. Beverly Burda, of course, was dead, one of only two fatalities to occur in Room 209.

During that difficult first visit to the hospital, Alfred and Mary Andreoli struggled to keep their composure as they chatted with their injured son. When at last they left the room to get a cup of coffee, they fell into each other's arms and wept. They were still red-eyed when they met with their family physician who had come to the hospital.

"What do you think?" Alfred inquired.

"I can't say right now," replied the doctor. "But he's in good hands."

At that point no one could foresee that Gerry Andreoli would remain in St. Anne's Hospital for the next four months and that he would undergo several painful skin-graft operations to repair his shattered body.

WHEN SISTER DAVIDIS accompanied Sister Helaine into the emergency room at St. Anne's, she was directed to sit in a corner of the busy room. She watched as doctors carted the critically burned Sister Helaine away to an examining room before taking her upstairs for surgery. Another doctor who had been attending to the arriving victims walked in and saw Sister Davidis sitting alone in the corner.

"Has anyone checked that one?" he asked, pointing to her.

"I'm all right," the nun replied. "I brought Sister Helaine in."

The doctor walked over and pinched Sister Davidis's wrist, taking her pulse. "Get a cart in here, fast," he shouted to an attendant.

After doctors administered a dosage of demoral to slow her rapidly beating heart, Sister Davidis was taken upstairs where she was admitted as an inpatient.

The nun thought all this attention was silly, for she felt fine. There was nothing wrong with her. She wanted to leave, sensing she was needed elsewhere. After about fifteen minutes of lying in bed, she called for the nurse. "I feel better now," she said. "I think I can go."

"No," countered the nurse. "The doctor wants to see you."

"I just saw a doctor."

"I'm sorry, sister, you're not to go."

The nurse began removing Sister Davidis's shoes.

"Shouldn't I undress myself?" the nun asked.

"No," replied the nurse. "We don't want you to move."

As Sister Davidis lay quietly in bed, her face blistering from the heat of the fire and her system fighting off shock, another, younger BVM nun entered the room.

"Sister," she wept, "we just lost Sister Therese."

"What do you mean 'We lost her?' " asked Sister Davidis, whose usually quick mind was unable to comprehend what the nun meant. "Why can't they find her?"

"She just died," said the nun. "She's dead!"

The news left Sister Davidis momentarily stunned. What in the world is happening? When a doctor entered the room a few minutes later, he examined Sister Davidis's burned left hand. It was covered with blisters, and portions of flesh were charred by third-degree burns.

"I don't think you're going to be able to use that hand for a while," he announced.

VICTIMS OF severe burns suffer a multitude of almost simultaneous afflictions. They are threatened with shock, infection, loss of vital body fluids, kidney malfunction, and heart failure. A single badly burned child becomes the subject of general concern and conversation in a hospital for weeks. But on the Monday night of the school fire, nineteen seriously burned children were admitted to St. Anne's, each requiring special care and observation.

Somehow the hospital to which five serious burns might be a disaster was now caring for four times that many. A laboratory that normally performed a hundred specialized blood-chemistry analyses in a month was running three hundred in three days. The medical staff banded together in teams to provide constant attention to the injured children, and nurses maintained their watchfulness around the clock.

Initially it was decided that the burned children would be treated with ointments, the traditional "closed method" of burn treatment. But soon doctors switched to the newer "open method," placing naked children between sterile sheets on special revolving bed frames known as "Strykers." It was also a waiting game. Medical science found itself taking a back seat to the slow process of nature. It would take time, but before long scabs would form where skin had been seared off the victims' bodies, providing a natural protective cover to keep out infectious germs. Only then could the painful ordeal of reconstruction begin.

SISTER ALMUNDA, the hospital's administrator, remained in the emergency room at St. Anne's for the rest of that Monday evening, leaving only once, when Archbishop Meyer arrived to visit the injured.

"Where are the children?" he asked the nun.

"Upstairs," she answered. "I'll take you myself."

Meyer was escorted into the surgical rooms, where doctors were busy repairing the damaged little bodies of the injured. He saw and heard everything—the crying, the screaming, the moaning. He went from bed to bed, from gurney to gurney, blessing each survivor. When he came back downstairs he appeared bewildered, and his hands were shaking. He looked at Sister Almunda. "Is that all?" he asked.

"No, not exactly," replied the nun. "We have bodies in the basement. I'm sure you don't want to see that room."

Meyer, however, insisted that he be taken down to view the dead. He was led into the basement x-ray room where twelve victims lay on the floor underneath sheets. After pulling back the sheets and viewing the remains, the archbishop nearly fainted.

IT HAD BEEN a long evening, but as the hours passed, order was eventually restored at St. Anne's. By nine o'clock the auditorium in the nursing school and the operating rooms upstairs were empty, with every child bedded down. The crisis, however, was far from over.

At 8:30 that evening Dr. Callahan convened a meeting of twenty-five weary doctors who had treated the injured. They gathered inside a lounge to make plans. Their basic problem was one of logistics: who was to treat the children and how? Their solution: temporarily suspend the private practice of medicine. Dr. Thomas

Moore, an internist, and Dr. Joseph Forbrich, a pediatrician, were appointed team leaders, and they enlisted the rest of the medical staff to carry out their orders. Doctors were assigned in groups of three, and each group was to be on duty for three to four hours, making continual rounds, checking the condition of each child, administering medications as needed.

By week's end eleven patients remained on the critical list at St. Anne's. Three of them died before the end of December. A fourth child finally succumbed to injuries the following March.

THE PANDEMONIUM at St. Anne's was repeated at the seven other West Side hospitals that received victims from the school fire. They included Franklin Boulevard (twenty-six admitted, three DOA), Walther Memorial (fourteen admitted, two DOA), Garfield Park (twelve admitted), Norwegian American (four admitted), St. Mary's (one DOA), Cook County (seven DOA), and the University of Illinois (one DOA). Because of its proximity to the school, almost twice as many children were admitted to St. Anne's as at the other hospitals combined, and it was within its walls where most of the drama had unfolded.

As the evening waned, many parents still had failed to locate their children. For them a trip home would be useless; their homes were empty, their children "unaccounted." For these parents there remained one final and dreaded destination. As hope began to fade, they drove sick with fear to the drab yellow building on West Polk Street, the Cook County Morgue. Here the grimmest of all scenes took place.

Adults began trickling into the morgue around 6 p.m. At first the scene was a mix of crying and whimpering. Agonized with uncertainty, the families could find comfort nowhere. In a desperate attempt to be told the inevitable, they pushed and shoved their way in a line, waiting to check in with expressionless attendants seated behind tables and desks.

Early on officials at the morgue decided to wait until all the dead had arrived before allowing anyone downstairs to begin identifying the bodies. During this period the families were seated in four large inquest rooms, then called up one by one and asked to provide the physical information that would help officials make a positive identification.

Meanwhile, downstairs a procession of black police squadrols containing the dead was backing into the basement parking garage. The officers driving the vehicles thought of their own children, silently wondering if the badly burned bodies would ever be identified. But experience had taught them otherwise, that through medical science, dental records, and what little clothing remained there were sufficient clues to provide answers, even where fire had turned skin to ash.

More than twenty priests from around the city as well as dozens of nurses and doctors from the giant grey monolith of Cook County Hospital across the street had been called to the morgue to help process the dead or comfort grieving relatives. Reporters with television and still cameras showed up to capture the pathetic scene on film. For the families, the terror was made worse by the waiting. Dressed in their work clothes, overcoats, and hats, they sat stoically, their faces stained by tears. Others wandered about the room dazed, gulping cups of coffee, chain-smoking cigarettes, staring out from behind sullen, blank eyes at the now unfamiliar world.

As the waiting continued, one group of parents gathered in a corner to recite the Rosary. There wasn't enough space for all to kneel, so most stood as the Reverend Alfred Abramowicz of the archdiocesan chancery office led the prayers. "As we say this last decade," Abramowicz prayed, "let us ask our Blessed Virgin Mary for holy recognition, realizing that she too lost her only son on the Cross." When he finished, the priest raised a wooden crucifix and gave his blessing to all those assembled. Some parents broke down when he approached them. A few looked on bravely, still hoping that somehow, somewhere, their child would turn up safe.

But downstairs, spread out in long rows on the cold concrete floor, were ninety stretchers, each covered by a white sheet, each containing the body of a child or a nun. They were nameless numbers waiting to be claimed.

MONSIGNOR ED PELLICORE was one of the first priests to arrive at the morgue, and he went straight to the basement. The large room resembled a crude dungeon. Bare lightbulbs hanging from the ceiling cast a yellow pall, and a cold, icy draft swirled about the interior, spreading the stench of death into every corner. Pellicore walked along the line of sheet-draped bodies, his footsteps echoing off the white concrete walls.

Slowly and hesitantly, the monsignor bent over to pull back a few of the sheets, looking to see if he could recognize the children who lay beneath. As soon as he did, he balked, and a sick feeling rose from the pit of his stomach. Pellicore had been a priest for many years, and he knew the look of death; it was never pretty. In this case it was awful. Some of the children, he could see, had died from smoke inhalation. Others were badly burned, some beyond recognition. Their bodies had no names, only yellow tags indicating whether the deceased was a "Boy" or a "Girl." Regardless of their condition, he recognized none of them.

When Pellicore looked up he noticed, for the first time, Cook County Coroner Walter McCarron, whose responsibility it was to identify each of the victims. At that moment McCarron was standing nervously in a corner, mumbling orders to one of his deputies. The coroner was dressed in a grey suit, and his bespectacled, bulldog face was balanced atop one of his familiar bow ties. He looked pale and shaken. If someone walked up and handed McCarron a bottle of whiskey, Pellicore thought, he'd surely drink it right there.

Even though Pellicore wasn't wearing a priest's collar, McCarron recognized him. The two men approached each other. "We've prepared for a hundred bodies," the coroner warned. "We're just about ready to let them downstairs."

Pellicore thought for a moment. It was unwise; he didn't like the idea. He knew these Italian families. To let them down all at once would cause a riot.

Instead he offered a suggestion. "You don't want these parents coming down here to look at each body just to find one child," he said to the coroner. "Why don't we get some articles of clothing—a belt buckle, a wristwatch or a ring or whatever we can find, and then tell the people upstairs what we have. If we find one of the kids wearing a Mickey Mouse watch, then somebody upstairs should be able to identify the child without having to look at all the bodies."

McCarron agreed with the proposal. "Okay," he said. "Whatever you say."

McCarron was an elected county official, a wealthy trucking executive from Oak Park who had a reputation as a handshaker. Although he was well schooled in the art of politics, he had no background for the coroner's position, no training as a medical examiner. Other than viewing homicide victims on an individual basis during his one term in office, he was totally unprepared for the task at hand.

While priests and nurses comforted the growing crowd of parents and relatives, Pellicore took over downstairs, helping in the identification of bodies. Gradually a semblance of order began to emerge from the turbulent scene. Bodies that were recognizable were laid in one row. Those who appeared beyond recognition were placed in another. Sheets were pulled back, and pieces of jewelry and clothing were removed from each of the deceased, then given a corresponding number. Attendants began going from body to body, scribbling down notes: "Boy. Approximate age ten. Black hair. Brown loafers. Brown corduroy pants. White T-shirt. St. Christopher's medal (silver)."

The notes and items were then taken upstairs and shown to the parents, beginning the gruesome process of identification.

FATHER JOSEPH OGNIBENE was among the priests who had hurried to the morgue, and when he arrived there early that evening he was near collapse. Our Lady of the Angels had been his first parish assignment following his ordination in 1952. It was also his first love. As he approached the morgue he tried thinking of happier times, but his memories were clouded by awful visions of that afternoon. It would get worse, for he was about to enter a world that would leave him with even greater nightmares.

When Ognibene entered the building, a policeman standing guard by the basement doorway nodded him through. Once downstairs he joined the other officials gathered inside the big room. On hand were several priests and nuns along with a handful of doctors, nurses, and morgue attendants. Uniformed police and plainclothes detectives stood off to the side, pens and notebooks in hand. The stench of death was everywhere. Ognibene reported to Monsignor Pellicore, who was busy issuing orders.

"Joe," the monsignor pointed, "go see if you can make out any of the kids before we start bringing the parents down."

It was a natural assignment, for Ognibene knew many of the students. Slowly, numbed with grief, he and two nuns from the parish, Sister Andrienne one of them, went from body to body, pulling back sheets, trying to recognize the tiny forms that lay beneath—boys and girls who only yesterday they had winked at or smiled to in church. It was a long, painstaking process, and in the end, after viewing all the remains, the trio could identify only ten of the victims.

Reporting his findings to Pellicore, Ognibene took a moment to collect himself. He was still trying to catch up with events. Everything had happened so fast—it was unbelievable, simply unbelievable. He looked back at the rows of white sheets covering the floor. He had never envisioned anything so horrible in his life. How could God let such a thing happen to little innocents like this?

His thoughts were interrupted when a tall, sandy-haired nurse noticed him rubbing his left arm. "What's wrong?" she inquired.

Ognibene rolled up his sleeve to reveal a bloodied patchwork of blisters and burns running up his arm.

"Those need to be seen," said the nurse.

The priest was walked across the street to Cook County Hospital where for the next hour a doctor in the emergency room tended to his wounds. Afterward Ognibene returned to the morgue, his arm bandaged. He remained there until well after midnight. Before leaving, he was finally tracked down by his brother, Sam, another archdiocesan priest assigned to the nearby Our Lady of Mercy Mission. Sam Ognibene was unusually excited. "Joe!" he yelled. "Call Mom! She thinks you're dead!"

Father Joe was confused. "What?" he said.

"It was on the news! The news showed your name on the casualty list as being dead. Go call Ma right now and tell her you're all right."

Joe Ognibene hurried to a pay phone to call his mother.

"Mom! It's me, Joe. I'm okay."

INSIDE THE morgue's inquest rooms, where death was the normal business of the day, the precise, orderly system fell apart. Overwhelmed by heartbreak and exhaustion, nurses and nuns who tried to console grieving parents broke down themselves. Newsmen wiped their eyes before snapping photographs. Tough, hardened, policemen wept like babies.

Soon the last of the dead had arrived, and with them the time to escort families downstairs. Where possible, officials decided to allow only men downstairs. They sought out fathers, grandfathers, uncles, brothers, cousins, and in-laws. Many were hardworking people who had witnessed the brutalities of World War II. Nothing would have prepared them for what they were about to encounter.

First the tormented relatives were led into an anteroom where they were asked to identify a piece of underwear, a necklace, a wristwatch or ring. Then they were walked into the large holding room and escorted along the rows of white sheets. When they reached a number that was thought to be their child, a sheet was pulled back to reveal a body. Screams of anguish confirmed the findings.

After locating his son among the dead, one father, dressed in blue work clothes, had to be brought out of the room while supported by two larger men who sobbed loudly. Another father was carried out by a policeman and a priest. Still another emerged bravely from the basement, simply nodding his head to a group of relatives huddled in a corner. He walked over to a table, removed his hat, then confirmed for a morgue attendant the positive identification. The clerk made an entry into a ledger, and another number had turned into a child. One by one, as the hours passed, they would all be identified and given a name to be buried by.

Lloyd Chambers identified the body of his nine-year-old daughter, Margaret, after calling his wife at home to see if the girl had worn a red ruby ring on her finger that day. She had.

Eighth-grader Lawrence Grasso was another child whose body was identified by the ring he had worn to school that day. He received it over Thanksgiving and had just become a member of the American Legion Alamo Post Drum and Bugle Corps.

Fourteen-year-old Mary Virgilio was adopted by her aunt and uncle and had come to Chicago as a World War II orphan. She was identified by the gold chain and crucifix around her neck.

Joseph Modica, aged nine, had escaped the school but ran back inside in search of his younger sister. He didn't know that she had been safely evacuated. An I.D. bracelet made of sterling silver was found on his right wrist.

Sister Mary Seraphica Kelley was identified by a curl of red hair from one of her students, Kathleen Carr, who had been found lying on the nun when the two were discovered buried together inside the ruins of Room 210.

Sister Mary St. Canice Lyng was wearing a religious medal she had been given the night before by Sister Andrienne.

ONE OF THE bitter ironies of the Our Lady of the Angels tragedy involved Captain Tony Pilas of the Fire Prevention Bureau. His only daughter, Nancy, was a student in Room 211.

Pilas had joined the Chicago Fire Department in 1937 and had served with engine, truck, and squad companies before being promoted to superintendent of field inspectors for the bureau in 1957. He was forty-four, a short, soft-spoken man of Italian descent. He and his wife, Ann, lived just two blocks from Our Lady of the Angels Church, where they were active parishioners. Pilas visited the school often, not in an official capacity but as an interested parent.

On the afternoon of the fire he felt uneasy and vaguely ill as he sat at his desk in Fire Department headquarters in City Hall.

"I've got a bum stomach," he finally told another officer. "I'm going home early."

Pilas checked out of the office shortly after 2 p.m., got in his car, and headed west on Chicago Avenue. As he approached Hamlin Avenue, he saw Engine 85 racing across the intersection. He decided to follow, turning north on Hamlin. Almost instantly he saw smoke issuing from the school. His progress was slowed by other vehicles and by people running across the street, but he managed to find a parking space north of the parish church. He jumped out of his car and ran back to the school.

Pilas first tried to gain access to the building at the back door on the alley side of the school. When he saw flames roaring up the stairwell, he ran around to the front doors on Avers and tried to climb the stairs there, but dense smoke and heat forced him back outside. He returned to the alley side, where he broke the fall of a youngster who tumbled out one of the second-floor windows.

Tears were streaming down his face when he ran back around to the courtway separating the two wings. By then Sister Helaine, his daughter's teacher, had been brought down a ladder from Room 211. She was lying against the side of the building, critically burned. Pilas crouched down next to her. "Sister," he shouted. "This is Mr. Pilas. Where's Nancy?"

"Oh, God bless Nancy," the nun moaned incoherently. "God bless Nancy and all the kids."

Tony Pilas knew then that his daughter was still inside the room.

Later that night his brother-in-law identified Nancy's body at the morgue. Pilas's wife had told him how Nancy always laced her shoes backward, tying the bow at the toe end. That's how the girl was identified; her shoelaces were tied backward.

ACROSS THE STREET from the morgue, inside his room in Cook County Hospital, Stanley Burda had drifted into a false sleep.

The thirty-seven-year-old army combat veteran recently had experienced a string of bad luck. Only days before he had been laid off from his job as a milkman with the Bowman Dairy. He was worried about paying his mortgage and supporting his wife and four children.

Compounding Burda's plight, on the day after Thanksgiving, while he was chopping wood in his basement, a piece of metal from the axe or a nail flew up and buried itself in his left eye. He had been taken to County, a public hospital caring mostly for the indigent, where doctors that Monday had operated to remove the metal chip from his eye.

As he lay in the hospital bed after surgery, Burda asked himself what else could go wrong. Not long after, a priest entered the room to inform him that his eldest child, thirteen-year-old Beverly Anne, had been killed in the fire.

After struggling with the news, Burda regained control. He thought of his wife and asked his doctors if he could go home. "I have to be with my wife," he told them. Reluctantly the doctors granted permission. But before he was allowed to leave, Burda was given a strange pair of eyeglasses fitted with pinhole openings and a special shield for the left eye. He was sent home but was advised not to cry.

"If you cry," his doctor warned, "the salt from your tears might scald your eye. If that happens, it could blind you."

On his way out the door, Burda said simply, "God's will be done."

MARY MALINSKI, sitting in her apartment on Lawndale Avenue, was beside herself with fear. Linda had failed to show up. But, thank God, Gerry, her son, had escaped the school unharmed. When Nick Malinski arrived home from his job at a manufacturing company in the suburbs, the couple began their frantic search. First they went to the parish rectory where the names of children who had been taken to various hospitals were being recorded in a ledger. Then they traveled to three hospitals. Still no word. Finally Nick Malinski said to his wife, "I'm going to the morgue."

After dropping Mary off at home, Nick, with his brother-in-law, drove east to the county morgue. When the pair arrived they checked in with an attendant. "I've been everywhere," Nick said. "I can't find my daughter. She has blond hair."

"What's her name?" the attendant asked.

"Linda Malinski," Nick said, nearly choking on his words.

The attendant picked up a telephone. "One moment," she said.

A few minutes later a nurse appeared. "Mr. Malinski?"

"Yes," Nick answered.

"This way, please."

Nick and his brother-in-law followed the nurse downstairs, where they found Linda in a row of bodies. The girl's features had been blackened by smoke, but she was not burned. She had suffocated to death. Nick walked upstairs to use the telephone. Mary was waiting to hear from him.

OSCAR AND CATHERINE SARNO were anxious. Two of their children, nine-year-old Joanne, a fourth-grader assigned to Room 210, and thirteen-year-old Billy, an eighth-grader in Room 211, were still missing. Ronnie, their ten-year-old, had escaped with only a burned leg. He too was assigned to Room 210 and had escaped the burning school by jumping out the window.

Earlier that day, when fierce heat and smoke forced the fourth-graders from their seats, Ronnie was not more than an arm's reach from his sister. "C'mon, Jo," he had yelled to her. "I'm jumping!"

As he went over the windowsill, he could hear Joanne screaming. "Ronnie! Don't jump!"

Incredibly, Ronnie Sarno had not been injured in his fall. He landed on his feet and flopped over onto his back, then got up and brushed himself off. He was taken home, coatless and shaken, by a friend of the family. When Catherine Sarno rushed home to their apartment on Chicago Avenue around four o'clock, Ronnie was on the couch. "Mom" he said, "my leg hurts a little."

Catherine drove Ronnie to Garfield Park Hospital where he was treated and released for a small burn. When she returned home she found her truck-driver husband, Oscar, pacing the living room next to a pile of freshly wrapped Christmas presents. "I went to the school," he said nervously. "I can't find Billy and Joanne."

The Sarnos had followed the advice of police who told them to wait at home for a telephone call. Later in the evening, when the telephone inside the tiny apartment did ring, it brought crushing grief. Billy and Joanne Sarno had been positively identified by another relative as being among the sheet-covered bodies lying in the county morgue.

AS NIGHT TURNED to early morning, a steady stream of hearses began pulling up to the back door of the morgue to pick up the dead and transfer them to local funeral homes. By 4 a.m. the bodies of eighty-three children—ranging in age from eight to fourteen—had been claimed by grieving families. The three nuns killed had also been identified and removed to a funeral home. The fire-ravaged bodies of four more children would remain unidentified for two more days.

In the confusion of the evening, at least one mix-up occurred at the morgue, which resulted in two families claiming the wrong child. One, a Polish couple whose daughter had been killed, learned that the body they had claimed turned out to be a boy. Although the boy's body was burned beyond recognition, the genitals were found to be partially intact, enabling funeral directors to determine gender. As the mistake became apparent, rather than call each of the bodies back to the morgue, the parents agreed to accept the boy's body and bury it as their own. Officials never learned which family had claimed the other misidentified body.

SHORTLY BEFORE midnight, as parents still agonized at the morgue, Hook and Ladder 35 was ordered to pick up from the school and return to its quarters. After the truck had been backed into the firehouse, Lieutenant Charles Kamin headed upstairs for a shower to wash the grime from his body and mull over his earlier decisions. His right arm was sore from burns, and the muscles in his upper body ached.

As the shower soothed his body and eased his mind, Kamin thought about the locked gate that had barred entrance into the school courtway. It left him frustrated. Surely, he pondered, they could've gotten more out if that damn thing had been unlocked. Why did churches and schools always lock their gates? They must have spent a whole minute trying to knock that thing down. How many lives had it cost? Had he known sooner that the gate was locked, he would have ordered his driver to ram it with the truck. So they wreck the truck and save the lives of three, maybe four more kids. Hell, the truck isn't worth anything compared to kids' lives.

Kamin had seen his share of death at fires. But this was beyond belief. Before picking up from the school, he had heard someone say the students died because they panicked. For chrissakes, he thought. Adults would panic too. That fire was hot. Super hot. And it was bearing down on them fast. What the hell do they expect people to do? They were fighting for survival. They wanted to live.

After his shower, Kamin changed into a clean shirt and trousers and walked downstairs to write his report. The firehouse was quiet. The men were sitting in the kitchen, drinking coffee, watching the news. No one could sleep. And no one was talking.

As he picked up his pen to write, Kamin could feel the pain shooting up his right hand and wrist. As he neared the bottom of his report, he entered the following: "There were approximately sixty-three children rescued by this company, some with the help of civilians and other firemen, some individually."

He did not specifically mention the eight children he had pulled from Room 211.

LATER MONDAY NIGHT, church bells across Chicago tolled in mourning for the school fire dead. Most of the grief, however, was concentrated inside modest frame and brick houses and apartment buildings in Our Lady of the Angels parish.

Inside the stricken neighborhood's little bungalows and two-flats, lights burned through the night as families and friends gathered to comfort the bereaved. Relatives of the dead arrived home carrying small coats and jackets they had taken with them to hospitals and the morgue.

In some of the homes, many still held out hope, waiting for the telephone to ring, praying it would bring news of a located child. Instead, when the phones did ring, it was usually relatives calling to offer condolences or ask for the latest information. Reporters assigned to the awful but necessary task of obtaining photographs of the victims for the next day's newspapers traversed the neighborhood, ringing doorbells, hoping their requests wouldn't be viewed as cruel or insensitive. Most families cooperated, providing portraits of their children's first Holy Communion or latest school pictures taken that fall.

Meanwhile, despite a darkened interior that resulted from power lines being knocked down during the height of the fire, an endless procession of faithful continued to stream through Our Lady of the Angels Church. The worshipers, many sobbing, included the grief-stricken families of the dead as well as their friends, neighbors, and classmates. At the front of the church, beside the altar, was a small vigil of lights—candles set in red and blue cups, each lit with a prayer for a dead child.

Across the street from the church, in the convent, the aggrieved sisters of the parish were trying to comprehend what had happened. Among them was Sister St. Florence, the principal, who kept reliving what she had seen. "I don't think I'll ever lose the picture of those children who jumped out the windows," she later told another nun who arrived by train from the order's motherhouse in Iowa, to be with the anguished sisters in Chicago.

Inside the rectory, priests were trying to persuade Monsignor Cussen to rest. The events of the day had proven too much. The pastor was distraught, his normally cool demeanor unmasked. "I heard nothing," he kept mumbling. "I didn't feel any explosion. I just heard a couple of boys yelling, 'Fire. Fire.' Then I saw everything."

One of the priests produced a bottle of whiskey and Cussen was handed a drink. The men were concerned about the pastor. They were determined to get him to bed—one way or the other. "Here," they said, refilling his glass, "have another one. . . . And another. . . . And another."

Finally, after four or five drinks, the pastor fell asleep.

AS WIND SWIRLED the stench of burnt wood and death, crowds of curious continued to file past the ruined school, hoping to get a glimpse of its charred shell. Fire Department light trucks illuminated the eerie scene, showing in the half-light the broken windows and partially damaged wall on the north side of the school. Sidewalks were cordoned off, and police stood guard at each door. Inside, arson investigators carrying large portable lanterns crept through the darkened corridors and up and down water-drenched stairways, sifting through the debris, looking carefully for clues they hoped would lead them to the fire's cause.

For the small, closely knit community, the events of that afternoon seemed almost apocalyptic. Nothing would ever be the same. In a moment nearly one hundred neighborhood schoolchildren had disappeared. And for those who survived, the innocence of childhood was forever lost.

The chief question being asked now was, How did it happen?

Seven

REMORSE

O N TUESDAY, December 2, 1958, Chicago awoke in grief. Banner headlines brought home the news to a shocked city, and under Mayor Daley's orders, flags on all public buildings were lowered to half-staff.

The fire's toll was appalling. Eighty-seven children and three of their nuns were dead; ninety other students and three more nuns were injured, some with fractured skulls, broken bones, smoke-damaged lungs, and terrible burns. It was the worst fire to hit Chicago in fifty-five years. Not since the Iroquois Theater fire of 1903, in which 602 were killed, had so many lost their lives in a single blaze.

Throughout the city's stricken West Side, a nightmare was continuing for many families. Funeral directors received weeping parents and prepared for scores of wakes and funerals. But with the grief, questions began to arise: How did the fire start? How did it spread so quickly? Why did it go unnoticed for so long? And why did so many die? As investigators sifted the ruins and pieced together conflicting reports, disturbing facts began to emerge.

Our Lady of the Angels School, like many schools of its day, had no sprinkler system or smoke detectors, and its fire alarm rang only inside the building; it did not transmit a signal to the Fire Department. The school's second-floor staircases were open, without fire doors, and the building had just one fire escape. Window ledges were thirty-seven and a half inches off the floor—too high, it was determined, for many of the younger children to climb over. Consequently quite a few of the dead were found stacked beneath the windowsills. Finally, with an enrollment of approximately fourteen hundred students in the main building, the school was considered to be overcrowded.

Just a day after the disaster, some officials, notably Captain Henry Penzin, commander of the Austin Police District, blamed the fire's rapid advance on "sloppy housekeeping" after police bomb and arson detectives discovered a five-gallon can of paint thinner in the basement boiler room. The charges of negligence gained support when investigators found piles of clothing, old newspapers, exam papers, cardboard boxes, boxes of paper, and other debris in the basement. The clothing, it was later learned, had been collected during the parish's annual clothing drive, which had begun the week before.

Still, the school had passed its most recent fire inspection in October. Although Chicago's 1949 municipal code required that all schools built after its passage be constructed of noncombustible materials and equipped with fire-protection devices such as sprinkler systems, fire doors, and fully enclosed stairways, structures already in existence were governed by a 1905 ordinance that mandated none of those modern safety requirements.

After the fire was extinguished, pumps were brought in to siphon water from the basement of the school, and within the next forty-eight hours—after debris had been screened and carefully examined—evidence remained to pinpoint the exact spot where the fire had started.

At the bottom of the isolated, seldom-used northeast stairwell, on the checkered, asphalt-tile floor, investigators found a grey metal rim buried beneath a layer of ash and sediment. The rim still encompassed a few inches of charred fiber edging from the base of a trash container to which it had been attached. When the floor was scrubbed down, a circular mark defined where the container had stood. Portions of the nine-inch square tiles directly beneath the barrel were virtually unmarred.

A section of baseboard molding one foot away from the container showed signs that the fire had burned there for a long time. The molding had been thinned out by severe charring. It was a telltale discovery. The deeply charred V-mark in the molding pointed to the base of the fire, where flames had been most intense at its start.

Because of the chimney effect of the fire coming up from the basement and the burn patterns on the walls, investigators were sure this was the point of origin. Next they turned to the more grievous question of the fire's cause.

Initially it was thought the boilers in the coal-burning furnace may have exploded, but a check showed that the heating system had been working properly. Faulty electrical wiring was also ruled out as a possible cause. And no evidence suggested that the fire was fed by an accelerant.

Investigators were checking out stories of furtive student smoking in the basement, but so far no solid evidence pointed to a discarded cigarette as a possible cause. The only other possibility for investigators to consider was that the fire had been set—either accidentally or intentionally—by an unknown person.

Although they lacked this crucial piece of the puzzle, officials reconstructed the fire's rapid progression. Sometime after 2 p.m. the blaze started in the ringed, thirty-gallon cardboard trash drum located at the bottom of the northeast stairwell. After consuming refuse in the container, the fire smoldered undetected, elevating temperatures in the confined, L-shaped stairwell space, where the lower parts of three walls were covered with heat-reflecting sheet metal.

When intense heat shattered a window at the bottom of the stairwell, a fresh supply of oxygen was sucked into the area, causing the smoldering fire in the waste drum to flash up. Flames quickly spread to the unprotected wooden and asphalt-tiled staircase, feeding off the varnished woodwork and walls covered with fourteen layers of paint—the top two layers composed of an extremely flammable rubberized-plastic paint that produced heavy black smoke.

Because the building was without a sprinkler system, the stairwell quickly turned into a chimney. Flames, smoke, and gases billowed up the stairway from the basement. A closed fire door on the first floor stopped the blaze from entering the first-floor corridor, and it continued unchecked up the stairway and swept into the eighty-five-foot-long corridor leading to the second-floor classrooms. Inside the corridor, the flames fed on combustible wooden flooring, walls, and trim, as well as the ceiling, filling the corridor with deadly columns of penetrating black smoke. Within a few minutes the small fire had grown into a raging inferno, exceeding temperatures of fourteen hundred degrees Fahrenheit.

While the fire made its way up the stairwell, hot air and gases in the basement had entered an open shaft from a disconnected drinking fountain in the basement wall and flowed two stories upward inside the wall. This hot air fanned out into the narrow cockloft above the second-floor ceiling, sparking serious secondary burning in this hidden area directly above the six north-wing classrooms packed with 329 students and six teachers. Those flames eventually dropped into the second-floor corridor from two ventilator grilles in the ceiling, further trapping the occupants from escaping into the hallway.

Some survivors reported that after classroom doors had been opened and quickly closed, they heard a loud whoosh, thought to have come from an explosion that accompanied the ignition of volatile fire gases that had built up in the corridor. When intense heat from the fire began breaking the large glass transoms over classroom doors, smoke and flames entered the rooms, spread across flammable ceiling tile, and forced the occupants to the windows.

This was the situation inside the north wing when the first fire company, Engine 85, pulled up at 2:44 p.m. As firefighters concentrated on rescue, the blaze on the upper story of the north wing grew steadily worse and eventually burned off one-third of the roof before being brought under control. Desperate as the situation was, in the decisive early moments of their arrival firefighters still managed to save 160 children, pulling them out of windows, passing them down ladders, catching them in life nets, or otherwise breaking their falls before they hit the ground.

One crucial and confusing circumstance for investigators was that the fire had burned undetected for so long—at least twenty minutes. The north side of the school had been heating like an oven, with fire spreading inside the stairwell, walls, and cockloft, yet no one realized the building was ablaze until it was too late.

FOR FIRE COMMISSIONER QUINN, the night had been long and exhausting. In all his years as a firefighter he had never encountered anything so terrible, and he was feeling uneasy. Already rumors were circulating that the Fire Department was guilty of slow response, that ladders were too short to reach the school's high, second-floor windows. It was not true, and Quinn knew he would have to set the record straight. If there was a delayed response, it surely wasn't the Fire Department's fault. If firefighters had been called sooner, the kids could have been saved.

Still, this was all theory, and before he met with the army of reporters bivouacked inside the City Hall press room, Quinn needed facts. Because he had not arrived at the school until after three o'clock, he ordered all firefighters on the still-alarm companies to report to his office first thing Tuesday morning to give depositions describing their actions upon pulling up to the scene.

For Quinn, the Fire Department was his life. He took pride in knowing that Chicago had one of the finest firefighting forces in the world, and he worked hard at keeping the department on the cutting edge of the profession. True, firefighters had saved 160 children at the school under hazardous conditions, yet in light of 90 deaths the number of rescues was little comfort. The fact that such an enormous tragedy could occur in Chicago and under his command was a hard pill to swallow.

As the weary, grim-faced firemen began trickling into his office shortly before nine o'clock, their minds still haunted by the sights and sounds of the day before, Quinn received them with little more than a grunt. He was visibly upset, his face as cold as stone. The men knew they were in for a grilling.

Being in charge of the first fire companies to reach the school, Lieutenants Stanley Wojnicki and Charles Kamin were shown in first. On hand inside the office were Quinn's top deputies, including Chief Fire Marshal Raymond Daley, in charge of the uniformed force, who had also been at the school.

Once all were in place, Quinn, sitting behind his desk, set down his glasses and rubbed his bloodshot eyes. "There's going to be a million reporters in here," he said gravely. "I don't want any bullshit. I want answers. That's why you're down here."

Kamin was asked to speak first. The thirty-six-year-old veteran related how he had immediately ordered his men to tear down the iron fence and begin rescue operations inside the courtway and on the alley side of the building. He also described the tense scene he had encountered while working atop the ladder at Room 211. "I reached in and pulled them out," he said. "I didn't have time to worry about the ones I dropped. Then it flashed. It was over real quick."

When Kamin finished, Wojnicki began his deposition. The lieutenant of Engine 85 was exhausted, still numbed by the agony and death he had witnessed the day before. Like most of the others he had been up all night and had not slept a wink. All night long he kept asking himself the same question: Did I do enough? Did I do enough?

Wojnicki was an unsophisticated but sensitive man, and his emotions were torn. He kept turning over in his mind the awful dilemma he had faced upon pulling up to the school. He knew if he had tried to save a few of those kids himself—raised a ladder and went up and started yanking pupils off the windowsills—and then waited for another engine company to come in and start water, he would have been hanged. His job was to get water on the fire as fast as possible. That's what he did.

Struggling to keep his composure, Wojnicki described how, after being directed to the correct location of the fire and positioning the engine on Avers Avenue, he stretched a hose line into the alley and began attacking the flames in the rear stairwell.

"You saw fire in the stairwell?" Quinn asked.

"Yes," Wojnicki answered. "It was roaring. It was going straight up. I figured it had to be the seat of the fire."

Quinn: "Did you try to get any of these kids out?"

"Not at that time. We were too busy with the line."

Quinn: "What do you mean you were 'too busy with the line'? You're saying you pull up and you've got kids hanging out of the goddam windows, and you didn't try to get kids out? You dumb sonovabitch! What the hell's the matter with you?"

Wojnicki was stunned. He had always respected Quinn, but at the same time the commissioner intimidated him. Still, he held his ground. "I knew I had the truck coming in behind me," he said. "We tried making those stairs, to get up inside there. There was just too much fire for us to get in."

Another deputy spoke up. "Lieutenant," he said, "you say you attacked the fire in the stairwell, that the flames were going up the stairs. Do you suppose you assisted in pushing the flames up the stairwell by directing your hose line in there?"

"No," Wojnicki answered. Suddenly he was feeling nervous. Where were they going with this line of questions? In appeal, he looked over to Chief Daley, a bulldog but a respected member of the department. "I think we saved a lot of kids by knocking down that fire in the stairway," Wojnicki pleaded. "I know we did. I don't know what else I could have done."

Daley could see that Quinn was upset. They were all upset. They weren't in the habit of losing ninety people in a school fire. As he listened to the facts, Daley concluded that Wojnicki had fulfilled his responsibilities as officer of the first engine company on the scene. He came to the lieutenant's defense. "Considering the circumstances," he said, "I don't know how the hell you did what you did do."

Daley gazed over to Quinn, trying to diffuse the tension. "That was his job," he said. "He did his job. For chrissakes, those people were grabbin' at him. What more do you want?"

Quinn, still angry, relented a bit. "All right," he said, rubbing his eyes. "Is there anything more?"

"After the fire was knocked down a little," Wojnicki continued, "we were ordered to put our line in the snorkel, then help remove bodies. We picked up about ten o'clock."

After listening to the lieutenants' stories, Chief Devine of the 18th Battalion gave his own account, explaining in his Irish brogue how he had deployed the first-arriving still- and box-alarm companies, then telling how he radioed for the 5-11 alarm when the roof went in. "We tried," he said, "God how we tried. But we couldn't move fast enough. No one could live in that fire. I saw four of them leaning over a windowsill, crying. We tried to reach them. Then suddenly they slumped, doubled over the sill. They were dead when we got to them."

After the remaining interviews were completed, Quinn walked over to meet Mayor Daley for a City Hall press conference. As he headed for the mayor's office, he felt for his men. They tried. They did their best. As fire commissioner, what more could he ask?

When the press conference started, Quinn described for reporters what actions the department had taken at the school, promising that additional facts would be forthcoming during the coroner's inquest scheduled to begin the following week. Still, Quinn wasted no time in blaming the high loss of life on the delayed alarm to the Fire Department. "That school was as safe as any in Chicago," he declared. "It had a fire escape and six exits. But the kids on the second floor couldn't reach them because of the smoke."

Nor, he noted, could they reach the school's fire-alarm pull stations, which resembled light switches and were located six feet off the floor.

The adequacy of exits at the school also was at issue. Exit adequacy—as determined by proper enclosure, provision of at least two ways out remote from each other, and sufficient exit capacity for all occupants to leave the building promptly—was an established principle in building construction and fire safety long before Our Lady of the Angels. Yet the school did not meet these safety standards. When asked by reporters why he thought the building had sufficient exits after almost one hundred children didn't get out, Quinn responded that the number of exits was "all that was required under the law."

Despite Fire Department records showing that Our Lady of the Angels School could be evacuated in three and a half minutes, the commissioner pointed out that the trouble began after students tried to enter the hallways but were forced back into their classrooms by intense heat and smoke.

"The layman doesn't seem to understand that once a fire gets going, it goes faster than you can run," he said. "All you need is one inhalation of superheated air and your lungs collapse and your life is snuffed out. If we had been called three minutes earlier, we could've gotten all those kids out."

Quinn did admit, however, that part of the blame could be placed on the city's 1949 municipal code, which contained no "grandfather clause" requiring the installation of sprinkler systems and fire doors in existing buildings such as Our Lady of the Angels School. He said he planned to push for a city ordinance mandating sprinkler systems and fire alarm boxes for all public buildings.

When Quinn finished, a grim Mayor Daley announced that he had ordered "full and complete reports" on the fire, and vowed to station a fireman in each of the city's public and private schools that were found to be lacking in fire protection. "A tragedy of this magnitude should not go without hope that we can somehow improve the protection of our children," the mayor said.

THAT SAME MORNING John Raymond awoke in Franklin Boulevard Hospital with a badly bruised hip and an injured back that made it hard for him to move. Severe smoke inhalation made it feel as if he had swallowed a jar of tacks. But he was lucky, for unlike other, more critically burned and injured students, his hospital stay would be relatively short: one week.

Lying in bed with an intravenous line in his arm, John still didn't know what had happened, just that he was in a bad situation. He remembered stumbling inside his aunt's house across the street from the school, falling down on a couch, then being picked up by a stranger who carried him to his car and drove him and a few other children to the hospital.

John was hungry—don't they feed you in these places? He had never been in a hospital, at least not since he was born. His mom hadn't come by. She was still busy with his dad in another hospital. One of his uncles had told John that his dad had been injured but was okay.

A newspaper deliveryman walked inside the room. "Here," he said to John, "have a paper. You can pay me tomorrow."

When John unfolded the paper, the bold, black headline leaped off the front page: NINETY DIE IN SCHOOL FIRE.

Ninety! How did it happen? Immediately John thought of his two brothers. He was still unaware that they had escaped unharmed. He riffled through the pages, scanning the death lists. Their names were not there. Thank God for that. They must be okay.

Other familiar names, though, filled the long columns: Wayne Wisz. Margaret Sansonetti. Annette LaMantia. Larry Dunn. John Mele. Joseph Maffiola. Karen Baroni. Joseph King. They were all kids from John's room. He saw another name: Frank Piscopo was his next-door neighbor. They were buddies, classmates, hung around together, walked to school together every morning.

John couldn't believe what he was reading. It was like a bad dream. He counted the names. Twenty-seven of his classmates were dead. He went further down the list. He saw his nun's name, Sister Mary Clare Therese. She was dead too.

John had never known anyone who died, and now it seemed like everyone he knew was dead. Yet he was alive. God heard his prayer. He had been saved. But why him and not them?

TO THE SOUTH, in Garfield Park Hospital, John's father was in turmoil.

Jim Raymond was still in shock from blood loss and too upset to answer lengthy questions. He had become physically sick and vomited when police tried taking an initial statement from the janitor as he lay in his hospital bed on the night of the fire. In the confusion outside the school, the elder Raymond had scuffled with several firemen who tried to subdue him and walk him to an ambulance when he tried to reenter the burning building to save more children. Finally, when all else failed, one fireman hit him over the head with a pike pole, knocking him unconscious. He was then rushed to the hospital, where he received stitches to close the gash on his head and the injured wrist he had cut after smashing out the window on the second floor.

Lying in his hospital bed, Raymond replayed the awful scene in his head. He thought about the smoke. He would never lose the taste of that smoke. It was peculiar. Thick. Dense. Hot. He could breathe coal smoke and wood smoke. But he couldn't breathe the smoke from the fire. When his thoughts shifted to the children who died, he began to weep uncontrollably, burying his face in his hands. He felt so responsible. If only he'd gotten there sooner, he could have gotten them out. As a parent he knew he was lucky. His kids had escaped. Johnny was hurt, but at least he was alive.

And how did the fire start? He must have asked himself the question a thousand times. The boilers were fine. He had checked them just an hour before the fire. Everything was fine. Maybe a kid was smoking down there. He'd seen cigarette butts in the basement in the past, but not recently. Besides, he always chased kids out of the basement when he caught them down there. He hadn't seen any that day. If one of the kids did start the fire, it had to have been accidental.

When a newspaper reporter asked the janitor what may have sparked the blaze, Raymond replied, "It had to be human hands. That's all I can say."

SITTING ALONE in the living room of his small home on 97th Street, Richard Scheidt was still mulling over what he had seen at the school fire. The Tuesday afternoon papers had just hit the streets, and Scheidt was feeling self-conscious. He looked at the large photo on the front page of the *Chicago American* showing him, his face in anguish, carrying the begrimed, limp body of a ten-year-old boy from the school. The stirring image had captured the essence of the tragedy and would appear in newspapers and magazines throughout the world.

Although Scheidt was identified, the boy in the photograph was not named. The caption asked readers for help. "Do you know who this boy is?" When the boy's aunt saw it, she phoned the paper, asking to speak with an editor. "That's my nephew," she said.

The youngster was given a name. He was John Jajkowski, a fifth-grader from Room 212. He sang in the boys' choir. He had been looking forward to Christmas. He wanted to be a priest.

Scheidt set down the paper. He was saddened. He had pulled nineteen children from the wreckage, all of them dead. He was still shaken.

Later that evening Scheidt's telephone rang. It was John Jajkowski's father who wished to meet with Scheidt, "just to talk." Scheidt was reluctant. He remembered the advice of his older brothers when he had first joined the Fire Department eight years earlier: "Don't get too involved. It's only a job."

Since then Scheidt had grown into a hardened firefighter himself, and he had seen his share of tragedy. He had worked the Barton Hotel fire on Skid Row, where twenty-nine men had died. And the blaze at the Reliance Hotel, where five firemen had been killed. And countless automobile accidents in which he had removed mangled bodies, and the "everyday fires" that snuffed out lives just as quickly.

Through the years he had learned to let go, to purge himself of the daily pathos that was part of his job. But this school fire was different. He would never forget it. It involved kids, and so many of them. It shook him. He was a father himself. Three of his four children attended parochial schools. It could have been him on the other side of the line.

Scheidt decided to make an exception. "Okay," he said softly, "I'll meet you. That would be fine. Whenever you like."

The next night Scheidt drove to the Jajkowski home on North Lawndale Avenue, three blocks from the school. John Jajkowski opened the door. The two fathers shook hands and sat together in the kitchen over cups of hot coffee. Other family members were present. Jajkowski's twenty-nine-year-old wife, Josephine, was under sedation in another room. The couple's remaining child, two-year-old Steven, lay asleep in a crib.

"Was he already dead when you found him?" Mr. Jajkowski asked.

"Yes," Scheidt answered.

When he returned home later that night, Scheidt looked in on his kids—three boys and a girl. They were sound asleep. He wondered what they would become when they grew up.

Scheidt was due to work at the firehouse the next morning. He woke up at six, wanting to call in sick. Instead he got dressed and drove to the firehouse.

DURING THE WEEK crowds of curious onlookers continued to flock past the closed school to see the ravaged building that had been a death trap. Police had barricaded the streets from automobile traffic, and pedestrians were barred from entering.

In the December sunlight the scene remained eerily quiet. But beneath the somber appearance, nerves were fraying. Some parents and relatives, angered by the helpless frustration of losing a loved one, lashed out at those responsible for the safety of their children.

"They only had one damn fire escape in the whole place."

"Why wasn't there a fire door on the second floor?"

"Why didn't they pull the fire alarm sooner?"

"Who was in charge?"

As the finger-pointing multiplied, parish priests began receiving death threats over the phone and in person, as did school janitor Jim Raymond. Police provided round-the-clock protection for them. Still, on the streets of the stricken neighborhood, kindness and sensitivity were the rule. One woman whose children had grown and moved away, walked up to a nun outside the parish convent and pressed some folded currency into her hand.

Community centers and Red Cross stations across Chicago were crowded with people who showed up to donate blood, some going as far as to offer parts of their skin to help treat the children's burns. At Cook County Jail, inmates lined up to donate blood, and at Stateville Prison in Joliet, inmates sacrificed cigarette and candy rations, donating what money they had to assist the families of the dead and injured. Labor unions and other organizations also contributed money, and soon donations began arriving from around the world to Mayor Daley's Our Lady of the Angels Fire Fund. By week's end more than $100,000 had been collected to assist families with medical and funeral expenses.

Newsmen were allowed inside the fire-wrecked school where, amid the ruins and reminders, they took photographs and cursed under their breaths. In some rooms textbooks sat open on charred desktops, and shoes left behind in the mad rush to safety lay in puddles on the floor. On the first floor the coatracks were still full. But little remained untouched on the second floor. Here most of the garments, like many of their young owners, had been destroyed by fire.

Meanwhile, as a task force of forty investigators—including fifteen juvenile officers—was sent on a sweeping inquiry into the cause of the fire, investigators probing the ashes remained stymied as to its cause. No evidence was found to suggest spontaneous combustion, and no specific ignition source was located. Samples from the school's charred walls and stairs, and remains from the thirty-gallon waste drum found in the basement, were taken to the police crime laboratory for inspection and analysis. Some officials still clung to the theory that a cigarette tossed by a student sneaking a smoke in the stairwell, or by workers making deliveries through the basement door, may have touched off the blaze. And, as much as they tried to discount the possibility, investigators were seriously beginning to consider arson as a probable cause.

County Coroner McCarron announced plans to hold a special coroner's inquest the following week. McCarron had named a sixteen-member "blue-ribbon" jury whose task would be to determine cause of death and investigate the fire's origin. Meanwhile, Fire Commissioner Quinn revealed that officials intended to question five hundred upper-grade students at Our Lady of the Angels School. Quinn said survivors would be asked:

What children were out of their classrooms in the period immediately preceding the fire?

Which children were assigned to dump waste paper in the basement on the day of the fire?

Which students smoked cigarettes?

Mimeographed consent forms were prepared in order to obtain permission from parents to allow their children to be questioned.

City Fire Attorney Earle Downs met with bomb and arson detectives to begin the arduous task of checking pupils against a master file containing the names of three thousand known juvenile fire-setters in the city. But by week's end the check had produced no tangible leads.

Police had hit a dead end. They still had no answers.

ON WEDNESDAY, December 3, positive identification was made on the last four bodies that remained at the county morgue. The bodies, all girls, had been burned beyond recognition.

One girl was dressed in the blackened remnants of a blue school uniform with a safety pin at the waist. A second, larger girl, wore a metal ring with a pink stone, and had red nail polish painted on her fingers and toes. A third body had on underclothing embroidered with a red clock and the word "Sunday." The fourth body had a prominent overbite, but other than that revealed nothing more than gender.

Positive identification was made possible only through family dental records. The four were identified as Lucile Filipponio, age eight; Diane Marie Santangelo, age nine; Bernice Cichocki, age twelve; and Rose Ann LaPlaca, age thirteen.

Initially the parents of two of the girls refused to acknowledge that the bodies were those of their daughters. They later accepted the assurance of dentists and physicians who said the teeth in the scorched bodies matched those on the victims' dental charts. The mother of the girl with the nail polish had never seen her use it, so the parents of this child also hesitated before finally claiming the body as their daughter.

In a twisted sequel to the tragedy, police were hunting for a man who telephoned the relatives of two of the dead girls, demanding a cash ransom for the safe return of each child. While the girls' parents agonized at the morgue over whether to believe the bodies belonged to their daughters, the caller told the aunt of one of the girls that her niece was still alive. "If you want her, bring $25,000 to 5520 West Diversey Avenue," the caller said. Police detectives sent to stake out the location discovered the Northwest Side address to be a vacant lot. They searched the area but came up with nothing.

The bodies of the three nuns killed in the fire were returned to the convent across the street from the burned-out school. Along with a basket of white carnations, three simple, brown coffins, each closed and adorned with a silver crucifix and nameplate, were

Our Lady of the Angels School (above) at the height of the fire. Word of the blaze spread quickly through the neighborhood, drawing parents and hundreds of others to the scene.

Firefighters carried the body of Joseph Maffiola, age 10, down ladder.

Three who were heroes (from left): Reverend Joseph Ognibene rescued several children and was burned in the process; he later defended the actions of school personnel. The cool head and quick thinking of Sister Davidis Devine helped save all but two of her eighth-graders, while the diminutive Sister Andrienne Carolan led groups of students to safety through perilous conditions. (Photographs of the nuns circa 1975.)

The firefighters (above, from left) persevered: Charles Kamin was forever haunted by the image of children trapped beyond his reach. Stanley Wojnicki's Engine 85 was the first fire company to reach the scene. George Schuller's obsession with solving the mystery of the fire led him on a trail of deception and betrayal. Fire Commissioner Robert J. Quinn (left) steadfastly defended the actions of his men.

Firefighter Richard Scheidt, his face etched with anguish, emerged from the school with the limp form of John Jajkowski, age 10. This photograph, published throughout the world, came to symbolize the nature of the tragedy.

In the aftermath, the main corridor of the school's north wing (above), with its open roof and burned timbers, showed the fire's speed and ferocity. In Room 209 (below), the only way out was through the windows.

Sheet-covered bodies awaited identification at the Cook County Morgue (above) while Mayor Richard J. Daley, flanked by Police Commissioner Timothy O'Connor (left) and Fire Commissioner Quinn, toured the fire scene in grim silence. A witness said the mayor looked like "a father shocked out of his skin."

Three who sought answers (from left): Private investigator John Kennedy traced the origin of the fire and was the first to declare it had been set by human hands. John Reid used a polygraph test to confirm the admission of the juvenile suspect, but Judge Alfred Cilella threw out the confession, calling it a "fantasy."

School janitor James Raymond carried the accusation of "sloppy housekeeping" to his grave. He was never vindicated.

The church was reluctant (from left): Archbishop Albert Meyer, new to Chicago, balked at assigning responsibility for ninety-five deaths to a young suspect. Monsignor William E. McManus, superintendent of schools for the archdiocese, preferred to label the fire an "accident." Monsignor Joseph Cussen, pastor of Our Lady of the Angels, was among the first to admit that the blaze was suspicious.

The front page of the *Chicago American* on Friday, December 5, 1958, the day many fire victims were laid to rest. "The kids aren't dead. They've graduated to a state of perfect joy," the editorial read.

The shrine at Queen
of Heaven Cemetery,
Hillside, Illinois,
where twenty-five
of the fire's victims
are buried.

A new Our Lady of the Angels School, built of steel and brick on the
site of the 1958 disaster, was dedicated October 2, 1960, and
blessed by Cardinal Meyer. It is still in use today, but no marker
commemorates the victims of the fire.

placed on the sidewalk outside the convent, where prayers were offered by Bishop Raymond Hillinger. As Hillinger recited the Rosary,
heartbroken nuns dressed in black and white joined hands in the December cold and prayed for the souls of their beloved sisters. When
the service ended, the coffins were moved inside to a small chapel.
More than two thousand mourners filed past the three coffins, waiting in a line that stretched half a block. Included among the mourners were parents whose children had died alongside the women.

On Thursday the three coffins were carried across the street into
the parish church for a solemn funeral Mass and eulogy delivered by
Archbishop Meyer and Monsignor McManus, superintendent of
schools. The coffins were carried by eighteen parishioners—six for
each—followed by a color guard of one hundred police and firemen.

Thinking about what he would say, McManus concluded that the
three sisters had given much of themselves to their students. In their
tragic, untimely deaths, it seemed only fitting that they had stayed
behind, dying alongside the children. When the fire broke out, the
nuns didn't think to save themselves. They didn't run. They didn't
panic. They didn't leave the children behind. They stayed with them,
all the way through the fire to the ultimate journey from earth to
heaven.

McManus decided not to question their judgment in trying to get
the children out or having them stay put inside the rooms. Nobody
could make that judgment unless they were actually inside those
rooms and knew exactly what the conditions were like. The nuns
may have opened the doors and saw the inferno in the hallway and
figured there was no way out. Or maybe they were wrong in not trying to run for the stairs. McManus concluded it didn't matter. What
had been done had been done. Now, as a community, they must
cling to their faith, to accept God's will and go forward.

Approximately one thousand mourners packed the church that
morning to hear McManus celebrate the funeral Mass. More than a
hundred grieving nuns filled the pews in the first three rows. Because there was not enough room inside the church to accommodate
everyone, many more mourners stood outside on the front steps and
sidewalks. Loudspeakers were set up so that those standing in the
cold, raw wind could share in the words of comfort.

In concluding his eulogy, McManus said, "Our three sisters died
magnificent deaths. . . . There is no mother who could have been

more unselfish, nor more heroic, than our three sisters who died with their children."

When the service ended, the coffins were carried outside and loaded into hearses, then driven to Mount Carmel Cemetery in suburban Hillside, a few miles west of Chicago. There the three were lowered into their final place of rest, in a special plot reserved for the Sisters of Charity.

BY WEEK'S END, fourteen of the ninety-three school fire injured remained in critical condition with severe burns and fractured bones.

At St. Anne's Hospital three critically injured children were clinging to life. One of them, Victor Jacobellis, lay in a coma, his prognosis poor. The nine-year-old fourth-grader had broken his neck and crushed his chest after jumping off one of the high windowsills in Room 210. The neurological damage had left him in a vegetative state. He was being kept alive by a respirator.

Nick and Emma Jacobellis had remained at their son's bedside since the night of the fire. As the week progressed, Victor's condition didn't change. Finally, on Friday, doctors accompanied Nick and Emma to a quiet room at the end of the hall. "I'm afraid there's nothing we can do," they said. "It's up to you, but we would recommend cessation of support. He's not going to come out of it."

Pragmatic Nick Jacobellis trusted the doctors' judgment. If there was any hope, they would have found it. This was not the way Victor would have wanted it. For all practical purposes, his son was already dead. Still, it was not an easy decision. But they were strong people. What else could they do? It was God's will. "Whatever you say," Nick said.

That evening Nick and Emma Jacobellis visited their son for the last time. They wept as a doctor turned off the respirator that was keeping Victor alive. After a few minutes, Victor expired. The fire had claimed its ninety-first victim.

SISTER DAVIDIS remained in St. Anne's for a week. After her release from the hospital she was met at the convent by members of the news media who had been waiting to ask her about the final minutes in Room 209.

As reporters and photographers began crowding into the convent's first-floor reading lounge, word of the press conference

reached Monsignor McManus, the archdiocesan school superintendent, who quickly became angry at the prospect of a nun facing an
open interrogation and answering questions in a way that might
prove embarrassing or damaging to the church. McManus and other
officials were worried about the legal ramifications of the school
fire; attorneys had already warned the chancery office about the possibility of lawsuits stemming from the fire. In the immediate aftermath, nuns and priests from Our Lady of the Angels parish were told
to remain silent. No one was to answer any questions.

McManus wanted the interview stopped. He telephoned the convent and asked that the press conference be called off. "It's too late,"
a nun told him. "They've already begun." McManus rushed to the
convent from his office downtown, entering—as one nun later recalled—"like a black cloud."

Meanwhile Sister Davidis, dressed in her black habit, conducted
herself with grace and sincerity, speaking slowly and deliberately as
she described for reporters the final moments leading up to the time
she and her eighth-graders reached safety by jumping out windows
or climbing down ladders and the drainpipe running along the outside wall.

"It happened in a matter of seconds," she said, "but it seemed
like thirty years."

"Sister," a reporter asked, "do you have any idea how the fire
started?"

"I have no idea whatsoever," the nun responded.

When another reporter suggested that a pile of waste paper
stored under the back stairwell helped the fire's rapid advance, Sister Davidis objected. "No," she said. "Sister Florence kept the
school immaculate. I know of no cases where waste paper was
stored under the stairwell."

After the question-and-answer session ended and the reporters
started to disperse, Monsignor McManus admitted that after all it
was probably a good idea for Sister Davidis to get her story out in
the open. She had nothing to hide.

In the days following the fire, the BVM nuns traveled in groups
to attend wakes for the many school fire victims. Bereaved parents
appreciated their presence and personal concern. But as time passed
the nuns sensed a gradual change in sentiment among people living
in the neighborhood around the school.

"I can remember riding the bus to St. Anne's Hospital to visit some of the children," one nun later recalled. "When we got on, everybody in the bus stopped talking. By then, the BVM habit had become famous. They knew who we were, and you could feel the criticism in their silence, as though they were thinking, 'Oh, so you're the ones who didn't get the kids out.'"

IN A TIME when American sensitivities had not yet been blunted by the assassinations of the Kennedys and Martin Luther King, Jr., and by the cruelties of the war in Vietnam being brought into the country's living rooms on color television, the news of the Our Lady of the Angels fire jolted the nation and the world. Newspapers across the country filled their front pages with headlines and photographs of the fire, and American television networks led their nightly newscasts with reports from Chicago.

Across Europe, newspapers and radio stations reported the tragedy at great length. In London the BBC called the fire "too awful for words." In the Soviet Union, though, the official Communist news agency Tass and Radio Moscow used the school fire to harangue the United States for spending too much money on military hardware and approving only "miserly allocations" toward school safety. The fire, they asserted, was "no accident."

Meanwhile, messages of sympathy poured into the city from around the globe, including cables from German Chancellor Konrad Adenauer and Pope John XXIII. Regarding the arson claims being advanced in some circles, the Vatican said: "It does not seem possible that anyone could take such action against innocent children. We refuse to believe this and are inclined to think it was an accident."

The repercussions of the Chicago school fire were felt in every American city, large and small, as officials nationwide reviewed their school fire-inspection programs. Fire officials from several of the nation's cities and from as far away as London dispatched representatives to Chicago to study the blaze and gather information to help prevent a similar tragedy from striking their communities.

In New York City, Fire Commissioner Edward J. Cavanagh ordered the immediate inspection of that city's fifteen hundred public and private school buildings. Fire inspectors were ordered to pay particular attention to basements, exits, waste disposal systems, housekeeping, and fire drill efficiency. "We conduct these regularly and we are certain our schools are safe and in fine condition, but we are taking this step as a matter of assurance to parents and others concerned," Cavanagh explained.

In 1957, 127 minor fires had been reported in New York City schools. In 1958 the number sat at 117. John J. Theobald, New York City's school superintendent, said he did not believe such a tragedy could occur in his city because, with the exception of four older wooden schools in Queens, all of New York's schools were "fireproof."

Yet within the first twelve hours inspectors in New York closed four schools and evacuated more than a thousand pupils. One was a Hebrew school in Brooklyn where fire officials found hallways and fire exits blocked with lumber, desks, and other obstructions. Windows were found to be fixed with iron bars. A second Hebrew school in Manhattan was found to be strung with ancient open wiring. Two public schools in the Bronx had sprinkler systems out of service, and in one of these, acetylene torches and oxygen tanks were found stored in the building's basement. By week's end, eighteen New York schools had been closed for safety violations.

Despite Chicago's public school officials labeling their fire-prevention program as the most "extensive efforts in a generation," Fire Commissioner Quinn ordered fifty lieutenants from the Fire Prevention Bureau to begin inspecting every public and parochial school in the city. Inspectors' biggest concern was a lack of panic hardware on school doors. And because of conditions found at Our Lady of the Angels School, inspectors also chose to target accumulations of rubbish, obstructed exits, and barred doors. Still, Quinn told reporters that no schools would be closed, and he cautioned parents there was "no need to become frantic."

"All Chicago schools are in good condition, but we just are not taking any chances," Quinn said. "If we find one that is in bad condition, we will station one or two firemen in there during school hours. This will apply to all school buildings."

But fire-protection problems were institutional as well as local; because of Chicago's current building code, scores of older schools and other public buildings in the city were without sprinkler systems and other fire safety devices. Everyone knew it would take more than one or two firemen stationed on the premises to impede the spread of any fire.

ON THE FRIDAY after the fire, a solemn requiem Mass was offered for twenty-seven of the dead children—eighteen girls and nine boys—in the Illinois National Guard Northwest Armory on North Kedzie Avenue. Wakes and funerals for the remaining sixty-one children killed were being held privately elsewhere throughout the city's West Side and in nearby suburbs. Some parents chose private services rather than play out their grief in public. They had endured enough, deciding to sequester their loss among themselves. Still, in deciding to hold the mass funeral, archdiocesan officials had deemed the rites as a tribute for all who had perished in the school fire.

Seven thousand persons attended the 10 a.m. rites at the huge grey armory abutting Humboldt Park, many arriving more than two hours early. Wheeled inside were twenty-seven coffins in white and gold, each pathetically small but different in size, provoking its own set of memories. Above the coffins, on the armory stage, was a portable altar surmounted by six candles and a crucifix. Archbishop Meyer, his face gray and contorted in sorrow, offered the Mass. Next to him, wearing a look of frozen grief, was Monsignor Cussen. Cardinal Francis Spellman of New York was also present.

In summing up the week of sorrow, Bishop Raymond Hillinger spoke to the congregation, referring to the slogan with which Chicago had recovered from the fire of 1871: "Today, this week, the motto 'I will' has meant 'I will be kind.' Chicago to us will always mean the city of the Good Samaritan.

"It would be folly to try to minimize the tragedy of last Monday afternoon," Hillinger preached. "The fire was ghastly. It was hideous. It was horrendous. But God is not mocked. He does not allow disasters to take place without reason. The heavenly Father in His providence governs all things. The blunt but consoling statement is that He will draw untold good from the purgatory of this week. From the ashes, love, phoenix-like, has risen. . . . "

During the Mass the choir sang Perosi's "Libera Me," usually sung at the rites of popes and cardinals. A chant of the Latin poem "Dies Irae," based on a prophecy that the world will be destroyed by fire, was also delivered.

After the final prayers, heartbroken parents and relatives were asked to rise from their seats in the front rows and wait for their child's name to be called: "Peter Cangelosi. David Biscan. Millicent Corsiglia. Christine Vitacco. Joseph Modica. Diane Marie Santangelo. Margaret Chambers. Joseph King. Aurelius Chiappetta. . . ."

The families—some silent, others weeping or fighting back tears—fell in line behind the coffins containing their loved ones as they were wheeled outside to waiting hearses before an honor guard of policemen and firemen. The funeral procession then moved across the West Side and into the nearby suburbs, to Queen of Heaven Cemetery in Hillside, where interment services were held in the raw, icy cold.

At the burial site, veteran news photographer Jimmy Kilcoyne was shaken by what he saw: "The mothers were throwing their bodies on caskets and sobbing like they never wanted to let go."

A memorial for all ninety-five victims of the school fire would eventually be erected on the burial site, a triangular plot known as the Shrine of the Holy Innocents, a section of the cemetery reserved for children.

ON THE SUNDAY after the fire, "The Angelus," a small weekly bulletin distributed to parishioners at all the Masses at Our Lady of the Angels Church, contained no mention of the fire. Within the thick, black border on the front page, there was a simple message in large type:
"Blessed Are They Who Mourn
For They Shall Be Comforted . . ."

BEFORE MONTH'S END, two more students—both fourth-graders from Room 210—died, bringing the death toll to ninety-three.

Kurt Schutt, the ninety-second victim, died December 8 in Edgewater Hospital. He had been transferred there from Franklin Boulevard Hospital to permit the use of an artificial kidney machine—the only one in the city at that time—to filter impurities from his blood. He had been burned over 80 percent of his body.

"Kurt was very brave," said a hospital worker who cared for him on the day of the fire. "I wanted to take off his glasses, which were blackened by smoke, but he put his burned hands up to hold them on. I let him keep them on."

Susan Smaldone, the ninety-third victim, died December 22 in St. Anne's Hospital. She suffered burns over 85 percent of her body, "but she was always in good spirits," recalled a member of the hospital staff. As the days passed, a massive infection took over her swollen body, and her vital fluids diminished rapidly.

Susan had a beautiful singing voice. She had come out of the fire still believing there was a Santa Claus. Before she died, she had written him a note reminding him to look for her in the hospital.

The holiday season, usually a time of happiness and anticipation, was a time of mourning and sadness in Our Lady of the Angels parish. Darkness, it seemed, was everywhere.

Eight

INQUEST

O N WEDNESDAY, December 10, Cook County Coroner Walter
McCarron convened his blue-ribbon jury inside the auditorium
of the Prudential Building in downtown Chicago, setting in motion a
public inquest into the fire that was to last six business days.

The building's management waived the $800-per-day rental fee
for the room and, at the coroner's request, arranged to have present a
doctor and two nurses in the event a grief-stricken parent might need
medical attention. Among the press contingent in the front row of
seats, behind a battery of newsreel cameras, were reporters from
local and national news organizations as well as correspondents
from England and West Germany. Crowded behind the press corps,
sitting elbow to elbow inside the wood-paneled chambers, were
three hundred spectators, including many bereaved parents.

Although nine days had elapsed since the fire, the circumstances
surrounding its occurrence were still shrouded in mystery, and those
in the audience had come seeking answers to a myriad of troublesome questions.

Jury members appointed by McCarron had varying backgrounds
in building construction and fire safety. They included engineers, ar-
chitects, business and insurance executives, and a labor union president. Roy Tuchbreiter, chairman of Continental Casualty and
Assurance Company, was named foreman. Technically the jury was
a fact-finding body whose sole mission was to determine cause of

death, but it also set out to investigate the fire's cause and origin and to look into the possible culpability—civil or criminal—of persons and agencies involved. Moreover, McCarron had outlined the inquest as an overall study of school fire safety which he hoped would highlight current deficiencies to help prevent a similar tragedy from ever repeating itself.

"This is a dark page in Chicago history," McCarron said in his opening remarks. "I hope something may come out of this to save lives in the future, not only in Chicago but throughout the country." Thus the inquest "upon the bodies of Joseph Maffiola, Karen Culp, Wayne Frederick Wisz, and the eighty-nine others who died in the fire at Our Lady of the Angels School" was formally set in motion.

THIRTY-ONE-YEAR-OLD Mrs. Udella Maffiola, whose son, Joseph, a fifth-grader assigned to Room 212, had been tagged as the first fire victim removed from the school, was accompanied to the stand by her husband, Mario, who sat next to her but did not testify.

For days now, the Maffiolas had been enduring a living nightmare—first by learning Joey was among the dead, then identifying him at the morgue, waking him at a friend's mortuary on Western Avenue, attending his funeral that Saturday, and finally watching helplessly as his tiny coffin was lowered into the ground at St. Joseph's Cemetery. Like the other parents in the hearing room, the Maffiolas were exhausted, physically and emotionally, but they were eager to learn what had really happened at the school.

McCarron sat down beside the couple and began the questioning.

"What is your name, address, and occupation?"

At first the tearful Mrs. Maffiola looked surprised. She didn't realize that the calling of at least three parents was a legal necessity to establish that the dead had been identified. "Mrs. Udella Maffiola, 614 North Springfield Avenue. I work at Motorola."

"What is your relationship to the deceased?"

"Mother."

"As I understand, you lost a little boy, or girl?"

"Yes, I lost my son."

"What is his name?"

"Joseph Maffiola."

"And his age, please?"

"Ten."

McCarron paused to offer her a paper cup filled with water. "No," she waved. "I'm all right."

The questioning continued: "Have you or your husband or any member of your immediate family—some one of you—made an identification of your son, is that correct?"

"Yes, sir."

"The corpus delicti has to be established," said McCarron. "That is why I asked that question."

"Yes," Mrs. Maffiola said. "He was identified."

"I am going to make it as easy as I can. Is there any comment, any statement you would care to make? As a mother, you have the right."

Mrs. Maffiola looked out at the audience. There was no comfort, no solace in sight. A mother's loss was something only a mother could understand.

"Well," she cried, "as a mother, we just hope and pray that it would never, never, never happen again. . . . We all have children to look forward to for the future.

"It happened. Who knows why. But it happened, and let us hope it won't happen again. I don't want it to happen again. If you have children, you don't want to send children to school. You do not want to be afraid of sending others to school. . . .

"My son didn't lose his life for nothing—that is the way I feel. I just hope nobody will forget about it. . . ."

Mrs. Olga Wisz was asked to appear as a witness. Taking the stand, the thirty-one-year-old mother was trembling, and tears rolled down her cheeks.

"I understand that you lost one of your children. Is that correct?" the coroner asked.

"Yes," she replied. "Wayne Frederick Wisz."

"A little boy?"

"Yes. Ten years old."

"Have you or any member of your family established identification?"

"Yes."

"Is there any comment, anything that you may have to say?"

"Please," she whispered, biting her lip, "build safe schools for our kids."

A third parent, Edward Reeb, made an equally brief appearance before the jury, confirming that he had identified the body of his ten-year-old daughter, Marilyn Patricia, at the morgue.

Fire Lieutenant Stanley Wojnicki was the next witness to be summoned. He was the only first-arriving firefighter called to testify.

Since the fire Wojnicki had been on an emotional roller coaster. Already he had begun to experience nightmares, waking up during the middle of the night sweating and screaming. As a former Our Lady of the Angels parishioner, the lieutenant had known many of the dead children and their families, and had attended many wakes. He had lived next door to the Vitacco family, whose daughter, Christine, was among the victims.

Dressed in his Fire Department uniform, Wojnicki sat down before the microphones, his face contorted, his hands shaking. "My name is Stanley Wojnicki," he began, "6346 North Tripp, lieutenant of the Chicago Fire Department, assigned to Engine Company 85."

His voice choked with emotion, Wojnicki stumbled through his description, reading from a statement he had given to investigators on the day after the fire. As he began his monologue, several parents in the auditorium broke into tears and were escorted from the room.

"On December 1, 1958, at approximately 2:42 p.m., we were given a still-alarm of fire by the main fire alarm office to 3808 West Iowa.

"On arrival, we pulled up with the fire engine, in front of the school at Iowa and Avers, and I immediately called the fire alarm office for a box-alarm of fire. I got off the engine and I seen children hanging out of the windows, screaming. Mothers and nuns were out in front of the school as this was going on."

After Wojnicki described how the fire was extinguished, McCarron looked to the jury for questions, but there were none.

Before being excused, Wojnicki, his voice still cracking, spoke again. "I want to say this. There would have been more deaths if we didn't act as fast as we did with the help of civilians and nuns and parents. . . . By the time I got my hose out, the truck was throwing up ladders. People don't realize the work of the Fire Department. We did the best we could. It is a scene that I will never forget in my lifetime."

Sergeant Drew Brown of the Chicago police bomb and arson

unit was called to relate what pertinent information he had to date. Wearing a dark suit and tie, Brown lugged his worn briefcase to the stand, extracting from it a thick stack of papers.

A low-key but expert interrogator, Brown, as the principal detective on the case, had been at the school from the Monday afternoon of the fire until 10 p.m. the following Tuesday, probing the ruins, looking for clues. He knew that 99 percent of all fires burned upward, so as soon as the fire was extinguished he went straight into the basement stairwell. Once the water there was cleared out, Brown examined the debris and confirmed his initial hunch that the fire had in fact started somewhere in the base of the stairwell. He had spent the last twenty years looking at fires, and this one had obviously started in that area. Still, he had so far been unable to fix the cause.

"On the evening of the fire," he began, "we proceeded to the hospital as part of our preliminary investigation. We talked to the persons there who had been involved in the fire. The same evening and the next morning we located youngsters who had been in the area of the stairwell where the fire apparently started. We talked to them about what they had seen, what they had smelled."

Brown said the police investigation had not yet produced any evidence of possible arson. "We have discovered no evidence that would indicate the fire was set," he said. "However, we have not ruled out the possibility it may have been a set fire."

Police had found evidence, Brown revealed, indicating that some material found in the basement may have been flammable. He told the jury of statements taken from two boys who were in the boiler room at the very time the fire was burning. Joseph Brocato and Ronald Eddington, both eleven years old and assigned to Miss Coughlan's classroom (Room 205), said principally the same thing: they had been in the boiler room at about 2:35 p.m., emptying wastebaskets into cardboard barrels. The janitor had rushed into the boiler room from outside, run into the basement chapel, run back through the boiler room, and when he got outside shouted to someone to "call the Fire Department."

The two boys, Brown said, "do not tell or do not say that at any time they saw the fire in the area that was on fire."

Dale K. Auck, a juror who was an engineer and secretary of the National Fire Protection Association, noted that there were three routes a person might take into the boiler room—one from the chapel, one from the door outside the boiler room itself, and a third from the northeast stairwell. "I wonder whether it is known," asked Auck, "what route these boys took to get to the boiler room, what route they took to get back to their classrooms?"

"They didn't go through the stairwell that had the fire in it," Brown said. "They went in through the chapel way, which leads into the boiler room. They didn't go through the area, none of them, where the fire was apparently burning."

Brown told the jury his investigation had been hampered by the numerous wakes and funerals, and because the entire student body of Our Lady of the Angels was being transferred to other schools.

"Today will actually be the first opportunity we will have to talk intimately and separately with everyone in that school," he said. "There is nothing specific we can tell you at this time."

"Well," asked the coroner, "you have ruled out arson, is that correct?"

"No, sir," responded Brown. "Definitely not. We have not ruled out arson."

ELMER BARKHAUS, the salesman who had first noticed the fire while driving through the neighborhood, was the final witness called during the opening two hours of morning testimony. Barkhaus told the jury how he had seen smoke, parked his car, and run into the candy store next door to the school.

"I asked her if she had a phone," said Barkhaus, describing his brief encounter with store owner Barbara Glowacki. "I wanted to report a fire in the school. She said she had no phone. I turned around and ran across the street and rang a couple of doorbells in a two-story building there. A lady from the first floor came out and said she had no phone but that she would run next door, get the phone and call the Fire Department."

"Did you say that the woman in the store had no phone?" asked McCarron. "I understand that she did have one."

"She said she had no phone," Barkhaus replied. "When I was running across the street, I heard her scream, 'Oh my God!' I looked around and there she was at the corner of her building, looking at the fire."

Under repeated questioning by McCarron, Barkhaus acknowledged that he had never placed a call to the Fire Department himself, but rather had informed neighbors of the fire, asking them to call.

"All you did was ask people to do it?" asked McCarron.

"That's right," he said. "Ask people to do it. . . . I don't know who it was that called."

AFTER THE morning hearing, the jury was driven to the fire scene to examine the burned-out north wing of Our Lady of the Angels School. The jurors were mystified that the blaze had spread so rapidly, because so many things about the building seemed adequate.

Stone-faced in their hats, overcoats, and dress shoes, they walked into the basement to inspect the ruined northeast stairwell, then climbed other stairs and viewed the partially collapsed roof. They visited the second-floor classrooms where snow had fallen on some of the desks below openings in the roof.

THE NEXT DAY three witnesses were called to testify.

Barbara Glowacki, the candy store owner, told how she had agonized alone in the alley while waiting for the fire engines to arrive. "Maybe I'm wrong," she said with a rapid German accent. "Maybe they did come fast, but to me it was like an eternity. It seemed like they never, never came.

"Another lady was standing there. All we say at that minute was, 'Why don't the Fire Department come?'

"Then finally, here one fire truck was pulling up, but he didn't come by us where it was needed. He stood on the corner, by Iowa Street.

"I am sorry to say, but now I know they did a great job.

"Then I remember one or two of the ladders going up, and I saw one of the younger janitors. I saw him running, and I saw our monsignor come running out. His eyes was crying. His face in horror at what he saw. And I saw one of our priests carrying a child in his arms."

McCarron asked Glowacki how long she had waited to call the Fire Department after Elmer Barkhaus left her store.

"Right away. . . . I dialed 'O' for operator. . . . I said, 'Our Lady of the Angels School is on fire.' I was screaming. I was very much upset. They said, 'We had somebody call in already. Help is on the way.' "

The appearance of Sister Mary St. Florence Casey, the school principal, on the witness stand aroused the sympathy of the jury. Dressed in a long black habit, the pale-faced nun appeared fragile and shaken, looking like a mother who had lost her children.

"Sister Mary St. Florence, who is the principal of the school . . . is under medication, and sick, and we will have to bear with her," McCarron announced.

"I was substituting in a third-grade room," she began. "Sister was ill.

"The day went along normally, and then sometime between two-thirty and a quarter to three, the fire bell rang. The children ran out normally from my room and from the other room on that first floor. There were three other rooms.

"Then I just retraced my steps back to this room where there is a stairway going up to the second floor. By the time I got back there, smoke, flames, and everything were right at my feet, and I could see the children from those seventh-grade rooms coming out and they seemed to be a little fearful because they couldn't see their way. Their faces were black with smoke, but I encouraged them to go down."

After escorting the students outside, the nun said she looked up and saw more students at the second-floor windows overlooking Iowa Street. "Just at that moment the hook and ladder came and put up ladders immediately and they were all rescued . . . and then I went out into the street and the hose and ladders were all at the Avers Avenue side."

Edward J. Hladis, an assistant prosecutor representing the Cook County State's Attorney's office, informed McCarron he did not wish to question the principal.

"The State's Attorney, for the record, does not want to ask any questions," McCarron repeated.

When James Raymond was asked to step forward, the mood inside the auditorium became charged. The janitor's appearance had long been anticipated. Since the fire, Raymond had seen his life held up for public scrutiny by the press. For more than a week newspapers had been reporting on his activities the day of the fire, telling how his four children had gotten out of the school and how he had been injured in the blaze while helping to rescue trapped occupants.

Because Raymond had been one of the first to discover the blaze and knew the school intimately, he was considered a key witness. Who but the janitor could provide the jury with more exact details of how the building was maintained? Also police were concerned about "several discrepancies" they found in Raymond's story, mainly involving the time he said he first discovered the fire and the time the blaze was phoned in to the Fire Department at least twelve minutes later. Raymond had initially agreed to take a polygraph test, but it had been canceled after the janitor's attorney, John Hogan, also an Our Lady of the Angels parishioner, decided against it, saying his client was too emotionally upset.

Raymond was clearly nervous. In the days after the fire, some newspaper accounts implied that the janitor was somehow responsible for the tragedy. Since the fire he had received death threats. He had stayed up late almost every night, sitting at the kitchen table with his wife, replaying the awful day in his head. How could they think he had anything to do with the fire when he had four of his own kids in the school?

Still, allegations of "sloppy housekeeping" swirled outside the hearing room as John Hogan delivered an opening statement for the record before Raymond's testimony.

"Mr. Coroner and gentlemen of the jury," Hogan began. "I have known Mr. Raymond for twenty years. He has asked me, as friend and counsel . . . to be of assistance in this course of the fire investigation. He is not asking me as a lawyer to defend him because he does not think that he has anything to defend.

"Mr. Raymond appears before you gentlemen of the jury as a witness. He is not, in fact or emotionally, able to give you a complete, unconfused account of the events that occurred at this fire.

"On December 1st, I found that Mr. Raymond suffered an injury to his head—a severe laceration and shock that prevented him from recalling everything clearly.

"He has been employed as a janitor since 1945. He had four children in this school. I have deemed it necessary to bring to your attention Mr. Raymond's present physical and emotional condition.

"If Mr. Raymond has made inconsistent statements on different occasions, it is unfortunate. However, I am sure you will understand what must obviously be his condition. If you will permit him, I am sure he will tell you all the facts he knows. We ask that you evaluate the testimony in light of the background as I have given it."

It was not the intention of the inquest to hurt anyone, McCarron replied. "This is a fact-finding body, and it is a question of finding out the cause of death or deaths, and anything relating to those deaths."

"The housekeeper of the school" was dressed in a dark suit, white shirt, and black tie, and looked haggard. He appeared with his left arm wrapped in a bandage and a black patch covering a spot on his head where he had been struck during the fire. Staring straight ahead, he began answering questions the way Hogan had told him to—answering yes or no but not elaborating.

Raymond told the jury he had been employed as "maintenance man" at the school for "a little over thirteen years." He related how he had been returning to the school from another parish property when, at about twenty minutes after two, he noticed smoke coming from the rear of the school.

"I immediately dashed there to see what it was, and the window was bright red. I didn't waste one minute. I turned right around and ran right into the priests' house and hollered to the housekeeper there, 'Call the Fire Department, quick!' And she did.

"And from there I dashed into the boiler room which is right across the way. There were two little boys in there with waste paper baskets. I told them to drop the baskets and get back. . . . I chased them right out. I don't know what room they were from."

The janitor then told how he ran upstairs, opened one window, broke out another, cutting his wrist, and helped lead students from Room 207 down the fire escape.

"By that time I was so full of smoke and I lost so much blood that I came down the stairs, and there were two firemen there. I wanted to get back up. I felt a big bump on my head, and the next thing I know, I woke up in Garfield Park Hospital. That was late in the evening."

A juror asked Raymond where he thought the fire originated.

"As far as I know," he said, "it could have started at the back stairway. That is where I saw the red window. Nothing touched the boiler room at all."

The coroner asked if any material was stored in the northeast stairwell.

"I don't know," Raymond replied. "We very seldom use it. I know there was an empty drum—a one-hundred-gallon drum of calcium chloride. I heard them talk about a drum. That was what the drum was, calcium chloride."

"Were there not papers and rubbish there?"

"Some said there was a stack of paper up in the corner. How they got there, I don't know."

"In the basement?"

"In the stairway."

"Do you know how the papers got there?"

"No, sir."

"How long had the papers been there?"

"I very seldom check there because we don't use that entrance."

As the questioning continued, it was obvious that police sergeant Drew Brown and the jurors were having difficulty reconciling the time discrepancy in Raymond's testimony. "Do you know what time the fire alarm was struck, Mr. Raymond?" Brown asked.

"All I know it was 2:42 p.m.," Raymond answered. "I don't remember the time from then on."

Brown persisted. "You are positive it was 2:20 when you first saw the smoke?"

"It was 2:20, 2:25. I am not sure of the exact minute or time," the janitor answered. "I know it was after two o'clock."

"How much time do you suppose you spent notifying the lady in the rectory?"

"About sixty seconds."

"I do not want to confuse you anymore," Brown said. "But would you explain to me once more how you know it was 2:20?"

"Well, I imagine I looked at my watch. Maybe my watch was five minutes fast or five minutes slow. I don't know."

If the janitor, as he insisted, had notified the housekeeper at once, then it was apparent he was confused regarding the time he first saw the reddened window in the northeast stairwell. On the other hand, if his recollection of the time was anywhere near correct, an intolerable lapse of seventeen minutes or more had occurred before the Fire Department was called. Raymond admitted he had not personally seen Mrs. Maloney, the rectory housekeeper, make the telephone call. "I didn't stay that long," he said.

"Mr. Raymond," asked the coroner, "you stated the stairs where the fire apparently started were very seldom, or infrequently, used. I should be interested to know what 'seldom' means. Does this mean they might not have been used for several minutes? Several hours? Several weeks? How often did people pass up and down that stairway, would you guess?"

"Well, I don't know. They may be using that four or five times during the day. I am not at the head of those stairs checking."

On the afternoon of the fire, Raymond said, he had last been inside the school basement about twenty minutes before two o'clock, "checking my boilers."

"When had you last been in the stairwell, where the fire is believed to have originated, prior to the fire?"

"I am not sure; maybe nine days."

"Do you know whether or not papers, piled newspapers, and clothing had been cluttered or were stored in that stairwell prior to the fire?"

"I wasn't there. I wasn't sure. Somebody told me there was a bundle of newspapers there."

The parish, Raymond said, had been conducting its annual clothing drive at the time of the fire, but most of the clothing, as far as he knew, was being stored in the church basement, which was separate from the school building—"unless somebody put a box of clothing that I didn't know nothing about or didn't see."

"Do you know the names of the last persons in the stairwell prior to the discovery of the fire?" McCarron asked.

"No."

"Do you know whether the boys who bring the waste paper down to the basement use that stairwell?"

"They wouldn't get into the boiler room if they came down that stairway with waste paper."

"Why not?"

"Because there is a door leading into the boiler room off that stairwell that is locked at all times."

The janitor was asked if he had ever noticed litter in the stairwell.

"I have at times," he said. "With over twelve hundred children there, there is bound to be a little bit."

"Have you ever chased them out of there?"

"All of them, when I catch them. If I see them, I chase them out because they have no business loitering or sitting on those steps."

"Have you ever noticed any smoking on the part of any individual in that stairwell?"

"No."

"Have you ever seen any evidence of any smoking having occurred there?"

"Yes."

"In what form?"

"Cigarette butt."

"Cigarette butts?"

"One."

"When was that?"

"About two months ago."

"Do you know how it happened to be there?"

"No."

"Did you make a report of it?"

"No."

Juror Dale Auck then asked if Raymond had an opinion of how the fire started.

"Well, if you want my opinion," he answered, "it was started by human hands."

"What do you mean by that?" asked Deputy Coroner Harold Marks.

"There are no electrical devices or anything in that stairwell," Raymond answered. "There is no way a fire could start by combustion or anything else or by itself."

"What makes you say it was started by 'human hands'?" Marks asked again. "By that, do you mean someone started this fire?"

"That is my opinion," Raymond answered.

"That," interjected McCarron, "is an opinion."

"May I ask the witness," Auck continued, "when he says by 'human hands,' does he mean by matches? By cigarettes? What?"

"Well," replied Raymond, "whatever a human hand would start a fire with."

Asked about fire drills, Raymond said he did not supervise drills but was usually present when they were held. The last drill, he said, had been conducted approximately thirty days before the fire.

"Did they evacuate the building?"

"They always do."

"Do you know how long it takes them to evacuate the building?"

"I think the last time they did a fairly good job and it took them about three and a half minutes."

"When they have fire drills, do they use the stairwell where the fire is believed to have started?"

"I think some of them did, yes."

Finally the jury made one last effort to resolve the question of whether Raymond had delayed in alerting the housekeeper about the fire. "When you saw this fire," Auck asked, "did you do anything to try to put it out or extinguish it yourself?"

"I figured it was so big, there was nothing I could do," the janitor said. "I didn't have nothing with me. Only my two hands. I was worried mostly about getting the children out of the school."

THE THIRD DAY of inquest hearings opened Friday morning, December 12, and James Raymond was recalled to the witness stand. He was asked if the outside door to the school's northeast stairwell was usually locked over the weekends.

"Every time I go home," Raymond answered, "I check the handle from the outside to be sure it is locked."

"Do you know whether or not that door was locked on the day of the fire?" McCarron asked.

"I am not sure whether it was locked or not," Raymond said. The hardware on the inside of the door "was just a small metal bar that you could flick up or down with your finger."

The janitor told the jury there were four fire extinguishers on each floor of the north wing, hung on the wall about seven feet off the floor, and two fire alarm controls, one on each floor in the south wing.

"There were no fire alarm devices in the north wing?" a juror asked.

"No."

"Or in the basement?"

"No."

The janitor also noted that "no big painting" work had been done in the school since summer. And a roll of "tar paper" that had reportedly been stored in the basement of the northeast stairwell was not tar paper at all, but floor covering, "just like asphalt tile. . . . I was going to cover a wooden table with it."

"But it had been in the stairwell for perhaps nine days before the fire?" McCarron asked.

"Somewhere around there. I really had no occasion to go through there."

Juror David Klafter, an architect, attempted to resolve speculation over debris in the northwest stairwell. "You disposed or burned up the papers that were accumulated every day, in the boiler, instead of letting them lie around in the basement?"

"That is correct," Raymond replied.

"At the time of the fire, there was no accumulation of paper or other rubbish?"

"The drums where the waste paper is dumped were absolutely empty at that time."

"I want to call your attention to an article in *Life* magazine, which came out today, which says that the basement where the fire started was crowded with barrels of refuse and stacks of newspapers, some dating back nearly two months."

"I don't recall seeing those," Raymond stated.

"Then this article is wrong?"

"To my knowledge, yes."

AFTER RAYMOND was excused, Nora Maloney made a brief appearance on the stand. Cook and housekeeper of the parish rectory for twenty-six years, she tried to clarify her role in reporting the fire.

"I was in the kitchen," she began. "I was making some sauce, and Mr. Raymond came in and said, 'Call the Fire Department! There is a fire in the school!'

"I couldn't think of the Fire Department number, so I called the operator and told her that 'Our Lady of the Angels School over on Iowa, was on fire,' and to 'Send the Fire Department.' And she said 'Wait a minute.' I think the next voice was a man, and I gave him the same information, and then the Fire Department came."

"Do you know about what time that was, Mrs. Maloney?" McCarron asked.

"I would say between 2:30 and twenty minutes to three."

"How did you arrive at that time?"

"I figure it was about that time. I had just started to prepare my sauce about 2:30. I didn't look at a clock at all, and I didn't look at a watch because I didn't have one."

Lay teacher Pearl Tristano was called for a brief statement. She related how, after smelling smoke, she conferred with lay teacher Dorothy Coughlan in the room next door, and how the two teachers evacuated their classes down the interior stairway after learning the principal was away from her office. "Then I ran and sounded the fire alarm," Tristano said.

"About what time was this?" McCarron asked.

"I would say between 2:35 and 2:40. I know it was after 2:30 because my boys had returned with the baskets they had emptied."

"Did you send any of your children downstairs with papers?" asked McCarron.

"Yes, sir," she replied. "There were two who went with baskets."

"When those boys came back, did they tell you that they had seen anything burning?"

"No, sir."

"Do you remember about what time you sent those boys downstairs?"

"About 2:25. They were back by 2:30."

Before she was excused, another juror asked her if all the rooms usually sent one or two boys down at about 2:30.

"Usually. We didn't keep the waste paper in the room overnight because it was a fire hazard."

"So there must have been a number of boys going up and down the stairs about 2:15 to 2:30?"

"Yes, I imagine there were several."

AFTER A WEEKEND recess, the jury continued its hearings on Monday morning, December 15, calling to the stand three city officials.

First Deputy Fire Chief Robert O'Brien, in charge of the Fire Prevention Bureau of the Chicago Fire Department, was a personal friend of Mayor Daley; the two had grown up together in Bridgeport. During his testimony, O'Brien—who would be killed three years later when a building collapsed on him during a South Side apartment fire—repeatedly reminded the jury that although the school was not "actually safe" it was "legally safe," because it did not have to comply with the city's 1949 municipal code.

Since the fire, O'Brien testified, the Fire Prevention Bureau, backed by fire companies throughout the city, had inspected 368 Chicago school buildings and found numerous fire safety violations, including a lack of panic hardware on exit doors, missing exit signs, and poor maintenance of fire extinguishers.

Our Lady of the Angels School, O'Brien said, had last been inspected October 7 by Lieutenant Henry Anselmo of the Fire Prevention Bureau, who reported it to be in "safe and legal condition." Anselmo had noted the absence of a fire door at the top of the northeast stairwell, but because the 1949 code did not apply, this did not constitute a violation. Anselmo also reported that fire extinguishers in the school were legally placed no more than seventy-five feet apart, but he failed to report they had been hung so high off the floor they would be difficult for an adult—let alone a child—to reach in case of emergency. The report cited no electrical deficiencies and nothing to indicate that rubbish had accumulated in the boiler room.

Legally, Anselmo could not describe the school as being overcrowded, and though he was aware that no fire alarm box was within one hundred feet of the school entrance, he made no recommendation to remedy the situation because the 1949 code did not apply to schools built before the law's passage.

More telling than Anselmo's report was a voluntary letter written to O'Brien after the fire by Captain Tony Pilas of the Fire Prevention Bureau. Pilas had made an informal inspection of the school two weeks before the fire.

"As a parishioner and a father," Pilas wrote on December 9, "I had the occasion to visit the school many times in an unofficial capacity. As a captain in the Fire Prevention Bureau, I naturally would observe the general condition of the premises on these visits, and at no time did I ever notice any fire-prevention violations. Two weeks before this tragic fire, where I lost my daughter, I was in the school." (Pilas's letter later made him a target for some of the parishioners whose children had died in the fire. "Some of the people were pretty bitter against me," he later admitted. "They wanted to cut my throat. They said the letter was a 'whitewash,' that I was in favor of the church and the city. But all I did was tell the truth.")

"If I remember correctly," O'Brien told the jury, "there was another inspection made in 1957, by the local Fire Department battalion chief. He was called on by the sister superior to witness a fire drill, and he said the building was evacuated in three minutes and thirty seconds."

O'Brien was asked what safety recommendations he would make for a building such as Our Lady of the Angels School. He listed enclosure of all stairways, installation of a sprinkler system and rate-of-rise detection system in which heat would activate an alarm, more exterior fire escapes, and elimination of transoms over classroom doors.

When asked about building overcrowding, O'Brien replied that when such conditions were noted by fire inspectors, they referred the matter to the city's Building Department, which was responsible for acting against such violations.

"Do you mean to tell me," asked jury foreman Roy Tuchbreiter, "that if you find overcrowding, you leave it up to the Building Department for any action that you deem necessary?"

"If it appears to our inspector, yes."

"Would you say, chief, that Our Lady of the Angels was, in its present condition, one of the most risky of school buildings in Chicago?"

"I would not consider Our Lady of the Angels in a bad, risky condition."

"Is it a combustible building?"

"Yes."

"There were children more than twenty feet off the ground?"

"Yes."

"It had combustible stairways?"

"Yes."

"It had small rooms?"

"Yes."

"It had, on occasion, fifty people or more in rooms?"

"Yes, sir."

Still, the jury could not budge Chief O'Brien's official stance that Our Lady of the Angels was a safe school.

"Legally safe," repeated O'Brien. "I think the big problem was lack of prompt attention to that fire. I think that fire was burning for a good twenty minutes before firefighters were called."

O'Brien was asked if his inspectors had "any inhibitions" in requiring "stringent standards" of such institutions as parochial schools.

"No," the chief replied. "We get the fullest support from the pastors of the archdiocese and also from the Chicago Board of Education."

When Fire Commissioner Quinn testified next, he quickly reminded the jury about the delayed alarm and the incorrect address first phoned in to the main fire alarm office.

"We did everything humanly possible to protect and get those children out of there, if there was any of them alive," he told the jurors. "There was definitely a delayed alarm."

Quinn confronted charges that Fire Department ladders were too short to reach the school's second-floor windows where children were trapped.

"The first-responding companies into these here alarms on a still-alarm fire is an engine company; it is not a ladder truck," Quinn said. "That engine company . . . they have a small ladder on there, either a twenty- or a twenty-four-foot ladder which is used for emergencies on maybe first, second floors, if it could reach them, also for the bridging of fences and so forth, to get in there where a fire may be in progress. That was the reason for that short ladder."

"Is there any provision in the code as to where an alarm system for sending an alarm outside the school shall be placed?" Marks asked the commissioner.

"According to the code," replied Quinn, "a fire alarm box should be placed one hundred feet from the main entrance of any institutional building or school, providing that the school or institutional building has been constructed after 1949."

"And in this instance, how far was the box from the school?"

"It was one block and a half away."

Quinn defended his department against charges of a delayed response. The delay in calling in the fire had been costly, but it was no fault of the Fire Department. "In the fireman's game, you either win or lose a fire in the first few minutes," he observed. "If you would have sent five hundred companies in there, they would have never accomplished what they should have accomplished because they never received the alarm properly.

"It wasn't the Fire Department, it was the people in that school building who never got the call into the Fire Alarm Office. . . . We cannot respond unless we are notified that there is an emergency, and, gentlemen, if you think for one minute that the Fire Department sits in a house after they receive a call, then you don't know the operations of your Fire Department. They are there day in and day out, waiting to go out through those doors on a fifteen-second notice."

"Commissioner," asked Deputy Coroner Marks, "if you had been given that alarm three minutes sooner, every child in that school would have been saved, is that right?"

"I would venture to say that, yes," Quinn replied. "Our records reveal 160 children were saved from this fire by the firemen."

George L. Ramsey, the city's building commissioner, concluded the day's hearing. The school building was not legally overcrowded, he explained, because the school was built before 1949 and did not need to comply with the 1949 municipal code requiring twenty square feet of classroom space for each student. Had the school been governed by the 1949 law, its capacity would have been limited to 232 students in the six classrooms on the second floor of the north wing. Instead those same classrooms held some 329 students and six nuns.

But Ramsey's answer did not satisfy juror Dale Auck. "People are people, whether they are in new buildings or old buildings," Auck insisted. "In fact, they burn up more easily in old buildings. Now let's face it, the school was overcrowded and seriously overcrowded, and you and I both know it."

"When you are dealing with buildings that are fifty, sixty, seventy years old, you must accept them under the ordinance in effect at the time they were built," Ramsey replied. "Changes are usually made as the result of tragedies such as this. Now is an opportune time to consider recommendations for changes."

ON THE FINAL DAY of the inquest, James Raymond was asked to give a separate statement under oath in the Illinois state fire marshal's office near City Hall. There he told the same story he had related under questioning at the inquest, but this time he revised his time estimate as to when he said he first saw the fire.

"I would say it was 2:30 p.m.," he told deputy State Fire Marshal A. Deneen Best.

"Had you been drinking that day?" Best inquired.

"No."

"That is your statement under oath?"

"Yes."

"Mr. Raymond, are you involved in this fire through any negligence?"

"No."

"Did you set the fire?"

"No. Four of my kids were in there, and if I didn't like kids, I wouldn't be there."

Nine

DOUBT

THE INQUEST drew to a close on Tuesday, December, 16. Sergeant Drew Brown of the police bomb and arson unit was recalled and asked if his expanding investigation into the fire's cause had revealed any new information.

"We have processed almost seven hundred youngsters by taking statements from each one," Brown said. "About thirteen hundred youngsters have been talked to to try to find the answer.

"We did find out there definitely had been smoking in the stairwell, and we definitely found out there was some delay in getting this alarm."

Brown's testimony responded to revelations that several older pupils—all boys—were seen smoking by other students in a washroom in the school basement on the afternoon of the fire. Another pupil also told police that in September he had seen boys smoking at the bottom of the northeast stairwell where the fire had started.

The sergeant said questioning of students produced "a boy who states he saw two youngsters in the stairwell smoking. This is the first time we have come across anyone who puts them right in the stairwell. And they were lighting matches."

"Did you get any information that would be helpful from the crime lab?" Coroner McCarron asked.

"We took a whole step from the back stairwell to the crime laboratory to distill the material to see if any gasoline had been used, if any volatile liquids could be obtained from it," Brown said. "They stated that water was all they could get out of this plank.

"We have submitted every bit of physical evidence available at the scene to the Police Crime Lab. Photos have been taken. We have revisited the scene a score of times. We have discussed this twenty-four hours a day with nearly everyone we could talk to. We talked to adults in the neighborhood, and it's status quo on the whole thing.

"We do not know yet whether it was arson, although the evidence—the balance of the evidence—must indicate that it was accidental." Later, after further questioning, Brown said he would classify the fire as one of "undetermined cause."

Wyatt Jacobs, an attorney representing the Catholic Bishop of Chicago, then examined Brown.

"You say you found some combustible material in the stairwell," Jacobs began. "Tell us what it was."

"We found some papers that children had written," Brown answered. "We found newspapers that dated back to October 20th. We found the remains of what appeared to be three cardboard boxes."

"Where was that located?"

"That one particular box was right under the window there the fire appeared to have its start. It was filled with whiskey bottles."

"Empty?"

"Yes, the bottles were broken."

"Did you find any evidence that there were matches in the well?"

"I didn't find any matches, no."

"You used this word 'arson' carelessly. Do you have any evidence at all?"

"I stated that this is an undetermined fire as far as we are concerned."

"Then you do not have any evidence that it was arson?"

"That is correct."

"But you are not ruling out arson at this time?" Deputy Coroner Harold Marks asked.

"No, sir," responded Brown.

After Brown was excused, Monsignor Cussen, the parish pastor, was summoned as the final inquest witness. As the clergyman approached the stand, McCarron asked for the cooperation of news photographers. "If there are going to be any pictures taken," he ordered, "take them before and after, but not while the witness is testifying."

The coroner then turned to Cussen. "Will you tell the jury and tell me what you know about this incident, please?"

"Well, that Monday afternoon," the pastor began, "I had been in the boiler room shortly before two o'clock. I was talking to the janitor.

"I returned to the rectory and I received a call that the truck from the Salvage Bureau had come out for clothes we had gathered from a drive the week preceding. We called the school and asked the sisters to send over some boys. She sent something like thirteen boys to help these men load the truck on the Hamlin Avenue side of the hall. They were just finished when one of the boys says, 'The school's on fire!'

"I ran through the hall and came out to the front just as the first engine—85—pulled up. I went in the first door of the school, the east door on the Iowa Street side. I went up to the second floor and we opened a window. Civilians followed. We got them organized and we took every child in that room but one."

The pastor said he then tried to get through to the north wing of the school where students were trapped, but was driven back by smoke. "It was heavy, kind of oily, and black."

"I came downstairs and then went over to the north end of the building," he said. "Youngsters were coming down the ladders. I did all I could there to aid these children. Some of them lost their heads and jumped. With the aid of civilians, we picked them up and brought them over to the place north of the school and set them there in the alley until the ambulances came along. That's about it."

"Monsignor Cussen," Dale Auck asked, "if there was an accumulation of material and debris in this stairwell, apparently someone knows when it was put there and how it happened to be there. Do you know who that person might be?"

"No, I don't."

"Have you any opinion as to the source of this fire, what started it?"

"No, I haven't. The only thing that bothered me was that it was more or less a flash fire; it went so very fast. I was in the boiler room about a half-hour before that, talking with the janitor. There was no sign of smoke."

"Is this stairwell a generally used stairs? I mean, there is no reason why people are not used to using those stairs?"

"No. They use it. We don't use it for entrance and exit to the school because it faces an alley and there is a great deal of danger because traffic is particularly heavy in that alley. It is open to anyone to use it. I have to use it myself when I have been in the building, going from the first floor to the second, or from the second to the first."

"The exit door at the bottom is closed?"

"No. It has to be open at all times."

"People coming out of public buildings have a tendency . . . to light up their cigarettes just before they leave. Is it possible an adult may have dropped a match or cigarette in the stairwell?"

"It could be, because it's off the alley. Anybody could get in there."

The pastor was then asked what procedures were followed regarding the sounding of the school's fire alarm. He said the school had had six fire drills since September.

"Can anyone sound the alarm?"

"Yes, sir."

"Could any teacher evacuate a room without asking permission?"

"Oh, yes, yes. In fact, that is what I thought this was when I came out of the church hall because of all the children on the south side of Iowa Street and the west side of Avers. I thought it was a drill until I saw the smoke in the back of the school."

"Monsignor, did you ever receive any notices from local governmental agencies with reference to violations?"

"No, I haven't. Not at any time. I think we were superior as far as good housekeeping was concerned because I have been more or less a crank on that type of work. The school was in good physical condition. It was an old building, yes, but we brought it up to date. It was well kept. The youngsters were very clean. In fact, they would even clean up the street in front of the school."

Cussen then asked to make a final statement. "I have been a priest for forty years," he said, "and I have been associated with children all that time. I do not think I will ever be satisfied until we find what caused this fire."

As the doors closed behind them, parents attending the inquest came away with little new information to help salve their grief. The cause of the fire was still a mystery, and several parents criticized McCarron's questioning as irrelevant, repetitious, or sometimes downright inept. Parents also were irritated over the reluctance of some city officials to pinpoint responsibility. Had a neutral observer listened to the testimony, he might have thought the inquest was designed simply to absolve the living rather than show concern for the dead.

IT TOOK the coroner's jury nearly three weeks to complete its findings. On January 7, 1959, the panel reconvened and announced its conclusion that Joseph Maffiola, Marilyn P. Reeb, and Wayne Frederick Wisz had: "Died on December 1, 1958, in Cook County Hospital from asphyxiation due to smoke inhalation and other causes, due to external violence caused when the deceased, together with ninety others, came to their deaths, victims of a fire of undetermined origin that took place in Our Lady of the Angels School, located on the premises commonly known and described as 909 North Avers Avenue, Chicago, Illinois.

"From the testimony presented, we, the jury, are unable to determine whether this occurrence was accidental or otherwise."

Roy Tuchbreiter, foreman of the jury, embellished these findings: "Judging from the evidence presented, the fire originated in the stairwell at the northeast corner of the school building and had been burning for some time before it was discovered. However, the exact point of origin cannot be established and we therefore have reached the conclusion that the cause of the fire is undetermined."

Attached to the jury's report was a list of twenty-two nonbinding recommendations for fire safety in school buildings. Among others, the report cited the following four suggestions:

—Provide an approved automatic fire sprinkler system in all school buildings;

—Enclose all vertical passageways with incombustible construction and protect all openings into them with approved fire doors;

—Provide approved fire barrier doors at all corridor and room partition openings;

—Provide an approved automatic internal fire alarm system whose components incorporate smoke and heat detectors, and which is linked directly to the Fire Department.

Our Lady of the Angels School would have to be graded as deficient with regard to the jury's key recommendations, but at that time, if the same safety standards had been applied throughout the nation, hundreds of other aging school buildings would have been considered equally deficient. Still, it took an unusual combination of circumstances to expose the vulnerability of Our Lady of the Angels School, including—as some investigators insisted—the unproven reality that the fire had been set.

In the end, because the school fell outside the 1949 municipal code, both the city and the Chicago archdiocese skirted criminal liability. Never was there any mention of convening a grand jury in Cook County to hear evidence of possible criminal negligence against either entity, despite the release of a scathing report on the fire by the National Fire Protection Association, whose authors clearly blamed city and archdiocesan officials.

The school fire deaths, the NFPA reported, "are an indictment of those in authority who have failed to recognize their life safety obligations in housing children in structures which are fire traps. Schools that lack adequate exit facilities and approved types of automatic sprinkler or detection equipment, which possess excessive amounts of highly combustible interior finish, substandard fire alerting means and poor housekeeping conditions must be rated as fire traps."

THE FINDINGS by the coroner's jury were immediately criticized for being too inconclusive and for failing to fix responsibility on any person or institution.

"It's like they wanted to wash their hands of the entire matter, sweep it under the rug," recalled John Trotta, whose thirteen-year-old son, John David, had died in Room 211.

Trotta had attended the inquest, listened to the witnesses, and came away feeling that he still didn't have the answers he was entitled to as an aggrieved father who had lost his only son. He had gone to the inquest hoping to submit a list of questions to the jury. "I gave them to the foreman of the jury, and you know what he says to me? He says, 'We don't want to do anything that will embarrass the archdiocese.' Can you believe that?"

One of Trotta's questions had to do with the time Jim Raymond said he first saw the fire and the time Mrs. Maloney, the housekeeper, called the Fire Department.

If Raymond was correct in saying he first noticed the fire at 2:30 p.m., and immediately notified the housekeeper, then why the twelve-minute delay? One possibility is that Raymond was wrong about the time. Another is that the housekeeper may have first tried to verify the fire report with the pastor or some other authority figure. Another more likely explanation is that Raymond, despite his claims to the contrary, may indeed have spent several minutes trying to fight the fire in the stairwell before running to the rectory.

"That was something we always suspected but were never able to pin down," recalled George Schuller, who, as a lieutenant assigned to the Chicago Fire Department's arson squad and photography unit, investigated the fire and photographed the building's charred ruins. But even if this was true, Schuller said, it would be a natural reaction for which he could not fault Raymond. "Everything went wrong there," he said."There was a delay in calling us, and then when we were called we got the wrong address and were sent to the rectory. But that first company on the scene did everything humanly possible. They called right away for a 2-11. But it was too late."

As for Raymond himself, the fire and the coroner's inquest took a terrible personal toll, one from which he never fully recovered. Before the fire he had been held in high regard. Afterward his reputation faltered. The point of the inquest was to gather information from key witnesses. Instead, for Jim Raymond, it was like a murder indictment.

"Those people were searching for straws," John Raymond, his son, later recalled. "My father was just a handyman janitor taking care of a lot of buildings. Nobody complained about his work before that. I think they were looking to rough someone up after this deal. It was the turning point of his life."

Others who knew the janitor also saw the "sloppy housekeeping" charges as off base. "He could always be seen sweeping up the floors and cleaning this and that," remembered Father Ognibene. "He had a big job, a lot of buildings to take care of. That fire didn't occur because of any negligence on Jim's part, that's for sure. Yeah, it was an old building, but it was a clean building."

Although allegations of the janitor's negligence were never proved, the stain they left upon Raymond's name lingered long afterward. In neighborhood taverns and coffee shops, not all those who talked were convinced that Raymond was merely a fall guy. Maybe he did have something to do with it. If not, why didn't he take a lie-detector test? And what about the trash in the stairwell? There were rumors he liked to drink. Maybe he tipped something over in the boiler room.

Nor was all the talk behind Raymond's back. Parents who passed him in the street muttered accusations, and there were occasional death threats. "I don't remember my father saying anything bad about it," John Raymond recalled. "My father was very quiet and remorseful. But I do remember hearing him crying all the time. He was shook pretty hard. I think what bothered him more than anything was that if he'd gotten there sooner, he could've got everyone out of the building."

Jim Raymond gradually withdrew from other people and became a loner. A beer drinker like many of his blue-collar friends before the fire, he turned to hard liquor. "He'd either go down to the corner and find his bar stool or just come home and find his bed," John Raymond said. "We'd find him there in the middle of the day, just lying in his bed. He became a very lonely man."

In time Raymond's life slowly fell apart. He never received true vindication. When a new Our Lady of the Angels School opened in 1960, a new janitor was hired to maintain it. Raymond was relegated to taking care of the church and rectory. In 1965, when Monsignor Cussen retired as pastor, Reverend Donald F. Kelley, a retired navy chaplain, was named as his replacement. By that time Raymond's drinking had worsened considerably, and a decision was made to let him go altogether. In 1968 the Raymond family moved to a suburb just outside Chicago. Jim Raymond never went back to work. He died of cancer in 1978 at the age of sixty-three.

WHILE THE INQUEST was in progress, many agencies and groups of investigators were examining the fire scene. The most comprehensive and credible report on the origin and cause of the school fire was made by John Kennedy.

A private fire and arson investigator based in Chicago, Kennedy had a brassy, cocky way about him that often annoyed his peers. He was a big man—six feet, four inches tall and weighing 230 pounds. He liked to smoke enormous Havana cigars and unabashedly fancied himself as "the world's greatest arson detective."

"When I hit a fire scene," he once commented, "I look for clues even most firemen don't know about. Every fire leaves 'fingerprints' that tell what happened—you just have to know enough about chemistry to read 'em."

Kennedy prided himself in pioneering the "Pointer System" in detecting the origin of a fire. "Fire travels upward once it starts," he explained, "so you look for the lowest point where there is evidence of burning. I perfected the method of tracing the path of a fire back to its source from a study of the burned flammables."

During World War II Kennedy rose to the rank of lieutenant commander in the navy, survived three ship sinkings, and later was transferred to intelligence with the responsibility for investigating fires within the naval establishment. After the war he became a special agent for a group of mutual fire insurance companies, making investigations that took him to virtually every state in the nation. Later he formed his own investigative agency, lectured at fire schools and seminars, and helped train police and fire department arson squads. Among his pupils were Lieutenants Jimmy Kehoe and George Schuller of the Chicago Fire Department.

On December 3, two days after the disaster, Kennedy had been retained by the Fireman's Fund Insurance Company to investigate the Our Lady of the Angels fire. The company was the insurer of the school building, the damage to which had officially been set at $125,000.

It took Kennedy more than three months to complete his findings, and on April 15, 1959, he delivered his report in the downtown office of the insurance company in the presence of Monsignor Cussen. The flamboyant investigator complemented his thick, typewritten report with copious photos of the interior of the school and with diagrams he charted on a chalkboard, showing the exact spot where the fire originated and the pipe shaft through which the hot air, gases, and smoke vented into the false ceiling above the school's second-floor classrooms.

"The manner in which the fire spread to the upper portion of the structure was most unusual," Kennedy said. "The fire evidently was smoldering for a long time, estimated to be at least one half-hour and possibly as long as forty-five minutes before the discovery and alarm at 2:42 p.m. This means the fire was burning as early as 2:12 p.m.

"The superheated gases and smoke which vented to the cockloft were forced to the west and accumulated in an area over the second-floor corridor at almost the exact center of the roof. You don't need a direct application of flame to wood to start a fire. All you need is a high enough temperature and wood will lose its ability to dissipate heat. This superheated air and smoke caused a second ignition sometime later when sufficient oxygen was admitted to this area beneath the roof.

"In addition to this principal method of spreading the heated gases, the hot air, smoke and later fire mushroomed up the open back stairwell to the roof area, and also entered a thirty-by-thirty-inch open ventilation grille in the cockloft almost immediately over the stairwell.

"It is quite evident the roof space over the center and east portions of the second floor of the school had been superheated long before the discovery and reporting of this fire. It is quite possible that, although witnesses do not report seeing any smoke or fire in the second-story roof area prior to discovery, a fire of severe proportions was actually burning in this concealed space at the time.

"It is reported that some fifteen minutes before discovery of this fire that the nuns and students in Room 208 and the room directly below had complained of heat in the rooms. It was undoubtedly the superheated gases and smoke passing up through the east wall of Room 208 and the room below which caused the temperature rise. There is little doubt that this is the manner in which the fire spread from the point of origin and caused a second and more serious burning beneath the roof."

None of this information was revelatory, but Kennedy now made one of his typically authoritative assertions. "The cause of this fire," he said, "is undoubtedly that of a human agency. It is very probable that this is a fire of incendiary origin.

"Although no definite suspects have been identified at this time, it is entirely possible that in the future some individual or individuals may be apprehended and charged with arson in connection with this fire."

Kennedy said he based his conclusion on the absence of "any machinery, equipment or any electrical wiring in the stairwell which could have malfunctioned and accidentally caused the fire. In addition, spontaneous ignition has been eliminated as have all the so-called 'natural causes.'

"This fire had to be set by a human being, either accidentally or intentionally."

Supporting his contention about the incendiary nature of the fire, Kennedy cited evidence he had discovered in the sacristy of the basement chapel.

"In the sacristy, a distance of about sixty feet from and with open access to the point of the fire's origin," he said, "I found several matches and a match book. These matches, some of which had been lit and some which had not, had been torn from the book and scattered about on the top of a wooden table. This was done in such a manner as to indicate someone had torn matches from the match book, igniting some of them and tossing them indiscriminately about this area. From the condition of the soot and smoke which had settled over the table, matches and match book cover, it was evident that this had been done prior to the fire and possibly immediately before the fire. The soot covered the top of the match book and matches, but the surface beneath them was clean."

After listening to Kennedy's explanations, Monsignor Cussen looked at the investigator and said, "Well, that's the only thing that makes sense of all the stories I've heard."

In his report Kennedy left no doubt there had been an accumulation of material at the base of the stairwell. "These materials," he said, "included two metal containers, a third container constructed of cardboard, a roll of linoleum, a brass scale of the platform type, a metal bookcase with adjustable shelves, a metal hand snow plow, some felt cloth which may have been used for rags or polishing, some newspapers—possibly as much as thirty pounds, more than three textbooks, a large wallpaper sample book, remains of a cardboard box, a roll of metal screen, and some bound test papers. These findings were confirmed by me. The items I enumerated are a minimum number of confirmed items found in the stairwell basement. There might have been more."

The fire had smoldered for at least a half-hour, Kennedy concluded, because of "the severe baking of the boiler room door which was caused by an even distribution of heat over a period of time and further corroborated by a similar-type baking of the door jambs of the girls' toilet room.

"The door to the boiler room was metal clad with wooden braces and although the wood was severely and deeply charred, the metal held and kept the fire from transmitting into the boiler room.

"The wooden door to the girls' washroom was burned, but from the nature of the burning, it appeared as though the door resisted the heat for some time before the fire burned through. This is due to the fact the fire was a smoldering type or covered fire, and did not receive sufficient oxygen to blaze up and cause more smoke, flames and other noticeable by-products that would have resulted in an earlier alarm.

"Instead, the fire continued to burn slowly and to generate heat. It was confined to the small stairwell area partly because of the closed doors to the boiler and girls' washroom and also because of the metal-clad surrounding walls. The smoke robbed the area of oxygen, preventing the fire from burning through and erupting."

In his investigation Kennedy said he had visited the police crime laboratory at least ten times to learn if any accelerant had been used in setting the fire. He watched as materials taken from the stairwell were analyzed.

"The tests proved negative," he said. "No accelerant was used."

Kennedy's complete findings were never disclosed to the general public, so parents of the school fire victims were never fully apprised of the facts. Because Kennedy was a private investigator hired to determine how the fire started, the information he collected during his probe was not shared by the archdiocese with anyone, including those most affected by the tragedy.

IN THE MONTHS following the fire, the tragedy at Our Lady of the Angels School slowly faded from public consciousness. Interest in solving the mystery waned. As time went on, the story of the school fire was no longer front-page news or the lead item on evening newscasts.

On March 10, 1959, Valerie Thoma, a cheery, fourteen-year-old eighth-grader who had leaped from a second-floor window with her clothing aflame, died in St. Anne's Hospital. She had been in Room 209 and had remained in the hospital since the day of the fire. Valerie suffered head injuries in her fall but had been taken off the critical list. She was undergoing skin grafts and other medical reconstruction when her body finally failed her.

William Edington, sandy-haired, thirteen years old, and an eighth-grader from Room 211, was the last victim to be claimed by the fire. He was burned over 80 percent of his body. Burns covered his back, his chest and abdomen, part of his legs and arms, the right side of his face, and his right ear. In the hospital he was the most polite child, and everyone loved him. Twenty-five times he went into surgery for skin grafts, with 6,000 square inches of preserved skin from donors used to cover his open wounds. Another 240 square inches were transferred from his mother's thigh and applied to his back. But in the summer his liver began to fail, and jaundice set in. On August 9 he died, 251 days after the fire.

With Edington's death the arithmetic was complete. The final death toll from the school fire reached ninety-five—fifty-five girls, thirty-seven boys, and three nuns.

IN AUGUST 1959 Monsignor Cussen granted his first newspaper interview since the fire and said publicly for the first time what many had long believed to be true. "There's no doubt in my mind that somebody set that fire," the pastor said.

Cussen had recovered from a stroke he suffered in May, brought on by the stress and anguish over the fire, and admitted he had lost fifteen pounds. It was the first in a series of strokes he would suffer later in his life.

"I used to wake up dreaming about it," he said, "but not anymore. I sleep better now. Since I've been sick, I've been able to get a good night's sleep. For a while they didn't think I was going to make it. Too much tension, I guess. But I feel a lot better now."

In the interview the pastor made another stunning disclosure not widely known by those in the parish—that someone had tried to set fire to Our Lady of the Angels Church that June, six months after the school tragedy. The fire had flickered out before causing serious damage. Burned pieces of a curtain had been found on the floor of a confessional. The arsonist had taken two candles from vigil lights in the church and placed them beneath a bench in the confessional. The curtain, removed from a door in the confessional, was set ablaze, but the fire died quickly in the small enclosure.

"There's some nut loose," Cussen said.

Ten

CONFESSION

A LMOST THREE YEARS PASSED, during which little new information about the fire emerged. Then, on October 26, 1961, a handwritten letter sealed in a plain white envelope with no return address was delivered to Fire Department headquarters in Cicero, Illinois. Its anonymous writer named a thirteen-year-old boy as the person who had set fire to an apartment building two days earlier in the suburb made famous in another era as the domain of gangster Al Capone.

This blaze in a building on West 21st Place had started in a pile of crumpled newspapers at the base of a stairwell. It was discovered early and caused little damage. When the town's fire chief, William Zahrobsky, turned the letter over to police, Captain Chris Rooney called in Lieutenant Victor Witt and youth officer Ron Richards.

"I think you better check into this boy's background," said Rooney, reminding the officers of another apartment building fire in the town the day before, October 25, on South 49th Court. This fire had been set in similar fashion—with newspapers being crumpled and ignited in a stairwell.

As they looked into the October 25 fire, the officers learned that the same boy identified in the letter had also been seen leaving that location. A woman who lived in the building across the street told police that at the time of the blaze the boy had come to her home to collect for his newspaper delivery.

"Can you smell any smoke on my jacket?" he asked her.

When the woman couldn't say for sure, the boy pointed to the building across the street. "There's a fire over there," he said. "You better call the fire department."

After the boy left, the woman found two books of matches inside her front door. They had not been there before he arrived.

The next day Chief Zahrobsky and Lieutenant Witt went to question the boy at Cicero public elementary school, where he was enrolled as an eighth-grader. After being summoned from his classroom, the youth walked into the principal's office and sat down in a chair. He was chubby, blond-haired, and wore thick glasses. "I had a feeling you were going to come and see me," he said, looking up at the men.

"Why do you say that?" Witt asked him.

"Because," he replied, "I was the one who saw that fire on 21st Place the other night. The firemen driving the pumper told me I did a good job, that I probably saved a lot of lives."

Witt was intrigued by the boy's candor. He looked at him for a second, then asked, "Are you in the habit of carrying matches with you?"

"No," the boy answered.

Witt asked the boy to stand up and empty his pockets on the desk. The boy complied. Among the contents were two books of matches and a cardboard box containing several wax-stick matches from the Playboy Club.

"Where did you get these?" Witt asked him.

"From my father's jacket pocket."

"Have you ever been in any trouble with the police?"

The boy thought for a second. "Once," he said, "in Chicago. I tried to derail a train and the police saw me and chased me. They caught me."

"How do your parents punish you when you do something wrong?"

Because he was a big boy, he said, his mother made him remove his pants, lie across a chair, "and then she strikes me with a cord from an electrical appliance."

"What kind of punishment does your dad dole out when you do something wrong?" Witt asked.

"He punishes me like a man."

"How's that?"

"Well, you know, with rabbit punches."

"Have you ever been punished for playing with matches?"

"Well, once. My father held my hand over the gas burner on the stove."

The boy was asked if he was afraid to tell the men about the two Cicero fires for fear of punishment by his parents.

"Yes," he replied.

"Did you set the two fires in those apartment buildings?" Witt asked him.

Hesitating briefly, the boy looked down, then nodded his head. "Yes," he said.

As Zahrobsky and Witt continued their conversation with the boy, he revealed that he liked to play with matches and was excited by the sound of fire sirens. Witt decided they should take the boy to the police station for further questioning. His mother was called at her job at an electronics manufacturer in suburban Northlake, and was asked to meet them there.

Once at the station, the boy was led into an interview room where Lieutenant Witt was joined by Officer Richards. When the two officers asked the boy about other suspicious fires in Cicero, he maintained he had started only the two apartment building fires. The officers did not believe him. Witt bent down to one knee and looked the youngster in the eye. "As far as the seriousness of the act," he said sympathetically, "it is just as serious if you started one fire or a hundred fires. Now, son, be honest with me, did you set any of these other fires in this area?"

"Yes," said the boy, admitting to several other fires in various locations. One of them had occurred October 9 in a three-story apartment hotel on Cermak Road. He said he had ignited that fire by stuffing newspapers and a cardboard box under the rear staircase, then lighting them with a match. This blaze was extinguished by the fire department without serious damage. He also stated he had turned in a false fire alarm on October 24, the night of the 21st Place fire.

When the boy's twenty-eight-year-old mother arrived, the officers explained the circumstances of the interview, telling her that her son had admitted setting a series of fires in the town. The woman, who was three months pregnant with her second child, did not look surprised.

"Why did you do this?" she asked him.

The boy did not reply.

Chief Zahrobsky showed the woman the matches that had been removed from her son's pocket. "Do you know, ma'am, how he may have obtained these?"

"Well," she said, "he has a habit of going through the drawers. He probably took them from his dad."

The woman told the police that her son was under the care of the Catholic Counseling Service and had been seen by one of its psychiatrists. The treatment, however, had not been continuous.

Witt placed a call to the Chicago offices of the Catholic Counseling Service, which confirmed the relationship. A counselor advised that she had made one contact with the family, and that an appointment made for further treatment had not been kept. When Witt related the particulars of the current case, the counselor scheduled a new appointment to see the boy. Satisfied with this arrangement, the police released the boy to his mother's custody.

"Please keep an eye on him," Witt asked the mother.

ON NOVEMBER 16, 1961, another apartment building fire in Cicero was started on an enclosed rear porch, and the same boy was positively identified as having been seen leaving the building just before the fire was detected. This time a seventy-two-year-old woman living on the building's second floor was hospitalized for smoke inhalation.

Officers Witt and Richards returned to the Cicero school to question the boy about the latest fire. He related that on the day and time in question, his mother had accompanied him on his newspaper route while he was making collections. But further questioning revealed a period of time in which he was out of his mother's sight. Working on this period, the officers continued their questioning him about the fire. After a few minutes the boy's alibi broke and he began to sob. "Yes," he admitted. "It was me."

The boy said he had gone to the rear porch of the building, removed some rags stored in a box there, then lit them with a match he claimed to have picked up from a Chinese restaurant on Madison Street in Chicago.

"What did you do after you started the fire?" Witt asked him.

"I went back on my collections," he replied.

"Why did you start that fire?"

"Because," he said, "I wanted to get even with the kid who lives there. He pushes me around a lot and I don't like him."

The boy's mother had been called, and when she arrived the two officers related to her the circumstances of the interview, informing her of the admission her son had just made. At first she didn't believe it.

"Speak to the boy," Witt said to her. "He'll tell you."

After the mother talked with her son privately, the two officers accompanied her and the boy to the Cicero police station, where a juvenile complaint was sworn charging him with the November 16 fire. But later, at a hearing in Cook County Family Court, the boy recanted his admission to police, denying he had started the fire. His mother also testified before the hearing officer that her son had been with her and that she could account for his whereabouts the entire day.

After hearing the evidence and testimony, the court found the boy guilty. He was placed under the supervision of the Family Court and once again released to his mother's custody.

MEANWHILE, in checking out the boy's background, Officer Richards began building a rather intriguing profile.

Along with his mother, the youth lived with his thirty-one-year-old stepfather and his sixty-five-year-old grandfather in a brick two-flat on Cicero's south end. The stepfather was employed as an assembly-line worker at a Chicago electronics manufacturer, and the mother worked full time in Northlake. Following the couple's marriage in 1959, the husband had adopted the boy, who assumed his new stepfather's last name.

The youth's school record was troubled. After moving with his family from Chicago to Cicero in December 1960, the boy was enrolled in St. Attracta's parochial school, but his parents withdrew him after only two months. In March 1961 he transferred to the Cicero public school, where his attendance record was poor and his behavior noted as "deplorable." His grades were very low, and his teachers regarded him as a "troublemaker" who always pleaded "for another chance" when he misbehaved.

Digging into the boy's earlier academic experience, Officer Richards made another discovery, and his interest in the boy heightened considerably. While living in Chicago in the late 1950s, the boy and his mother resided in a small frame cottage on North Springfield Avenue, and under his mother's maiden name the boy attended the local parish elementary school. It was Our Lady of the Angels.

A check of attendance records confirmed that on the day of the fire—Monday, December 1, 1958—the boy had been in class, a ten-year-old fifth-grader assigned to Miss Tristano's classroom, Room 206. Richards also learned that while a student at Our Lady of the Angels, the boy would leave his classroom at every available opportunity, asking his teachers to use the washroom or go to the principal's office.

"He was a chubby little blond-haired kid, tended to fantasize, was not athletic, but smart," Richards later recalled. "He wasn't the only kid we ever questioned about starting fires. But knowing he went to Our Lady of the Angels, I admit I got excited."

Richards called Sergeant Drew Brown at the Chicago police bomb and arson unit. "I need to get some background on the Our Lady of the Angels fire," Richards told him. "I think we may have something for you."

ON THE MORNING of December 21, 1961, Cicero firefighters were called to the boy's home on South 50th Avenue after a fire broke out in the basement. Firefighters arrived shortly after 9:30 a.m., extinguishing the blaze in about thirty minutes. The basement sustained serious damage, and the whole building was filled with smoke.

In speaking with the woman who lived on the building's first floor, fire officials learned that the boy had been seen in the basement shortly before the blaze erupted. "When I smelled smoke, I opened the back door and he was right there," the tenant told Chief Zahrobsky. "I've seen him down there before, sometimes with a lighted torch. I'm deathly afraid of him."

Zahrobsky located the boy in the house next door, where the Fire Department's inhalator squad was treating the youngster's grandfather for smoke inhalation and a possible heart attack after he was rescued by firefighters from the family's second-floor apartment.

"Son," said the chief, "would you come outside with me for a minute?"

"Sure," the boy replied.

Once outside, the chief asked the boy to sit in his Fire Department sedan, and the youngster complied gladly. Firefighters were picking up their hose lines and clearing the house of smoke when the boy's mother arrived home from work. "What's he doing in that car?" she yelled to Zahrobsky.

"I asked him to wait for me there," said the chief. "You can join him if you like."

She opened the back door and slid in next to her son.

After the fire operations were completed, the chief returned to the car and drove the boy and his mother to the police station for questioning.

"Son," the boy was asked, "did you start this fire?"

"No," he replied. "I was taking the garbage out when I smelled the smoke."

EXCEPT FOR his short-lived interrogations by Cicero police, because he was a juvenile the youth had at no time been taken into extended detention or locked up. Instead, after each questioning he was released to the custody of his mother.

On January 8, 1962, police again visited the Cicero school where the boy was a student. This time they wanted to question him about another suspicious fire on December 30. The blaze at the Town Hall Bowling Alley on West 25th Street, located a block and a half from the boy's home, had killed four men. One of the victims, Walter "Sunny" Smith, aged twenty-three, lived with the boy's family as a boarder. A coroner's jury had ruled the deaths "accidental," and foul play was not suspected. Authorities listed the fire's cause as "unsolved," though police suspected the boy was responsible.

But under questioning by Lieutenant Witt and Officer Richards, the boy denied any knowledge of the fire, insisting he had been home watching television with his parents. His mother verified the story. "He was with us," she said. "He didn't go out all night."

The following day the boy and his mother were asked to return to the Cicero police station, where officers—joined by investigators from Chicago, among them Sergeant Drew Brown—requestioned the young suspect using a tape recorder. During this exhaustive interview the boy again broke down and admitted to setting a rash of fires both in Cicero and Chicago, in basements and on back porches. He said he had set his first fire when he was five years old, holding a match in front of a spray paint can in a garage near his home on Chicago's West Side. The paint, he said, "ignited like a big torch" catching the garage on fire. The fire had been extinguished after a neighbor noticed smoke.

"I love to watch fire trucks," the boy said. "I have a siren on my bicycle and I ride around with it on half the time. I like to set fire to garbage cans. I like to light a twig or a stick and carry it around from can to can like a torch. Sometimes the can burns like a rocket.

"When I set a fire, I stay in the neighborhood sometimes. I play ball or play with the kids. When the Fire Department comes, I run back and watch."

When questioning turned to the Our Lady of the Angels fire, the boy grew tense and his face became flushed. But he quickly regained his composure and vehemently denied setting the school fire. "I don't know who started it or how it started," he said.

Police believed the boy was lying. "Son," Brown inquired, "who was your teacher when you went to Our Lady of the Angels?"

"Miss Tristano," he said. "She pushed me out the window."

"You jumped from the window to save yourself?"

"She pushed me out. She pushed all the kids out. I did a belly-flopper and landed in a fireman's net."

Later that same afternoon Sergeant Brown and Officer Richards met with Miss Tristano, who by then had become an instructor at a local Catholic college. Tristano related to the officers how, after smelling smoke, she had led her students to safety by taking them down the interior stairway in the school's south wing.

She disputed the boy's claim that she had pushed him out the window. "None of my students left by the windows," she said. "When I smelled the smoke, I took him and the others out into the hallway and down the stairs. I am quite sure I pushed no one out."

"Do you remember this boy specifically?" Brown asked the teacher.

"Yes," she replied. "He sat in the right front seat where I could watch him. He was a problem boy. Any kind of mischief you can imagine, he was in."

"Do you know if he left the room that afternoon for any reason?"

"He was in my room when the fire broke out. I remember him being there at least ten minutes before the fire." But, Tristano said, "three years have elapsed and children often went to the washroom. I just can't remember."

After the interview, Brown hastily returned to his office and checked his records on the school fire. Contained in the file was a statement the boy had given detectives on December 12, 1958, in which he reported being evacuated down the stairs along with his classmates from Room 206.

INFORMED OF their son's admissions, his parents contacted an attorney for advice. Dino D'Angelo suggested they take the boy to the offices of John E. Reid, a prominent Chicago polygraph expert, and have the youth submit to a lie-detector test. The parents agreed and said they would pay for the examination themselves, ensuring that they would receive the results rather than have Reid turn over his findings to the police and fire officials.

On January 12, 1962, the mother brought the boy to Reid's office in downtown Chicago. Reid was at lunch. While they waited, Robert Cormack, one of the firm's staff examiners, interviewed the mother for a half-hour. She complained that fire investigators had been harassing and pestering her son and interfering with his education, interrogating him at school every time there was a fire in Cicero.

She did admit, however, that the boy had set some fires. She then produced a list of addresses and dates of eleven fires that had occurred in Cicero and Chicago, including those about which the boy had frequently been questioned.

"I want him to take a lie test to find out once and for all which fires he set and which ones he didn't set," she told Cormack. "I think he started one or two of them, but not all of them." She did not tell Cormack that her son had attended Our Lady of the Angels, or that the police had also questioned him regarding the school fire.

Cormack asked if she thought her son was getting sexual gratification out of setting fires. "He doesn't seem to realize he's setting fires," she said, "and after he sets them, he has a guilty feeling and remorse."

Knowing his problem, the mother said she regularly drove her son back and forth to school and did not allow him to be out of the house unless he was accompanied. She also told Cormack that the boy was being seen by the Catholic Counseling Service.

During the course of her conversation, the mother related that her son had been born in 1948, in Cleveland, Ohio, an illegitimate child conceived after she was allegedly raped by her stepfather when she was fifteen. The child was born in a home for unwed mothers, and it was planned that the baby would be put up for adoption. But after being unable to agree to the arrangement, the mother decided to keep the boy. She later settled in Chicago, where she had relatives, and the boy's natural father moved to California. Her new husband, she said, had bought the boy "all kinds of sports equipment," but because her son was not interested in sports, the equipment had gone unused.

When John Reid returned to the office, Cormack briefed him on the facts, and Reid took the boy into a separate room to interview him further before administering the polygraph. A tall, slender, well-spoken man with a professional air about him, Reid was a lawyer and former Chicago police officer who had walked a beat before building a national reputation as a polygraph expert. He knew the thirteen-year-old boy would not be the most reliable subject for a polygraph test, so he tried to get as much information as possible before the test, letting the idle lie-detector apparatus serve as a silent threat to the boy to tell the truth.

"Son," Reid began, "I want you to talk to me and tell me the whole truth before we hook you up to the lie detector."

"I will," the boy answered. "I'm not going to lie."

"Good."

Reid began by asking the boy about the fires he was alleged to have set in Cicero, and the youngster openly admitted to igniting four apartment building fires, including the blaze at his own home. He also admitted setting fire to the garage on Ridgeway Avenue in Chicago, "near where I used to live," when he was five years old, and further related to Reid the facts of another fire he started in Chicago, inside the hallway of an apartment building near Springfield Avenue and Ohio Street. In starting this fire, the boy said, he had spread newspapers in the hallway, squirted them with lighter fluid, then ignited the papers with a match. "The firemen came and put it out," he said. To this point the boy had not mentioned that he had attended Our Lady of the Angels School in 1958, or that he had been questioned about the school fire.

"Do you have any others as bad as me on this test?" he asked Reid.

"Yes, we do," Reid replied. "We have much worse. We have had murderers sit in that same chair."

The boy paused, then spoke again. "Sometimes," he said, looking down at the floor, "after I set fires, I feel so bad that I wish I wasn't even born." Another pause. "Is it only boys or girls that set fires?"

"Boys or men mostly," Reid said.

"Then why wasn't I born a girl?"

Reid didn't comment. Instead he asked, "What school do you go to?"

"Cicero Public School. It's a grade school."

"What grade are you in?"

"Eighth."

"What religion are you?"

"Catholic."

"But you don't go to a Catholic school?"

"I used to," said the boy. "I did go to St. Attracta and before that, when I lived in Chicago, I went to Our Lady of the Angels School."

Reid was dumbfounded. Our Lady of the Angels?

"Son," said Reid, trying to mask the sudden excitement in his voice, "were you at Our Lady of the Angels at the time of the fire?"

"Yes, I was."

"I want you to tell me the truth," he said. "Did you set the fire at Our Lady of the Angels School?"

"No, I didn't," the boy responded. "But on the afternoon it happened, I was coming back to school with this other kid, and I said, 'I got some matches in my pocket and I could burn down the school and we wouldn't have to go to school no more.' "

"Did you really have matches with you?"

"No. But I told my friend that I did."

"Son, I want you to make sure you're telling me the truth because I'm definitely going to include the Our Lady of the Angels fire on the lie test. Now, I'm asking you again. Did you start that school on fire?"

"No, I didn't."

Reid decided not to ask more questions about the school fire before administering the polygraph. To ensure that the machine would work on the boy, Reid gave him a standard control test. After fitting the boy with pulse, respiration, and blood pressure monitors, Reid presented him with seven numbered playing cards, all face down.

"I want you to choose one card but answer no to each question I ask you," Reid instructed.

"Okay," said the boy. He looked interested and inquisitive, and not the least bit intimidated.

When Reid asked him whether cards one through four were his chosen card, the boy answered no, and little movement was noted on the polygraph. Then Reid asked him whether he had chosen card number five. Again, as instructed, the boy answered no, but this time the polygraph showed considerable movement on the blood pressure and pulse recordings—indications he was lying.

"Son," Reid said, "it's clear to me that you took card number five."

"Gee, that's right!"

"Good," Reid said. "It appears that the machine is working on you."

"Good," said the youth, his boyish curiosity still apparent.

"Okay," Reid said, "let's begin the real test. Remember, just answer the questions by saying yes or no. Understand?"

"Yes. I understand."

Reid decided to lead the boy back to December 1, 1958. "Now, let's start. Did you set fire to Our Lady of the Angels School?"

"No," the boy answered.

Reid looked at the machine; its movements were identical to those registered after the boy had answered no to question five of the control test. He's lying, thought Reid. Still, he decided to ease off a little, to let the last question hang over the youngster's head.

"Did you set fire December 30, 1961, to the Town Hall Bowling Alley in Cicero, Illinois?"

"No," said the boy. "I was home watching TV with my parents."

The machine's response regarding the bowling alley fire was not clear. Reid set down his pencil and looked the boy in the eye.

"Son," said Reid, showing the boy the polygraph reading, "I think we've got something to talk about here. The machine indicates you were not being truthful for the question I asked you regarding the Our Lady of the Angels fire."

"It says that, does it?"

"Yes, it says that. I don't think you're telling me the truth about the Our Lady of the Angels fire." Reid paused for a moment. "Your mother wants the truth. I want the truth. You told me you're a Catholic boy. You know telling a lie is a sin. There are ninety-two children and three nuns looking down at us right now from heaven who want the truth. Now tell me, did you set the school on fire?"

The boy looked suddenly to the floor, shifting his eyes back and forth, turning in his chair. "Well," he said nervously, "I didn't set the fire. But I'll let you know who did."

"All right," Reid said. "Go on."

"See, me and this kid, he came home with me at lunchtime, and when we were walking back, he says, 'Lookit, I got some matches that I found at your house. I can set the school on fire and we'd have a couple weeks off.' "

It sounded to Reid like the boy had created an alter ego, that in fact he was describing himself. "Son," he said, "I don't think there's any other kid at all in this case."

"Well, do you think that's so?"

"The lie detector has shown that."

"Well, I guess so. I guess I better tell you the truth."

"I guess you better."

Suddenly the "friend" in the earlier story changed to the person of the suspect himself. The boy began describing to Reid how he had left his classroom on the afternoon in question, obtaining permission from his teacher to use the washroom. He had gone downstairs to the boys' lavatory in the school basement. He said he had started the fire on the way back to his room, tossing three matches into a waste drum filled with paper at the bottom of the empty northeast stairwell.

"Are you sure," Reid asked, "that you actually started a fire with the three matches?"

"Oh, yes," said the boy. "I saw them start up. I stayed there for a minute and watched the flames get bigger and bigger, then I ran back to my room.

"I didn't want it to be such a big fire, nobody to get hurt. I thought the janitor would find it and he'd put it out. I thought it would be bad enough just to give us a couple days off from school. I didn't know so many kids were gonna be killed."

"Why did you set the fire?" Reid asked him.

An edge of bitterness crept into the boy's voice. "Because of my teachers," he said. "I hated my teachers and my principal. They always were threatening me. They always wanted to expel me from school."

John Reid was amazed. He was convinced the youngster was telling the truth. He asked the boy to draw a pencil sketch of the basement and northeast stairwell, and the youngster pinpointed the exact spot where the fire had started. The sketch showed the boy had excellent recall of the building's interior.

When he finished, he set down his pencil and looked up to Reid. "I can't tell you how glad I am to get this off my chest."

BECAUSE OF the enormity of the boy's confession, Reid left the youngster alone for a moment and walked to the reception room to inform the boy's mother what he had been told. Upon hearing the news, she didn't seem very surprised, and Reid quickly determined that all along she had suspected her son of setting the fire.

"I would like to call my husband," she announced.

"Yes," said Reid. "I think you should. I would also advise you to contact a lawyer, that is, if you don't already have one."

After showing the mother to a telephone, Reid stopped to confer with one of his staff associates, George Lindberg, also an attorney. Reid briefed Lindberg on the facts, and for a moment the two men immersed themselves in thought. The case was complicated, especially because of the confidential nature of the conversation. Still, it would be a good idea to take a statement from the boy, to get the confession on record. Reid looked thoughtfully at Lindberg. "George," he said, "he's got the history. He was in the school. I think we should get it down on paper and see where we go."

LATE THAT AFTERNOON Mildred McGuffie, a secretary in Reid's office, began taking a lengthy statement in shorthand from the boy in the presence of Reid, Lindberg, and a third staff associate, Stephen Kindig. The boy's mother remained in the waiting room.

Reid began the questioning.

Q: Did you go to Our Lady of the Angels School at the time there was a fire there?

A: Yes.

Q: What year was that?

A: 1958.

Q: Do you recall the date of that fire?

A: It was on December 1st.

Q: . . . What grade were you in?

A: Fifth.

Q: Do you recall your room number?

A: 206.

Q: What was your teacher's name?

A: Miss Tristano. I don't know if I could spell it or not.

Q: When you went to Our Lady of the Angels, did you usually come home for lunch?

A: Yes.

Q: Did you go home for lunch on the day of the fire, that is December 1, 1958?

A: Yes.

Q: What time did the fire start?

A: Around three o'clock.

Q: Was that a.m. or p.m.?

A: Three o'clock in the afternoon.

Q: Did you come back from lunch with anyone?

A: Yes, my boyfriend.

Q: What is this boy's name?

A: I don't remember, but I think it was Bob.

Q: Where does Bob live?

A: I don't know the exact address. It's on the opposite side of the street. Our number was 508 North Springfield and he was on the odd side of the street.

Q: I suppose you talked to Bob when you were coming back with him.

A: Yes.

Q: Do you recall at this late time what you talked about?

A: Murders and horror pictures.

Q: How old was this lad you call Bob at the time?

A: Nine at that time.

Q: What grade was he in?

A: Fourth at Our Lady of the Angels School. I never seen his teacher.

Q: So you talked about murders and horror pictures and stuff like that?

A: Yes.

Q: Did you say anything about your school when you were coming back?

A: I told him I had matches in my pocket and I said I was going to burn down the school so we wouldn't have no more school for a couple of weeks or days and that we'd have a vacation.

Q: What did Bob say?

A: He thought I was kidding.

Q: Were you actually kidding?

A: Yes.

Q: Did you think anything more about burning down the school after that?

A: About a quarter of three that same day.

Q: What did you do?

A: I asked my teacher if I could be excused and went to the washroom. After coming from the washroom, I went to the chapel [in the basement] to see if anyone was in there. Then from the chapel I went back to this here can like the janitors have. It was made out of cardboard and had steel rims on it and I didn't see anybody no place, and I used three matches and I lit the thing and I ran back upstairs to my room.

Q: After you went to your room, what did you do?

A: I went back to my seat and was talking and goofing around, bothering kids and then my teacher opened the door and there was smoke coming and she ran to the fire alarm upstairs and she turned it in for the school so everybody could get out to know what it was. Then she got all us kids over to the window and [we] had to wait until the firemen could get through there first with the net and she pushed us out the window and she jumped out herself.

Q: What did you do after you got out?

A: I stayed around and watched the fire for a while and then I ran to my [Cub Scout] den mother's house because she was going to have a den meeting. . . .

Q: . . . Just before we started this statement, you made a drawing for Miss McGuffie, Mr. Lindberg and myself, is that right?

A: Yes.

Q: Will you point this drawing out to Mr. Lindberg, who is sitting right next to you, and tell him again what you did after you left your room at Our Lady of the Angels School on December 1, 1958?

A: I went downstairs to the boys' washroom. Then after I went to the washroom I came out of the boys' washroom and went to the chapel to see if there was anybody in there and there wasn't anybody in there so I walked back to the can.

Q: What kind of can was that?

A: The can was a cardboard—it was a round cardboard rubbish can for papers and it had metal rims on it for the top and for the bottom. I looked around and I didn't see anybody. I threw three matches in the can and then ran up the stairs to my room.

Q: Did you light these matches?

A: Yes.

Q: Did you see whether or not they caught fire?

A: Yes.

Q: Did they catch fire?

A: Yes.

Q: In the drawing here it seems as though you have the can located under the stairs, is that where it was?

A: Yes.

Q: Was there anything else under the stairs?

A: Two or three little rooms for the janitor to put his brooms, brushes and stuff like that.

Q: What was your reason for setting this fire?

A: What do you mean?

Q: What did you do it for?

A: Well, I thought we'd get a couple of days off from school because of the fire.

Q: Did you see flames in the can before you left to go back to your classroom?

A: Yes.

Q: Did you have any special feeling at the time you started this fire at Our Lady of the Angels School?

A: Just that I didn't think it was going to hurt nobody.

Q: What was in this can that you threw the lighted matches into?

A: School paper from all the rooms—all kinds of paper and the papers that kids throw out that they didn't need.

Q: Was it full to the top?

A: Yes.

Q: Did you tell anybody about Our Lady of the Angels fire before?

A: No.

Q: Why are you telling us about it now?

A: I wanted to get it off my chest.

Q: Why didn't you tell it to anyone before?

A: Afraid my dad was going to give me a beating and I'd get in trouble with the police and I'd get the electric chair or something.

Q: Why are you thinking about the electric chair?

A: On account of what my dad told me.

Q: Was he referring to anything particularly?

A: No.

Q: How did your father start talking to you about the electric chair and so forth?

A: A couple of days ago it was a picture I seen—Wednesday, I think—a picture of a guy. He got sent to the chair for nothing—he didn't do it and my dad kept telling me things about it and about the gas chamber.

Q: This picture you are speaking of, where was that picture?

A: On TV.

Q: Who played in that?

A: Edward G. Robinson.

Q: I want to get it clear in my mind as to how your father talked to you about the electric chair. You said he brought it up after seeing this Edward G. Robinson picture the other night, but did he say anything about that to you before this?

A: No, except for that one fire I set at 1906 49th Court in Cicero.

Q: When was that?

A: I don't know what day it was. It was on the night I was collecting for my paper route. I think it was around Thanksgiving in November.

Q: What did he say to you then?

A: He said the next time I set any place on fire and if you kill somebody and if the police don't get you and give you the electric chair, I'll come after you myself personally and kill you.

Q: Did you believe your father would do this?

A: Yes.

Q: Before this past November and before the statement that you said your father made to you about the electric chair, what was the reason why you didn't tell anyone about Our Lady of the Angels fire?

A: I was scared to.

Q: Who were you afraid of?

A: I was scared of my dad. Not my mother, but my dad would give me a beating.

Reid concluded the interview by bringing the boy back to the present, ensuring for the record that the statement was not in any way coerced or given under false pretenses—that the boy was confessing willingly and knowingly.

When the interview concluded, the boy was left alone in the examining room. Reid and his staff went into another office to begin transcribing the statement into typewritten form.

Meanwhile the boy asked for something to read, and he was handed a few magazines. Picking up a November 1961 issue of *Look* magazine, he began flipping through its glossy pages. When he came upon a color photograph showing the Kennedy family posing in front of a Christmas tree inside the White House, he stopped. The tree in the photo was set next to a grand staircase with bright red carpeting running up its steps. The boy unzipped his trousers, removed his penis, and began to masturbate.

Unknown to the boy, the scene was being observed by Stephen Kindig of Reid's staff, who had been posted to monitor the boy through a two-way mirror to ensure that the youngster did not try to injure himself or attempt suicide by jumping out the window. Kindig went to summon Reid. "John," he said, "I think you better come with me. I want to show you something."

When the two men returned to the mirror, the boy was still masturbating—fondling himself with one hand and turning pages with his other, often returning to the photograph of the White House Christmas tree. The two men watched as the boy masturbated for four one-minute periods. He did not ejaculate. Finally, appearing as though he feared someone might walk in on him, the boy placed his penis back into his pants, zipped up his trousers, then ripped the page from the magazine, folding it in half and stuffing it into his pants pocket.

Reid knew that arson was often a sexually motivated crime, and after watching the boy's actions he was convinced that the youth was receiving sexual gratification from starting fires. Reid concluded that the boy was dangerous.

THE BOY'S STATEMENT covered eight typewritten pages. At the bottom of the final page, Reid, Lindberg, Kindig, and Mildred McGuffie signed their names as witnesses.

When the boy's stepfather arrived at Reid's office early that evening, he and the mother were provided a copy of the boy's typewritten statement and informed of their son's admission regarding the school fire. The stepfather rose from his chair, incredulous. "He told you what? Why that little sonovabitch. Where is he?"

"Calm down," Reid said from behind his desk. "Legally, he cannot be punished."

Reid explained that despite the admission, the boy could not be charged with a crime. The Illinois criminal code of 1961 stipulated that a juvenile under the age of thirteen was "incapable of committing a crime" and therefore could not be held criminally liable until reaching the age of thirteen. Because the boy had been only ten years old at the time of the school fire, he was immune from prosecution. Still, Reid considered the boy a danger to himself and to society. "It's obvious he needs psychiatric treatment," he said. "I think we should give this information to the authorities."

The stepfather could barely control his anger. "He made that up," he said. "After that fire, he told us one of his friends, a fourth-grader, showed him some matches and said he was gonna burn down the school."

Reid thought for a second, recalling that the boy had developed an alter ego during the interview and had attempted to place blame for the fire on this nonexistent person.

Again the stepfather spoke up. "I thought this was to be confidential. I don't want it going any further."

Reid said he favored full disclosure.

"If you give this information to the authorities," argued the mother, "they'll bring out all the other fires that happened in Cicero, and he was older then. He could get in trouble for that."

"I think you've got a moral responsibility as parents to get help for the boy," Reid countered. "If you don't do something now, who knows what he might do? He might start a fire later on, in a hospital or a hotel or God knows where, maybe kill somebody, and then he'll have to bear the full brunt of the penalty. At least by informing the authorities now, he'll get proper psychiatric treatment while still a child."

The mother looked nervous. "What about the newspapers?" she asked. "Can't we do it without all the publicity?"

"I cannot assure you of that," Reid answered. "But I promise you that as far as I'm concerned, I will not make any statement whatsoever."

"If this comes out," said the stepfather, "they're gonna put him in jail forever or tie him to the electric chair." He rose from his chair, visibly upset. "All right," he said, "I've heard enough. I want to see him. Where is he?"

Reid escorted the parents to the examining room where the boy was waiting. As soon as the man confronted his stepson, his anger boiled out of him. "Goddammit!" he shouted. "Did you set that goddamn fire? You tell me now!"

The boy backed against the wall, frightened. "No!" he exclaimed.

"Then why did you say so?"

"Because," he pointed to Reid, "he told me to."

Reid asked the boy to leave the room and then scolded the stepfather for his emotional outburst. After the two men regained their composure, Reid told him, "If you don't bring this thing to the attention of the authorities, I will myself."

The stepfather thought for a second. "Give us a little time to talk to our lawyer," he said softly. "He'll get in touch with you over the weekend."

"Okay," Reid said.

FOR JOHN REID, the situation presented a terrible dilemma. The results of the test were supposed to be confidential. If he took them to the authorities, he would be violating the parents' trust. Yet considering the enormity of the confession, coupled with the fact that the cause of the school fire had never been officially determined despite an enormous amount of money spent to investigate it, Reid felt obligated to clear up the mystery surrounding the deaths of ninety-five people.

The next day, Saturday, January 13, Reid contacted one of his

colleagues, Fred Inbau, a Northwestern University Law School pro-
fessor specializing in legal ethics. After listening to the facts of the
confession, Inbau considered the tenuous legal issues of privileged
communication versus the public's right to know the truth. He also
considered the boy's own plight, realizing that by disclosing this information to the authorities, the youth could receive the proper psychiatric counseling he so desperately needed.

Seeing as how, under Illinois law, the boy was immune from
criminal prosecution because of his age, Inbau advised Reid that as
an attorney and member of the bar it was his duty and responsibility
to inform city officials of these developments.

"I would advise you to tell them," Inbau said.

Reid next telephoned attorney Dino D'Angelo and disclosed the
information he had obtained from the boy on Friday, asking D'Angelo to convey the same information to juvenile authorities. He also
advised him of his conversation with Inbau. D'Angelo said he
would confer with his law partners over the weekend and discuss the
matter with the boy's parents, then contact Reid on Monday morning.

Late Monday Walter Dahl, one of D'Angelo's partners, called
Reid and told him that after discussing the matter with the boy's parents, the attorneys were not convinced that the youngster had set the
school fire and therefore had decided not to disclose the information
to the authorities.

"And we hope you won't either," Dahl said.

Reid ignored the plea and called Judge Alfred Cilella of Family
Court. Reid knew the boy was to be brought before the judge in regard to the Cicero fires, and he thought the judge should know about
the youth's admission about the school fire. But Cilella quickly ter-
minated the conversation. He told Reid he did not want to disqualify
himself because he would likely have to hear the case, adding that
the boy was already under the jurisdiction of Family Court for another Cicero fire.

Meanwhile, word of the boy's visit to the polygraph laboratory
had leaked, and that same Monday Reid received telephone calls
from police Sergeant Drew Brown and from George Bliss, a leading
investigative reporter for the *Chicago Tribune*.

Brown said the information had come to him from, among other
sources, Monsignor William Gorman, chaplain of the Chicago Fire

Department. "Can you at least confirm for me," Brown asked Reid, "that this boy has confessed to you the crime?"

"If anything is forthcoming," Reid replied, "it will probably come from the attorneys for the family."

Bliss, though, seemed to know the situation well, and he pressed Reid to go on record and provide details of the boy's confession. "We've had a reporter, Weldon Whisler, out in Cicero for the past month and a half checking the kid out," Bliss advised. "We know all about the questioning he's been through and we know about the interrogation of his fifth-grade teacher [Miss Tristano] too."

The *Tribune*, Bliss said, had been tipped off by Cicero police. When he told Reid his newspaper had contacted Judge Cilella and was going to print the story without using the boy's name, Reid confirmed that he had talked to the boy and had administered a lie-detector test. But he refused to disclose his findings. "I cannot comment," he said.

The story of the boy's alleged confession made front-page headlines in Chicago's newspapers the next day, January 16: "Information that a 13-year-old boy has confessed setting the fire at Our Lady of the Angels School, which took the lives of 92 children and three nuns, was given yesterday to Judge Alfred J. Cilella of Family Court," the *Tribune*'s story read. "Judge Cilella promised an investigation of the report that the boy signed an eight-page confession under questioning by John E. Reid, head of John Reid and Associates . . . a nationally known expert on lie detectors.

"Cilella said if the confession is found to be accurate, the boy should be taken into custody.

"Suspicion that the boy might have been responsible for the school fire began to grow when investigation showed he had been a pupil there at the time of the fire. He attended school there, however, under a different name. . . ."

ON WEDNESDAY, January 17, 1962, the boy, accompanied by his attorneys, surrendered to Cook County juvenile authorities at the Audy Juvenile Home in Chicago. There, with the approval of Judge Cilella, he was held incommunicado, and investigators were not allowed to interview him.

Cook County State's Attorney Daniel P. Ward asked Reid for his complete files on the case, and later that day a conference was held among all investigators who had worked on the school fire. After the conference, a delinquency petition was filed in Family Court charging the boy with the three fires he was alleged to have set in Cicero on October 24, October 26, and December 21, 1961. But authorities did not have enough evidence to charge him in the Town Hall Bowling Alley fire, and the petition made no mention of the Our Lady of the Angels fire.

If the boy was found delinquent for any of the Cicero fires, he would be placed in the custody of his parents (amounting to probation) or a psychiatric treatment center, or be incarcerated in an Illinois Youth Commission penal institution.

Ward did, however, indicate his intention of filing a second petition charging the boy with the Our Lady of the Angels fire, even though he knew the Illinois crime code forbade the conviction of any person under the age of thirteen at the time of the committed offense. Even so, by charging the boy, officials were hopeful that a judicial ruling could find the boy responsible for the school fire, the cause of which was still listed as "undetermined," and thereby lay the mystery to rest.

The boy was not scheduled to be in court until early February. Meanwhile Judge Cilella ordered him to be examined by a team of psychiatrists to determine if he was fit to stand trial. The report submitted to the judge by Dr. John V. P. Steward, the court-appointed psychiatrist who examined the boy along with three consulting psychiatrists, included the following: "We are in agreement that the boy is aware and has full knowledge of the nature of the proceedings initiated against him and is capable of cooperating with his attorneys. . . . He is not mentally defective nor psychotic. Psychological tests indicate a full scale intelligence quotient of 110, placing him in the bright category."

Chicago police and fire investigators had reviewed the boy's confession (obtained from the state's attorney), cross-referenced it with evidence obtained at the time of the blaze, and reconfirmed that the boy was present in school on December 1, 1958. They concluded that the young suspect was the person who had set fire to the school. Chicago police also tracked down a number of the boy's former classmates from Room 206, questioning them as to whether they recalled him leaving the room on the afternoon of the fire. None could remember. When Miss Tristano, his teacher, was requestioned, she reiterated her earlier comments, saying she was unable to recall if she had granted the boy permission to leave the room and use the washroom, or if he had sneaked out of the room without her being aware of it.

In a legal maneuver to allow them to question the boy themselves, Chicago investigators issued an amended petition in Family Court charging him with arson in connection with the school fire, including the petition of the boy's confession that he had started the blaze. The judge accepted the petition, but when the boy's attorneys objected to his being questioned, Judge Cilella again sided with the defense, and the request to interview the suspect was denied.

FAMILY COURT hearings on the boy's case began on February 8 and were continued twice. Because the case involved a juvenile, the three sessions were held behind closed doors; access to the courtroom was restricted to attorneys, witnesses, the boy's family, and the press.

When he was called to testify before Judge Cilella during the first court session, the young suspect, on the advice of his attorneys, entered pleas of not guilty to all counts and denied he had ever started any fires.

At the second session John Reid was called as a witness and asked about the confession the boy was alleged to have made to him. Reid told the court he was convinced the boy was telling the truth about the school fire, describing for the judge how his secretary typed out the statement, which was then read and corrected by the boy, who initialed each of its eight pages. "He told me he set fire to Our Lady of the Angels School, and he drew a pencil schematic sketch of how he set the fire," Reid testified. "My observation is that the boy set the fire and I believe sincerely that he did."

When Reid finished, attorney John J. Cogan, a member of the boy's defense team, objected. "Your honor," said Cogan, "we would ask that the court strike from the record the testimony Mr. Reid has just given pertaining to this boy's alleged confession on the grounds that the defense feels this alleged confession was obtained by Mr. Reid involuntarily and under color of coercion. Mr. Reid's observation and opinion regarding what he 'believes sincerely' is not fact and should not be construed as such."

Cilella agreed, ordering that Reid's remark be stricken from the record.

Still, Chicago authorities introduced into evidence the burned rim of the fiber trash container in which the boy said he tossed the three matches, and photographs showing the stairwell floor where the circular mark of the trash barrel had been found. Neither the barrel rim nor the photographs had ever been revealed to the general public. Chief James Kehoe of the Chicago Fire Department's arson squad and police Sergeant Drew Brown both testified that, in their opinion, the school fire started exactly where the boy said he had set the blaze.

At the final court session the boy was recalled to the witness stand and, under questioning by Cogan, recanted his confession that he set fire to the school. He said he signed the confession after Reid told him that if he did so, he could go home.

"I was frightened and tired," he explained.

As for the pencil sketch he drew in Reid's office showing the layout of the school basement and the path he allegedly took to the northeast stairwell, the youth testified that he had merely drawn what Reid had told him to. (While the boy was in his office, Reid had determined the school's interior plan in a telephone call to investigator John Kennedy.)

When the session ended, Cogan asked the court for a directed verdict in favor of the boy, arguing that the school was not a dwelling and therefore the boy could not be charged with arson, only with burning a building, for which the three-year statute of limitations had run out. Cilella, however, disagreed, admitting into evidence the boy's rough pencil drawing of the school basement.

JUDGE ALFRED CILELLA took pride in his image as a wise and fair jurist in Family Court matters. He had a reputation as being tough on offenders, and he never balked in imposing discipline on youngsters who had veered into a life of delinquency. But this case was different. Instead of helping to rehabilitate the boy, Cilella knew that if he found the youth responsible for the school fire, it would be tantamount to issuing a death sentence. Our Lady of the Angels was in an Italian neighborhood. He himself was Italian. If he ruled that the boy had started the fire, what would be accomplished except to place a deadline on the youngster's life?

Even though the evidence was circumstantial, Cilella was convinced the boy had set the school fire. The facts showed the boy was obviously sick and a danger to the community, a person in need of psychiatric treatment. It was quite plausible he had not intended to harm anyone; he never expected the fire in that trash can to do what it did. Still, the evidence coupled with the polygraph test, the boy's confession to Reid, and the drawing he made of the school basement, was overwhelming.

And what about Reid? His stature and reputation as a polygraph examiner was first rate, his credibility flawless. If Reid had formed an opinion that the boy was guilty, he was likely correct.

Then there was the issue of the archdiocese. Cilella was a devout, lifelong Catholic, an active member of the Knights of Columbus DeSoto Council on Chicago's North Side. He felt a sentimental responsibility to the church in which he had been reared, and to its archbishop, Cardinal Meyer, a quiet, reverent, studious man who avoided the limelight and held a genuine concern for his people.

A finding of guilty against the boy would surely create a legal headache for the archdiocese, and the archdiocese, Cilella figured, had already taken enough hell for the fire. If it were ever proven that one of its own schoolchildren had started this tragic fire, the church could be held negligent for failing in its duty to supervise the boy while he was under its guardianship, thereby creating an environment that enabled him to sneak off and start a fire that killed ninety-five people.

No matter which way he ruled, Cilella knew it would not bring back the children who died in the fire. As a judge on the Family Court, his job now was to help rehabilitate this boy—a delinquent, mischievous thirteen-year-old—a habitual fire-setter with an extremely troubled background.

Eleven

DECISION

O N MARCH 13, 1962, Judge Cilella rendered his decision. As the verdict was announced, the boy sat pensive in the courtroom next to his attorneys. His parents were not present.

Reading from his twenty-one-page opinion, the judge began his reasoning. "The child testified under oath in open court and denied [setting] the Our Lady of the Angels fire," he said. "It is true he similarly denied setting the Cicero fires. However, his testimony was given on different days, with a week intervening.

"His denials of the Our Lady of the Angels fire, when considered in light of all the other evidence, were quite convincing. His similar denials with respect to the setting of the Cicero fires were not convincing."

The judge overruled the earlier defense objection by admitting into evidence the school fire confession the youth had given John Reid, determining that the statement had been given voluntarily. But, he held, the confession was "contradicted by all of the circumstantial and physical evidence which was adduced in open court."

The only similarity to known facts about the origin of the fire, Cilella observed, was the boy's statement that he had set fire to the cardboard trash barrel in the basement of the school. The boy said the barrel was under the staircase, but Chief Kehoe and Sergeant Brown had testified that it was near the foot of the staircase. (On this point the judge was later disputed by investigators who claimed the boy's description of where he started the fire was generally, though not precisely, correct.)

Another "discrepancy" Cilella found in the confession concerned the boy's description of how he had jumped out the window into the fireman's net. "The court finds this fantastic and incredible. This was not substantiated by his teacher or in the statement" the boy gave police eleven days after the fire.

"Under these circumstances, the court cannot speculate as to which of the material portions of the statement are true and which are false. The court is not convinced that the statement is true."

Cilella also took issue with John Reid. "The court is troubled by certain of the circumstances surrounding the giving of the statement. This is particularly true of Reid's assurances that the results of his examination [of the boy] would be held in confidence."

Reid, the judge said, "knew that statements made to him could not be held in confidence if the process of the law demanded their disclosure. His representation to the child that his signature was needed on the statement in order that Reid might complete his file was transparently false. In short, the child and his parents were misled."

Still, after dressing down Reid for the way he had obtained the confession for the school fire, Judge Cilella made a complete turnaround and accepted the confession Reid had obtained for the Cicero fires.

Concluding, the judge declared, "Upon the evidence before it, the court does not have an abiding conviction that this child set the Our Lady of the Angels fire. Such being the case, the court will not burden this child with the judicial determination that he is responsible for that tragedy."

So ended the best case investigators could muster in their quest to resolve the school fire mystery. For setting the fires in Cicero, Judge Cilella ordered the boy sent to the Star Commonwealth boys' center in Michigan. There the boy received psychiatric treatment to help cure him of his fetish for starting fires. He remained at the Michigan center until his release in 1965, when he entered military service and was sent to Vietnam.

Ironically, the youth's release order from the Michigan boys' center was signed by Walter Dahl, one of the lawyers who had defended him during the juvenile proceedings, and who by 1965 had become a judge on the Cook County Circuit Court.

AMONG THOSE interested in the case, opinion remained divided as to whether the boy had told the truth during his interrogation by John Reid. Despite Judge Cilella's ruling, the boy's description of how and where the fire started—details only the fire-setter would have known—corroborates much information compiled by investigators that had never been previously released. Investigators had never revealed the exact spot inside the school where the fire had originated. Nor had it ever been revealed that the blaze had in fact started in the ringed, thirty-gallon trash container. All news stories had reported in a general manner that the fire had started under the stairs in the northeast stairwell. In fact the fire's origin was eight feet from the base of the stairwell, in the exact spot the boy had indicated in his pencil sketch of the basement. The only obvious discrepancy noted in the boy's statement was the way he described his escape from the burning school building.

Also telling are the similarities between the apartment building fires the youth set in Cicero and the manner in which the school fire started—blazes which began in papers at the bottom of staircases. They further support the beliefs of Reid and other investigators who were convinced the boy was truthful in his confession.

Private investigator John Kennedy, though, remained noncommittal. "I'm not saying he did it, but this boy was there," Kennedy said. "He had the opportunity. He was a pathological fire-setter. He told things about the fire that only we, on the inside, knew to be true. What the boy said corroborates how I think it was set." Kennedy recalled that before 1962 "I was the only one with the courage enough to say officially that it was a set fire. I was all alone in the wilderness. Some people thought I was trying to take negligence off the Fire Department's back. Others thought I was investigating for the school and trying to absolve the pastor. But they were wrong. It's just that I came up with an answer some of them didn't want to hear."

John Reid, of course, could not be swayed in his conviction that the boy actually did start the Our Lady of the Angels fire. "One thing I could never figure out was the archdiocese doing what they did," Reid said during an interview in 1976. "They didn't want any of their kids being responsible for that fire. They sat on the judge. They sat on everybody.

"I know when I'm getting a false confession and I know when I'm getting a right one. I've been in this business since 1940, opened my own office in 1947. Over the years I've quizzed thousands of people. I've had more than three hundred murder confessions. If an examination is conducted properly, you get a pretty good reading on whether a person is being truthful or deceptive.

"The fluency of the boy's story was quite regular," Reid said. "He could tell me where he went after he came upstairs from the school basement. He told me about going to the Cub Scout meeting at his den mother's house and how the woman became upset because she had heard about the fire at the school. His story seemed to flow very easily."

When asked about the boy's obvious falsehood in claiming he was pushed out the classroom window by his teacher, Reid dismissed that part of the boy's statement as "fantasy." "I think the kid wanted to tell somebody about setting the fire. He was ripe for it at the time."

OFFICIALLY the Chicago archdiocese never attempted to resolve the cause of the fire, choosing instead to leave the question hanging. And though it could never be confirmed that Judge Cilella's decision to exonerate the boy was influenced by the archdiocese or any other outside interest, a powerful political relationship shared between city and church, in conjunction with the legal system, appeared to be at work.

George Lindberg, Reid's associate who witnessed the boy's confession and who went on to become a federal district judge in Chicago, offered an interesting slant on the case. "The information we obtained," Lindberg said, "is that the cardinal [Meyer] did not want this boy to bear the stain of being responsible for ninety-five deaths, and that the judge, therefore, was prevailed upon to throw the confession out. So it appears that Cilella's decision was predetermined."

Lindberg denied emphatically that the boy's confession was coerced by Reid. "He is dead wrong," Lindberg said. "I assure you that this was not a forced confession. Was he culpable? Absolutely.

There is absolutely no question in my mind that he did it. He furnished details that only the fire-setter would have known. My view is that other than being there and seeing him light the matches, we got [through the interview and polygraph test] the next best thing."

A close family friend of Judge Cilella's remembers the pressure he faced at the time of the hearing. "Al was a Catholic and he felt obligated to the church," replied the source, who asked to remain anonymous. "Afterward he took a real beating. His wife was incensed when he decided to let the boy off the hook. She really tore into him. 'How could you do this? How can you look at yourself in the mirror when you know he's guilty?' That sort of thing.

"After that happened they used to argue a lot at the dinner table. He took a real beating from all corners, and it had a very detrimental effect. It wasn't long after that he got sick and died. The stress was incredible. Privately he knew the boy was guilty. He wrestled with it and second-guessed himself for the rest of his life."

Sister Andrienne Carolan knew the boy well. She taught him religion for four years and had counseled him on occasion at Our Lady of the Angels School. "He was the kind of boy who would say anything to get attention," the nun recalled. "He didn't know who his real father was, and he was searching for a masculine image. He loved Father Ognibene and Father McDonnell, not so much because they were priests, but because they were masculine images in his life. He was a practical jokester and used to do some dumb things, but I can't say he would ever want to deliberately hurt somebody. In fact, if he misbehaved in class he'd be the kid who'd come up to you and say, 'Gee, Sister, I'm sorry I goofed off today.' "

Others remember the boy differently. Robert Lombardo was a student in the suspect's classroom. He recalled how, on the morning of the fire, he and another classmate were sent by Miss Tristano to look for the boy after he left to use the washroom and failed to return to the classroom in a timely manner. After going down to the basement, the pair located the boy in chapel of the north wing, leaving open to speculation that the youth may have considered starting a blaze earlier that same day.

"We found him right in front of the altar," recalled Lombardo, who went on to join the Chicago Police Department and earn a Ph.D. in criminology. "He had obviously come out of somewhere.

Whether it was in the boiler room or the back stairway behind the chapel, I don't know.

"We called to him, 'Hey, Miss Tristano wants you back in the room. C'mon, let's go.'

"We grabbed him and he pushes away. He runs off. He's gone. He took off running back behind the altar, to the stairs. We chased him a little but he was gone. We weren't looking to wrestle with him or fight with him. We went back upstairs to the room and told her he didn't want to go back to the room.

"On the same day we chased him around, when we were going home for lunch, he said to us, 'One of these days I'm gonna be famous. One of these days you're gonna read about me in the papers.'

"Of course we didn't know what he meant. We didn't pay any attention."

Although Lombardo said he could not recall if the boy had left the room later that same afternoon, at least one other former student from Room 206 said she distinctly recalls seeing him leave the classroom shortly before the fire broke out. "I remember him raising his hand, right around two o'clock, asking to use the washroom," she said. "He left that room and when he came back it wasn't long before Miss Tristano noticed the smoke and had us evacuate."

In 1958 Lombardo's family lived around the corner from the boy's home, near Ohio Street and Springfield Avenue. Lombardo hung around with the boy. "He came from a bad family situation," Lombardo said. "He used to get beat a lot by his stepfather. His mother was not very nice to the other kids in the neighborhood. We all played together—all of us kids in the neighborhood who lived nearby. We were all juvenile delinquents—stealing lightbulbs from street signs and throwing them, and eggs from the dairy over on Ferdinand Street. But that was as far as it went.

"But he was the little firebug of the neighborhood. I remember he set the mailbox on fire at Hamlin and Ferdinand. He's standing there one day throwing matches in it, starting it on fire."

Lombardo's family lived in the same Chicago apartment building the boy admitted setting fire to when he was interviewed by Cicero investigators. "It was a big court apartment building with an enclosed back porch," Lombardo recalled. "He set it on fire and it was blazing like crazy. It didn't destroy the building, but the Fire Department had to come and put it out."

Lombardo remembers being interviewed by police in 1962, after the boy was identified as a suspect in the school fire. "I told them of the incident with him in the basement," he said. "Nothing ever came of it. I thought for sure somebody would come back and question us again about it. But nobody did.

"We always thought the authorities, the police, would take care of it, make it right. It's like your parents. When something was wrong, your parents always made it right. That's how we looked at the fire. If someone set it, the police were like your parents. They would find out and make it right."

IN THE DECADES after the fire, the "boy" became a man and settled into the life of a truck driver living in a Western state. In the course of two brief interviews he revealed how, after being released from the Michigan youth center, he spent two years in Vietnam during military service. But he was reluctant to talk about the events that changed the course of his life in late 1958 and early 1962.

He did, however, remain emphatic in denying that he had set the Our Lady of the Angels School fire. "I don't want to open old wounds," he said. "As far as I'm concerned, I was a student at the school and that's all. I asked the teacher if I could go to the washroom that day. That was it.

"I got my ass in a bind for setting fires in Cicero. I had experiences like a lot of kids have, setting fires in back alleys or in garbage cans. When they brought me in, it was like the law trying to pin a crime on the first guy they think did it."

He was still bitter over the way he had been treated in the hearings in Family Court. "Ever hear about child abuse? That's what I'd call it. They had me in the Audy Home in solitary confinement for three months, in a little room."

And what about the damaging admissions he made to John Reid?

"He said to me, 'Look, it's coming out wrong on the polygraph. If you ever want to get out of here, you'd better give the right answers.' I wanted to get home. So I signed some things and then my parents looked at me, horrified.

"I was wrongly accused, and I went through hell because of it. When you're a little kid and spend as many hours as I did in that polygraph office, you'll sign anything. Reid started the whole thing. He instigated it."

The man said he didn't care to talk in greater detail about the school fire. "I don't feel like saying anything about it, because it happened so long ago and I don't really remember. If I say something, I might say something wrong. I want to forget about it, and besides, who the hell is gonna say they're sorry at me?"

DOUBTS ABOUT the boy's culpability were first nurtured in the mind of fire investigator George Schuller in 1962, following the close of the Family Court hearings. Despite the persuasive evidence showing that the boy had a history of setting fires, that he had been in Our Lady of the Angels School on the day in question and had left his room shortly before the fire erupted, Schuller, a member of the Chicago Fire Department photo unit and arson squad, still harbored uncertainties about the young suspect's confession.

Schuller was a lifelong resident of the city's South Side. Before joining the Fire Department in 1950, he had served with the navy in the Pacific during World War II. Something about the case didn't set right with him; he wasn't convinced the kid knew all that much about the fire. Although he couldn't put his finger on it, Schuller wasn't satisfied that the cause of the school fire had been resolved.

The fire had had an enormous effect on Schuller, one he would eventually take with him to his grave. On the afternoon of December 1, 1958, he had raced to Our Lady of the Angels School from City Hall with another Fire Department photographer, Don Walpole. They reached the scene just as firefighters began bringing bodies out of the building. Schuller worked through the night, taking interior and exterior photos of the school, paying special attention to the burned-out classrooms in the north wing and to the basement stairwell in the northeast corner of the building. He used up all the film he had in one camera and had to borrow another camera to finish his job.

Schuller photographed each classroom, the stairways, and the hallways. The images jarred his emotions. He could see dead children piled three and four deep alongside the windows on the second floor. He remembered seeing a brand-new shoe lying amid the debris. In all the commotion and excitement, it had become hard to think rationally, and when he saw a firefighter carrying the body of a boy accidentally bump the child against a wall, Schuller yelled at him, "Hey, damn it, don't hurt that kid." He knew his words made no sense—the boy was dead—but that's what seeing all those children had done to him.

Schuller photographed as many details as he could, including a clock in one classroom that had stopped at 2:47 p.m. He focused his camera lens on charred woodwork, overturned desks, debris that had accumulated in the stairwell, broken transoms, burned timbers in the cockloft, the basement heating system, books that lay open on desks, and the iron fence in the courtway that was eventually cut down with an acetylene torch. He took photos of a half-inch fire hose still folded neatly in a bracket near the front stairway, an unused fire extinguisher, portions of the sodden roof that had caved in over the second-floor corridor, and squares of acoustical tile that dangled haphazardly from classroom ceilings.

Schuller had stayed at the school until well past midnight, then had gone to his South Side home to wash up and snatch a few hours' sleep before returning to the scene the next day. For the next three weeks he returned to the school day after day, searching, probing, taking pictures, scribbling notes, and listening to conversations among other investigators, a number of whom leaned toward the theory that the fire was intentionally set. It was an opinion Schuller subscribed to from the start. "Damn it, Ann," he confided to his wife one night. "I know in my heart it was a set fire. But proving it is something else."

So Schuller, who had risen to the rank of captain with the arson squad, quietly maintained his vigilance with the hope that someday he would uncover the complete truth about the tragedy. Although his duties with the Bureau of Fire Investigation required constant attention to a variety of arson cases throughout the city, Schuller could never totally shake the school fire from his conscience. Finding its cause became an obsession.

Schuller figured all along that it was probably some troubled kid who started the fire. Over the years he spent hours at the fire academy, poring over records, studying the names of students who had attended Our Lady of the Angels. If a young fire-setter was apprehended in the city or suburbs, he would check to see if the name matched that of any student enrolled in the school in 1958.

In 1970 Schuller was named supervisor of the Bureau of Fire Investigation, with the rank of battalion chief. By then, he was one of the few remaining officers of the bureau who had worked the Our Lady of the Angels fire.

On a wintry night in February 1971, Schuller's life took a strange twist. He was called in to investigate a 3-11 fire which heavily damaged a North Side supermarket at Racine and Wilson avenues in the city's Uptown neighborhood. Arson was suspected. After finishing his on-scene investigation, Schuller began to pick up his gear when a young woman stepped out of a nearby tavern. She had dark hair and a pretty face but was noticeably overweight.

"Hey, fireman," she said, "you look cold."

Schuller's helmet and fire coat were coated with ice. "Yes," he answered, "I am. That was quite a fire."

The woman stepped closer. "I know who set it," she said.

Schuller laughed to himself. "You must've had one drink too many," he replied.

"No, I wasn't drinking. My brother set that fire."

"Your brother set that fire?"

"Yes, he did."

Schuller looked closely at the woman. Maybe she was telling the truth. "Listen," he said, "I'm cold and tired and I don't know if you're bullshitting me. It's getting late. If you're serious, why don't you call me at the fire academy at nine o'clock tomorrow morning."

The chief's hands were so frozen he couldn't unbutton his turnout coat. Instead he asked the woman for a scrap of paper and blew on his hands before jotting down his office telephone number.

"Here," he said, handing her the paper, "call me at this number."

The woman did call, and so began a strange odyssey for George Schuller in his personal quest to solve the mystery of the Our Lady of the Angels School fire. When the woman met with Schuller the next day, she appeared unkempt and sloppily dressed, and was suffering the effects of a bad cold. She implicated her brother in setting the supermarket fire, saying he lived with her and her husband in their nearby Uptown apartment on Malden Avenue. She said he had used pop bottles filled with gasoline to start the fire.

After checking out other details of her story, Schuller asked her to speak with detectives of the police bomb and arson unit. She did, but the detectives seemed disinterested and brushed her off. "I think you're wasting your time, George," one of the detectives told Schuller. "You fight the fires and leave the detective work to us. Forget about her. She's goofy."

As long as the police didn't care to pursue the matter, there was little more Schuller could do with the lead his informant had given him. "You know," he said, showing her to the door, "we can't live without fire. We heat our homes with it. We cook with it. But when it gets out of control, it can kill."

"I know all about that," the woman replied. "I remember the Our Lady of the Angels fire." The school fire had occurred twelve years earlier.

"Why does that stick in your mind?" Schuller asked quizzically.

"Because," she said, "we lived kitty-corner from the school."

Schuller was intrigued. "Why does that concern you?" he asked.

"Because my older brother set that fire," she said matter-of-factly.

Schuller was stunned. "Your older brother?" he said. "Where is he?"

"He's in Menard," she replied, referring to a state prison in southern Illinois. "He's doing time for arson."

When the woman gave Schuller her brother's full name, he fought to keep a straight face. He didn't wish to appear overanxious. He knew the Bureau of Fire Investigation already had an extensive file on the young man. He was twenty-three and had been sentenced to prison in 1965 for setting thirty-three separate fires in Chicago, including a November 1964 blaze in a six-story warehouse on Illinois Street that left one firefighter dead and five others injured. The warehouse was located adjacent to the firehouse of Engine Company 42, whose firefighters were away battling another fire the youth had set earlier the same Sunday in a hardware store around the corner. At the time of the warehouse fire, the youth was seventeen and had been on parole for just two weeks as a result of a May 1963 rooming house fire he had set in the same near north neighborhood that killed two men.

If the woman was telling the truth about once living near Our Lady of the Angels School, Schuller could not figure out how her older brother, who had a long history as a troublemaker, could have escaped the notice of investigators who had combed the neighborhood around the school immediately after the fire, looking for just that type of problem youngster.

Reviewing the files on the woman's brother, Schuller was unable to confirm that the family had lived in the building across the street from Our Lady of the Angels School at the time of the fire. He did learn, however, that the youth at the time attended St. Mary's Training School for dependent children in Des Plaines, a suburb northwest of Chicago. Records at the school did not reveal whether the boy had been released to his mother during the critical period that extended from Thanksgiving Day through the first week of December 1958.

Schuller discovered that the boy had run away from the training school a number of times and had numerous demerits not only for being "out of bounds" without permission but for disobedience, stealing, smoking, and fighting. In a fit of anger, the youth had once tried to stab another resident of the school with a pair of scissors.

After soaking up all the information he could from the imprisoned arsonist's file, Schuller made further contact with the sister, asking her to meet with him again. He wanted to show her a photograph he had taken outside Our Lady of the Angels School on the day of the fire. It was a crowd shot, and in it was an unidentified youth with a worried look on his face. The boy was dressed in a checkered flannel shirt and appeared to be about ten or eleven years old. When the woman studied the photo, she pointed to the youth in the crowd. "Yup," she said, "that's my brother."

Schuller was intrigued. Although he had checked many sources, he had never been able to confirm the identity of the boy in the photo. He asked the woman if she would tell Fire Commissioner Quinn (thirteen years after the fire he was still commissioner) about her belief that her brother had set the school fire. She agreed. Schuller briefed the commissioner on what the woman had revealed to him, so when they met he came directly to the point.

"Tell the commissioner," Schuller said, "who set the Our Lady of the Angels School fire."

The woman looked at the pictures on the walls, then at the man sitting behind the desk. "My brother did," she replied.

Quinn jumped up from his seat, slapping both hands on his desk

top. "What did you say, young lady?" he exclaimed. "Will you re-
peat that?"

"I told you. My brother set that fire. He was the one who burned
the school."

Quinn was incredulous. "Jesus, George," the commissioner said.
"Don't let her out of here until you get a complete statement from
her."

After repeating essentially the same story she had related to
Schuller, the woman signed a statement and returned to her North
Side apartment. Not long after, Schuller discovered that the woman
and her husband had moved out of the city. They left no forwarding
address. Schuller tried unsuccessfully to track her down. They had
disappeared.

Schuller's position as director of the Bureau of Fire Investigation kept him busy with more than nine hundred suspicious fires
each year. He could no longer allow the school fire to consume his
attention. Commissioner Quinn, despite his early enthusiasm over
the woman's revelation, had arbitrarily let the matter die. "I didn't
think the woman was right mentally," Quinn later admitted. "The
guy was in prison anyway, and if he did set the school fire, he
couldn't have been brought to court. In Illinois you can't prosecute a
kid for setting a fire if he's under thirteen."

Still, for Schuller the woman's story seemed plausible, and he
wasn't about to let go of it completely. In the mid-1970s he began
corresponding with the inmate at Menard and eventually made four
trips to the prison in downstate Illinois. The prisoner was tall and
lean, with long brown hair and long sideburns. He had a long chin
and a sheepish grin. During extended correspondence with the prisoner, Schuller compromised himself on more than one occasion—
by sending the suspect money and even offering to buy him a small
television set. Wittingly or unwittingly, Schuller also coached the
prisoner on certain aspects of the school fire. In the end, he finally
obtained the prize he sought: a signed confession in which the con-
vict admitted to setting the school fire.

In his confession the man wrote that on the afternoon of December 1, 1958, he had walked across the street from his home and
sneaked into the basement of Our Lady of the Angels School to escape the cold and smoke a cigarette. He claimed he had tossed the

cigarette butt into a trash container and left the building. His family did not see or hear from him for the next two days.

When the prisoner was paroled in 1979, he appeared on a Chicago television program with Schuller, who by that time held the rank of division fire marshal. The parolee's name was never used, and with his back to the camera he was asked the following question: "Did you set the Our Lady of the Angels School fire?"

He replied: "I did start the fire. And like I told the chief [Schuller] before, it was a pure accident that it was set, and I had no intention of hurting anybody. I did go down in that basement and start the fire, but it was a pure accident."

The man had been eleven years old at the time of the fire, so legally he was immune from prosecution. But his confession on television stirred up a hornet's nest in City Hall. Commissioner Quinn had since died, and Acting Police Superintendent Joseph DiLeonardi and the city's new fire commissioner, Richard Albrecht, challenged the validity of the parolee's statement. "We get people confessing all the time," DiLeonardi told reporters after a morning meeting with Mayor Jane Byrne.

Although the Our Lady of the Angels case had never been officially closed, privately police bomb and arson officials were certain the fire had been started by the Cicero youth who confessed in 1962 to John Reid. So too was DiLeonardi, a brash, flashy, fast-talking former chief of detectives who had spent most of his police career investigating homicides.

Police investigators assigned to check out the new confession wasted little time getting the truth out of the thirty-two-year-old ex-convict who had saved all his prison correspondence with Schuller. The letters were damaging to Schuller, because he had passed along information that helped the parolee put together a believable confession. In short order the police had the one-time prisoner admitting that his story was a hoax, that he had conned Schuller from the start.

Twelve

RECOVERY

F OR THE CHILDREN injured in the school fire, the road to recovery was often long and painful, the suffering great. But so too were their courage and fortitude, traits manifested through youthful innocence and a determination to survive.

Eleven children and one nun—Sister Mary Helaine, the eighth-grade teacher from Room 211—required repeated skin grafting to replace the skin that had been seared off their bodies. Because the school fire occurred before the advent of regional burn centers, each hospital was left to treat its own burn patients. On the night of the fire, a critical decision was made at St. Anne's Hospital, where most of the fire victims had been removed, to treat all their burns by the "exposure" or "open method."

First introduced in 1949 in Scotland and later pioneered in the United States at Brooke Army Medical Center in San Antonio—which dispatched a team of burn specialists to Chicago to assist in the treatment of the school fire victims—the open method simplified burn treatment and helped reduce the risk of infection, often a life-threatening complication for burn patients. Instead of being swathed in warm moist dressings—which encourage the growth of bacteria and must be changed every few days—the patient lies naked on a sterile sheet. Nature then takes over, covering the open wound with a thick brown crust, creating a natural barrier to the entrance of germs.

As practical and effective as it is, the treatment still presents complications, and meticulous attention to sterile techniques must be followed. Nurses treating the children were required to don sterile gowns and masks as they entered each room. They wore sterile gloves when they touched a burn. It would have been easier and safer to bar all visitors, but doctors recognized that the youngsters needed their parents, so they too were masked and gowned before being allowed inside their children's rooms.

Parents of burn victims often found their naked children strapped onto circular-framed beds resembling large canvas slings, each designed to relieve continued pressure on the youngster's uncovered burns. Because in many cases the burns covered both sides of their bodies, the children had to be turned constantly, as often as every two hours or sooner. The special beds were called Stryker frames— "the most uncomfortable bed in the world," recalled one fire survivor. Two nurses were required to turn the bed over. When turned upside down, the beds were only a foot or so off the floor, so the hospital's staff had to ensure that the floors were kept as clean and dust-free as possible to keep dirt, bacteria, and other particles from entering the raw, uncovered burn areas on the children's bodies.

Added to the children's discomfort was the cold. The skin is the largest of the body's organs, and its covering helps regulate body temperature. Deprived of the natural insulation of their skin, their bodies untouched by blankets, many children complained of being hot on the outside and cold on the inside. Rooms were kept warm by adjusting the heat, and nurses created ingenious tents by draping sheets and electric blankets over the bars above each Stryker frame. Another major medical concern involved maintenance of fluid and electrolyte levels to prevent the children from falling into shock. Because the fluid levels of burn patients fluctuate markedly, physicians treating the children had to check levels on each patient up to six times each day.

Worst of all was the pain. Each time a nurse had to turn a child, touch a wound, pry it gently loose from a sterile sheet, or change a dressing, the pain was excruciating. Consequently many children were administered morphine and other painkillers to ease their discomfort. "Every time you took the linen off, you pulled off some of their skin," recalled Henriette Rocks, a nursing nun at St. Anne's who at the time was known by her religious name, Sister Kathryn.

On December 1, 1958, Rocks, a blond-haired farm girl from downstate Streator, Illinois, was a thirty-one-year-old nursing supervisor in charge of the hospital's surgical recovery ward where twenty children, most in critical and serious conditions, were admitted. Rocks had been a nurse for almost eight years and was regarded as "seasoned" by her peers at the busy West Side hospital. Never, though, had she faced a more challenging crisis. The demands were great, and for more than a month she and her staff of nurses worked day and night to administer medications, monitor vital signs and fluid levels, change dressings and linens, coordinate with housekeeping staff, scrub floors to reduce the risk of infection, and simply be there to help ease the youngsters' fears.

"With the children," Rocks remembered, "you tried to relate to them the best you could and try to explain what had happened. But we really didn't talk about it much. In those days things were glossed over. Now what you try to do is reach the person and try to bring out their feelings. You try to support them in a much different manner. We tried to support them by not admitting what was going on. We tried to shield them, protect them."

Encouragement for the children, Rocks recalled, came from many different sources and from all over the world in the form of letters, gifts, and visitors. Often big-name entertainers—Jack Benny, Pat O'Brien, and Ed Sullivan among them—would stop by St. Anne's to visit the youngsters. It was good for the children to be remembered, for hospitalization was a lonely, isolating experience. Yet for Rocks and other members of the hospital staff, the visiting guests also created headaches. Even though the visits helped raise the children's spirits, they also affected the nurses' ability to isolate the burn victims from added risks of infection.

"Basically we had to protect them from people," Rocks said. "We had every type of entertainer coming in. We had clowns. We had cowboys. We had all these reporters coming in. Everybody had to dress properly. They had to wear gowns and masks.

"I was looked on as a real 'bitch' because I was yelling at people all the time, trying to keep them away from those children and make sure everything was clean, that they were protected. This included the families. They didn't understand it at the time. What those kids needed most was to be held and hugged and reassured. But you couldn't touch them. It was really a terrible thing. And I was put in the position of being the 'bad person' trying to protect them, and nobody was understanding why I was doing it."

Susan Smaldone, with more than 80 percent of her body burned, was the most critical case to be admitted to Rocks's ward. She had no skin. She was absolutely raw. For twenty-one days the little nine-year-old clung to life before finally succumbing December 22 from an overwhelming infection and kidney failure.

"With Susie," Rocks said, "what you wanted to do was take her and hold her. Every once in a while she would say, 'Oh, it hurts.' Especially when you were moving her. It was excruciatingly painful for her. All the time. You hoped she was going to make it, but you knew she probably wouldn't."

On the evening Susan died, Rocks had left the floor early, around six o'clock, after working a twelve-hour shift. She had something to eat and then retired to her quarters inside the hospital. She was putting her head on the pillow when she received a call notifying her that Susan had died. Rocks got dressed and went back up to the floor. Susan's parents had been at their daughter's bedside.

"I took them into a room and we talked for some time," Rocks recalled."Her mother was a British war bride, and she really had a beautiful outlook on life. They told me about Susie and how she had epilepsy and was more or less near her parents all the time because they didn't let her go out. Things revolved around her. They came back again after New Year's Day and we talked. The gist of the conversation, since the fire happened, was that although it was a horrible tragedy for their family, it brought them closer. They were looking at their other children differently. They said they knew they had an angel in heaven now. But they wanted to come back and thank me for everything I did for her. It was a wonderful meeting with them. I saw so much bitterness among other parents, and to see these two act the way they did was very inspiring for me.

"I felt so close to Susie and even now I still do. I feel she's my little angel in heaven. Every once in a while I say things to her."

Another patient in Rocks's care was Michelle McBride, the feisty, brown-haired thirteen-year-old from Room 209 who would later write a book about her lengthy hospitalization and recovery.

Over 60 percent of Michelle's body was burned, and on December 19 she was wheeled into an operating room where she remained under anesthesia for two hours. Skin was transferred to her right shoulder, the back of her right knee and her right hand, and areas around joints in danger of permanent stiffness if scar tissue were allowed to form.

Michelle underwent seven skin-grafting procedures, the last performed two and a half months after the fire. Because only a small amount of her unburned skin was available, her surgeon, Dr. Paul Fox, used grafts the size of postage stamps on her lower legs. Instead of moving the skin in a single sheet, he cut it into one-inch squares, placing them a half-inch apart over her calves. Because skin grows outward, the gaps eventually filled in. Michelle was discharged from the hospital in March 1959, but she faced a life of suffering and adaptation. She was forever plagued by arthritis and stiffness of joints, and years later still required use of a cane. During the summer months, rising temperatures and humidity brought painful, smarting reminders of her reconstructed body. "The fire not only robbed me of a childhood," she later commented, "it also robbed me of an adulthood."

Another patient in the same ward, a nine-year-old girl, was among the most horribly burned children to survive the school fire. The tip of her nose and part of her lip were the only unburned areas of her face. She was unable to close her burned eyelids or mouth. The backs of both her hands and forearms were burned as well. St. Anne's had no plastic surgeon on its staff, so it called in a consultant, Dr. Clarence Monroe. On New Year's Day 1959 he started a delicate series of skin grafts to give the girl a passable face. Eight operations were performed at St. Anne's, another ten at Chicago's Presbyterian–St. Luke's Hospital, where the girl had been transferred in March.

Even with the skin grafting complete, the road back to normalcy was not easy for her or any of the children. Doctors informed the girl's parents their daughter would never look normal, but thanks to the operations she could at least now close her eyes and mouth. In time she also learned how to play the organ with her grafted hands. But years later, as an adult, she rarely ventured outside her home in an affluent Chicago suburb, preferring to avoid the stares of the outside world. On those rare occasions when she left her home, her face was heavily masked with cosmetics—items of luxury for some women to enhance beauty and hide subtle signs of aging, necessary tools for her to camouflage her disfigurement.

GERRY ANDREOLI, another "burn," endured fourteen operations in which skin was grafted onto his arms, face, back, and hands, each painful ordeal lasting three to four hours. During the first month of his hospitalization, Gerry's parents stayed at St. Anne's, keeping an around-the-clock vigil, watching and agonizing as their pitifully burned son, his body naked save for his bandaged areas, lay motionless in a Stryker frame. At night the parents slept on couches in a closed-in porch and were furnished with extra blankets. They went home only to shower and change clothes. Relatives operated their store and took care of their younger children.

The Andreolis retained many sharp memories of their long stay at St. Anne's. They remembered telling a young nurse to remove a large mirror from Gerry's room. "It was right in front of him," Alfred Andreoli recalled years later. "We didn't want Gerry to see himself."

Early in Gerry's hospitalization the Andreolis heard complaints from the children about the food they were receiving. Proper nutrition is important for burn victims, and it is essential that they eat often to replace vitamins and proteins vital to the healing process. One day the physician in charge of Gerry's case entered his room and asked the boy if he was hungry.

"Yes," Gerry answered.

The doctor turned to Gerry's father. "There's a steak house on North Avenue," he said. "Get the biggest steak you can find and bring it in every day."

"And that's what I did," Mr. Andreoli remembered. "I'd get a filet, bring it in, and feed it to Gerry. He couldn't feed himself because his hands were burned. He couldn't even go to the toilet by himself."

Other parents were allowed to bring in food and feed their injured children. "It relieved the nurses and gave the parents time to be with their kids," Mr. Andreoli said. But if the patient was bedded in a Stryker frame, the feeding process became a chore. It took about forty-five minutes to turn a child from an upside-down position near the floor to a position where they were lying on their backs, face up.

"At mealtime," the senior Andreoli recalled, "some of these kids would be face down on a Stryker frame. Their faces would be a foot off the floor. The kids couldn't wait forty-five minutes to be turned.

The food would get cold. It was pathetic to see a mother lying on the floor, on her side or back, with a plateful of food, feeding it to a kid lying upside down."

After his condition stabilized, Gerry began the first of his fourteen skin-grafting operations. Each time Gerry would go to surgery like a trooper. Later in the day he'd be returned, sometimes unconscious, sometimes screaming. For his parents, the reaction to his pain was tormenting. They felt helpless. "We'd be in the room and hear these screams," Mr. Andreoli recalled. "He'd be down the hall maybe three hundred feet away. All we could do is bite our lips and say, 'There's Gerry.' "

As the process continued, the rawness of Gerry's burn was replaced by the rawness of his skin grafts. Donor sites on his body used to take transplanted skin for grafts became new open sores. Much like placing a patch on an inner tube, in order to prepare an area to receive a skin graft doctors first had to create a granular texture over the skin bordering the area to be covered. Sheets of skin from donor areas were then thinly shaved from Gerry's buttocks and legs and cut into small squares. The colorless layers of skin were then meticulously stitched onto the raw, sterilized burn areas with the hope that the little patchworks of transplanted skin would take hold, regenerate, and grow together to form new sheets of skin to cover the open burns.

When the skin was removed, donor sites became new islands of smarting pain. After a skin-grafting procedure was completed, the newly covered wounds would be dressed and bandaged. Donor sites were covered with sterile sheets of rayon, exposing them to the air. Large scabs would form. The scabs itched, but they could not be scratched. As soon as the donor sites healed, the process would be repeated.

On and on it went, for three grueling months—changing dressings, lying motionless on his Stryker frame, being prepped for skin grafts, wheeled into surgery. Only when he was released from the hospital on March 7, 1959, did his parents tell Gerry that his girlfriend, Beverly Burda, had died in the fire.

After his discharge Gerry was required to return to St. Anne's for physical therapy three times a week. Therapy is another critical stage of the healing process for burn victims, consisting chiefly of active and passive exercises to rejuvenate muscles. Hydrotherapy—

placing burn patients in large tubs of swirling water to facilitate healing and stimulate muscle—was another element of the process.

Often Gerry's father would accompany him on the trips. One day in the spring, Alfred Andreoli asked a nurse if there were any other students from the fire still in the hospital. "Yes," the nurse responded. "There's a girl in the orthopedic ward."

"Thanks," Mr. Andreoli said. He looked to his son. "C'mon, Gerry, let's pay her a visit."

The girl was Irene Mordarski, and the visit that day was the start of a long relationship that would bring Gerry and Irene to the altar of Our Lady of the Angels Church eight years later to exchange wedding vows.

FOR IRENE MORDARSKI, recovery from her injuries was as long as it was arduous. She was confined to her bed until June 1959 and was hospitalized longer than any other school fire survivor save for the Edington boy, who died in St. Anne's that August.

Irene had two pins placed in her hip. She remained in traction for four and a half months. She underwent additional hip surgery in April and considerable skin grafting at various intervals. From time to time she was haunted by bad memories. Like many of the injured children in St. Anne's, she suffered from psychological trauma. She would wake up screaming in the hospital, often mistaking the dark of night for smoke. She was always planning an escape route and knew exactly where to go in the event the hospital caught fire.

When Irene was finally discharged from the hospital she immediately became a visible reminder of the fire, as did many of the children, hobbling through the neighborhood on crutches, marked by scars on their faces, necks, arms, and hands.

Irene was a captive of her own injured body, and more operations on her hip lay ahead. She couldn't play. She couldn't exercise. She couldn't run. She couldn't swim. She couldn't roller skate. She couldn't ride a bike. Later, at dances, she'd sit and watch as other teens moved around freely. The fire had robbed her of a normal adolescence. In addition to her physical limitations, she and her peers were affected psychologically. It would be years before she could strike a match. She couldn't look at candles. If her parents took her to a movie, she'd insist on sitting near the exit doors. The nightmares, it seemed, never ceased.

Still, life went on, and the friendship between Irene Mordarski and Gerry Andreoli that began at St. Anne's Hospital gradually blossomed in the years following the fire. Gerry attended Lane Technical High School on Chicago's North Side; Irene was a year behind Gerry at Madonna High School. When Gerry was a senior, he took Irene to Lane Tech's prom at the Aragon Ballroom on the city's far North Side—their first big date away from the neighborhood. Irene's mother made her a new dress.

That fall Gerry entered college at the Illinois Institute of Technology on Chicago's South Side and spent the next year and a half living on campus. "I was away from her longer than I wanted to be," he said. "It was hard for both of us. Eventually, I got a car so we could see each other on the weekends. Then I started working and went to evening classes, so we saw more of each other."

Irene still had difficulty walking. She had gone through several operations on her broken pelvis. In 1963, almost five years after the fire, she received a total hip replacement. Her left leg had become shorter than her right leg, which caused her to limp. She was never without pain.

Years later Irene recalled her early plight. "From the day of the fire until the early part of June," she said, "I never got out of bed. I was never on my feet. They had a pin about eight inches long right through my ankle, and I was in traction. They operated on my hip and did plastic surgery on my legs. While I was in traction, my left foot became bent, and to this day it's a size and a half smaller than my right foot. Whenever I buy shoes, I have to buy two pairs, one pair larger than the other."

Irene recalled taking her first steps in June 1959. "My mother was there," she said, "and I'll never forget the expression on her face. I guess she thought I'd just get up out of bed and start walking. The doctors and nurses were overjoyed I was up on my feet and my mother tried to act happy, but I could see the grief and shock in her face.

"I was on crutches throughout the eighth grade. I went to John Hay public school. Then I was operated on again in 1960, and they put me in a body cast so I had to take my first year at Madonna High School by telephone. The telephone company set up an intercom from my bed at home to the school. It seemed strange talking to classmates I never saw. I felt like I was missing my teenage years, that I was growing up without being young. It seemed like I was always in braces or casts or on crutches."

On March 22, 1967, Gerry took Irene to dinner at Pitzaferro's Restaurant on Chicago's Northwest Side. He had brought along an engagement ring but hadn't told her about it. He was twenty-one years old, she was twenty. They were in love. He asked her to marry him. She said yes.

They were married in August of that year in Our Lady of the Angels Church, and moved into a home on Chicago's West Side. Now they live in a well-to-do suburb west of the city, have two boys and two girls, and have grown into a loving couple with a genuine kindness and gentleness rooted in the suffering they experienced as children.

Irene endured a second hip replacement in 1973 and a third in 1993. She has been told to expect at least two more hip replacements in her lifetime. Gerry, ever protective of his wife, remained worried about the future. "Irene can't do things normal people can do," he said. "If she does any strenuous housework one day, she can hardly move the next day because she's in such pain.

"Both of us received settlements from the school fire, but you can't put a price on pain or a mother's inability to give her children the care she thinks they should have. I'm worried about Irene's problems later in life. Arthritis, for one. A broken hip can bring never-ending problems. I'll never be free of worry that one day she could be permanently disabled."

More than thirty years after the fire, white scars were still evident on Gerry's neck and on the right side of his face. Irene still favored her left leg when she walked, and at times required a cane. The injuries Irene suffered led Gerry to become interested in the profession that provides him with his livelihood. His business card reads: Dr. Gerald T. Andreoli, chiropractor.

ON JUNE 23, 1959, the first lawsuit was filed in Cook County Circuit Court on behalf of five children injured in the school fire. In their complaint the plaintiffs asked for $1,750,000 in damages against the Catholic Bishop of Chicago and the City of Chicago—$350,000 for each of the five students. The suit alleged that the Catholic Bishop had "carelessly, negligently and deliberately operated the school so that the same was highly dangerous to life and limb, and constituted a fire trap for the students attending." The suit also charged that the City of Chicago had "engaged in a pattern of conduct which consistently and regularly exempted the school from maintaining reasonable standards of safety."

A second lawsuit, filed July 8, 1959, sought $30,000 in damages on behalf of a father whose daughter had died in the fire. It was the first suit seeking compensation for a wrongful death in the fire.

One of the astonishing sequels to the school fire, however, was the refusal of a large majority of parents whose children were killed or injured in the blaze to bring legal action against the archdiocese. Their reluctance was in some measure a reflection of the times when church authority was still regarded with considerable awe among the faithful. It also could be attributed to the failure of the city's power structure to fix responsibility for the tragedy. Some parents, however, remained passive strictly out of respect for the dead children. "Why should I sue?" lamented one father. "It won't bring my son back."

Only three of a possible ninety-two wrongful death suits were filed against the archdiocese, and only nineteen of a possible seventy-six personal injury suits were filed.

One person who had detailed knowledge of all the personal injuries incurred in the school fire was Cornelius J. Harrington, Jr., a bright young lawyer with the prestigious law firm of Kirkland, Ellis, Hodson, Chaffetz and Masters, which represented the Catholic archdiocese. "I spent about a year at the school gathering information on all the injured children," Harrington recalled. "It was something I agreed to do after talking to Cardinal Meyer. We invited families in for interviews and asked them to bring updated medical reports on their children.

"Donations to the school were pouring in from all over the world. They had bushel baskets full of money and checks out there. These funds were used to help pay all the immediate hospital and medical bills.

"Meyer told me, 'I think we should try to settle not only all the suits that are filed, but we should also compensate every family whose child died or was injured regardless of whether they filed a suit or not. The question is: How do we go about it?' "

Harrington thought the courts should decide, and he did not foresee any difficulty in providing equitable settlements for families whose children had died in the fire. "At that time," he said, "juries did not award large settlements in cases of wrongful deaths of children. The average settlement by a jury was about $10,000. Under Illinois law the maximum for wrongful death of a child was $30,000."

In personal injury cases, however, there was no ceiling on the amount of compensation a child might receive. Harrington knew the awards could be astronomical unless some agreement was reached between the archdiocese and the attorneys for the plaintiffs. He visited with Judge Harold G. Ward, head of the law division of the Cook County Circuit Court, seeking his counsel in working out settlement procedures.

"I told him the cardinal wanted it to be fair for everyone and showed him a list of suits we had on file at that time," Harrington recalled. "Most of them were for minor injuries. I told him of the difficulty we were experiencing with some families refusing to file suit. He said to me, 'Well, I don't know how you can get people to sue if they don't want to.' "

Harrington talked with Chief Judge John S. Boyle, seeking his advice. Boyle suggested that settlements be negotiated in pretrial hearings by a panel of judges acceptable to both sides. Eventually a formula for the discussion of settlements was ironed out in a meeting among Harrington, Boyle, and Burton Joseph, the twenty-nine-year-old lawyer representing a committee of attorneys who had by 1965 brought fifty-nine lawsuits against the archdiocese—forty wrongful death and nineteen injury suits. Each side submitted a list of six sitting judges experienced in personal injury cases. From these twelve judges, Boyle selected Ward, Thomas C. Donovan, and Henry W. Dieringer.

In the spring of 1965 the judges began holding pretrial hearings. They heard each case separately, evaluated the potential jury verdict, and made recommendations for settlements accordingly. The judges had access to complete medical reports from hospitals and physicians, along with all the data compiled by Harrington. They took into account the pain, suffering, and disability of each child. The panel did not have to consider medical expenses amounting to approximately $1 million, which had been covered to a large extent by Mayor Daley's Our Lady of the Angels fund, by grants from Catholic Charities, and by other voluntary contributions.

Cardinal Meyer died in April 1965 after surgery for a brain tumor, and the following June, John P. Cody was named archbishop of Chicago. "When Cody finally came to Chicago," Harrington recalled, "this is the first thing we hit him with." In September, Cody, whose father had been a deputy fire chief in St. Louis, agreed to the settlements recommended by the three-judge panel. The total came to $2,996,400, including attorneys' fees.

"The money to be paid," Cody announced, "will be borrowed from Chicago banks and no special solicitations will be made. This I consider to be a moral obligation of the archdiocese and we shall meet our obligations. In accordance with the wish of the late Albert Cardinal Meyer, in which I concur, the proposed settlement includes those who did not file suit as well as those who did."

The judges' recommendations stipulated an award of $7,500 to parents of each child who died. Recommendations for personal injuries ranged from $350 to $350,000. In response to the first suits filed in June 1959, seeking awards of $350,000 for each of five injured children, the recommended settlements were: $3,500, $3,500, $14,000, $28,000, and $31,000.

The largest settlement recommended by the panel was awarded to a fourth-grade student regarded as one of the most seriously injured of the survivors, a girl whose face had to be virtually reconstructed through plastic surgery. Hospital, nursing, and doctor bills for the girl, amounting to more than $12,400, had been paid for out of the school fire fund established by Mayor Daley.

In the final breakdown the archdiocese agreed to pay $690,000 for ninety-two child death cases and $2,256,525 for seventy-six personal injury cases. Attorney fees were $26,875 in the injury cases and $23,000 in the death cases.

JOHN TROTTA was one parent who accepted the $7,500 death settlement. Like many parents who had lost children in the blaze, the money was of little consequence to him, and he was reluctant to sue the archdiocese. Trotta was nonetheless disturbed by the manner in which the settlements were reached.

"Here we are in this little room in the City Hall building downtown," he recalled of the final court hearing with the three-judge panel. "There were three of them sitting on one side of the table, and I'm on the other side.

"So help me God, this is how it went:

" 'What is your name?'

" 'John J. Trotta.'

" 'You were the father of?'

" 'John David.'

" 'Your address?'

" 'The same.'

"It all must have taken about two and a half minutes. And you know what they're doing? They're marking the information down in one of those little two-column journals the old grocer used to keep when your mother went to the store.

"It was either take their offer of $7,500 for the death settlement, or go into court. That was it. This is the hearing they were going to have to discuss with you . . . the whole bit. To me, it was a travesty.

"Remember, this was seven years after the fire. You talk about justice delayed being justice denied. This thing wasn't only delayed, it was detoured and sidetracked."

Monsignor McManus, though not directly involved in the litigation or settlements, sympathized with the parents. "Would I understand parents who would say, 'No amount of money could compensate for what happened to my child'?" he asked. "Of course I would, especially after the whole situation about shortcomings in fire safety in the schools was revealed."

In 1970 the Our Lady of the Angels Fire Fund set up in the wake of the disaster by Mayor Daley was transferred, under court supervision, to the Chicago Community Trust, one of the city's oldest and largest public trusts. The First National Bank of Chicago was named as depository. In Daley's words, the fund had been set up "to relieve the suffering caused by the fire." Some eleven thousand contributions were received from all over the world; the balance eventually amounted to $640,000, including interest and investment income.

For the next twenty-four years, fire survivors who required continuing treatment for their injuries could draw money to cover medical costs. Then, in 1994, the bank moved legally to close out the fund. Cook County Chancery Court Judge Edward Hofert, after considering the bank's petition and hearing from fire survivors, ordered that the fund's remaining $140,000 be distributed among six claimants who had come forward seeking money to pay bills for continued medical and psychiatric treatment.

As of mid-1995 a dozen or so survivors were still undergoing treatment for injuries sustained in the fire, or required continued use of medical aids such as special shoes, canes, cosmetics, and physical therapy. Now that the trust money is gone they must pay for their care themselves—through insurance, if they are covered, or by digging into their own pockets. They receive no assistance from the Catholic Archdiocese of Chicago.

In the end, the financial toll from the fire at Our Lady of the Angels, including funeral and burial costs, court settlements, insurance benefits, medical care, and the cost of constructing a new school building, reached an estimated $5.5 million.

THE HOLOCAUST at Our Lady of the Angels School clearly helped to bring about improved fire safety measures in schools throughout the country. Public outcry was swift, and Chicago newspapers echoed the fears of parents by waging editorial campaigns urging city and archdiocesan officials to act promptly to upgrade the city's aging schools.

Immediately after the fire Chicago was in "a state of terrible turmoil," Monsignor McManus recalled. Although McManus—as the archdiocesan school superintendent—had attended every inquest hearing, he was not called to testify. Still, he realized something had to be done to prevent a public panic.

"Parents were screaming all over the place about safety," he recalled. "And pastors were screaming about the cost of safety. Nobody knew what to do. And the things the Fire Department were now noting in their fire inspections had been there before, during all the previous inspections in all the schools before the fire. But all of a sudden, everything they could find in the schools was wrong. And there was plenty wrong, no doubt about it. But we got a lot of very negative publicity."

McManus sought advice from a local safety consulting firm, which recommended that the archdiocese install approved sprinkler systems in all its schools. The Catholic school board was at first open to the idea, but when McManus told the board it would cost the archdiocese $8 million to $12 million to implement such a plan, its members nearly choked; the cost estimate was almost fifty times greater than what the church was paying in liability insurance. Nevertheless, for a school like Our Lady of the Angels, the cost breakdown for a sprinkler system seemed nominal—about eight dollars per parent, the same price as one football helmet used by the school's football team—a reasonable price, it seemed, for a child's life.

Debate on the matter was short-lived, for on January 21, 1959, just two weeks after the coroner's jury released its findings, the Chicago City Council, steered by Mayor Daley, adopted retroactive amendments to the city's building code requiring automatic sprinkler systems in all city schools—public and private—of two or more stories in height and of ordinary frame construction with wooden floors and joists. Most such buildings had been constructed before World War I, when steel and concrete came into common use. Another change required that all school buildings be equipped with internal fire alarm systems directly linked with the city's fire alarm office, and placement of fire alarm boxes within one hundred feet of the main entrance. Fire drills were required monthly and had to be witnessed by Fire Department personnel.

The Illinois General Assembly that convened in 1959 directed the state superintendent of schools to consult safety experts and draft needed changes to cover all schools in the state. A steering committee produced a bulky, two-volume set of building and safety standards regulating everything from the brightness of exit signs to the proper installation of furnaces. The next year the General Assembly enacted the standards into the Life Safety Code of 1960.

Legislation also allowed individual school districts in Illinois to levy a special homeowner tax to pay for life-safety improvements without the need for a referendum. Ironically, the tax legislation did not cover parochial schools, and Chicago, where the Our Lady of the Angels fire occurred and where schools in later years would fall into notorious disrepair, was exempted.

As noble as the new state law was, its authors failed to provide adequate oversight. Numerous Illinois school districts over the years exploited the tax provision by broadly interpreting the definition of "life safety." Instead of limiting themselves to expending the tax money on specific life-safety items—such as exit signs, emergency lighting, sprinkler systems, furnace repairs, and the enclosure of stairways—school boards stretched the safety definition to permit the use of tax money to fund new gymnasium floors, new school lockers, remodeling of auditoriums, new carpet, the repair of swimming pools, and new bleachers at athletic fields.

One school district used safety tax money to convert a shower and locker room into a faculty dining facility, and a gym into a school cafeteria. Yet another school district earmarked $44,000 to resurface a running track. That project was never realized, but the district used the funds to replace chalkboards, improve an athletic field's drainage system, build a learning center, and renovate a teachers' lounge.

In the parochial school system, raising money for school fire safety proved to be problematic from the very beginning. Everyone wanted safer schools; how to pay for them was another matter. Parish pastors have always felt handcuffed by limited, shrinking budgets, and new expenses are never welcomed.

In Chicago's Catholic school system at the time, Monsignor McManus recalled "a lot of grumbling" from some pastors inside the archdiocese who remained opposed to spending money to put sprinkler systems in their schools, despite the enormous public outcry that resulted immediately after the Our Lady of the Angels fire.

"I knew the sprinkling people saw a bonanza that they never anticipated," McManus said. "We had to be careful so that we would not be overcharged and given sprinkler systems that didn't meet the specifications, so the pastors could be assured of getting a good sprinkling job for their money, that it would work."

Because the new safety requirements required the outlay of millions of dollars, changes did not occur overnight. In Chicago the City Council had set December 31, 1963, as the deadline for compliance, but the deadline was extended one more year to accommodate financing and other logistics. The amended deadline was met, and—as far as installed fire alarms and sprinklers, safety lighting, and supervised fire drills were concerned—the schools were brought up to code. But other problems of aging schools, such as the enclosure of stairwells and the general condition of multistory brick and wood-joist constructed school buildings, remained unchanged for years. Still, according to a nationwide survey published in 1960 by the National Fire Protection Association, major improvements in life safety were made in 16,500 school buildings in the United States within one year of the Our Lady of the Angels fire.

AS THE CONCERN for fire safety produced concrete results, so too did plans to build a new Our Lady of the Angels School. The gutted remains of the old school were razed in late February 1959, and construction on a new school building began that June.

In the interim, beginning the week after the fire, more than twelve hundred students from the parish school were bused each day to four neighboring parochial schools. Monsignor Cussen and Monsignor McManus also made arrangements with the Chicago Board of Education to rent thirty-seven classrooms in the nearby Hay, Orr, and Cameron public elementary schools to accommodate students from Our Lady of the Angels as construction proceeded on the new school.

Monsignor McManus recalled that first morning—Tuesday, December 9, 1958—when displaced students from Our Lady of the Angels assembled outside the parish church to board chartered buses. "That was heartwrenching," he said. "The children were assembling by classroom. In one class there were just three kids left who weren't dead, burned, or seriously injured. So it was very traumatic for those kids. It was a bitter cold day. When the kids came back at four o'clock in the afternoon that first day, the parents were all there to meet them. They were still terrified. They didn't want to let those kids out of their sight."

The children were uneasy as well. Most of the schools they were sent to were older multistory structures—buildings that resembled their burned-out school. Some youngsters were frightened by the thought of climbing stairs and sitting in classrooms two and three stories up. And there were new nuns and lay teachers to contend with. One fire survivor who temporarily attended classes at Our Lady Help of Christians School recalled that "In the beginning, the nuns were very rough. They were always probing your mind. If you were daydreaming, they'd call you up and ask what was the matter. I think they were trained to look for trauma."

Fire survivor John Raymond recalled that while he was in class at the Orr public grammar school, building engineers were cleaning the school's heating system when, without warning, the furnace kicked on, sending fumes throughout the building. John and other children from Our Lady of the Angels didn't wait for the fire alarm before leaving their seats and fleeing the building. One girl in John's room was so hysterical he had to carry her out the front door. "And they couldn't stop us," he said. "The teacher just let us go. She could see the panic in our faces. She knew exactly what was going on."

The decision to replace the old Our Lady of the Angels School with a new one came within days of the fire. Monsignor Cussen, still badly shaken from his experience, had vowed the day after the fire to construct a new school building in memory of those who had perished.

"The first decision we had to make was whether we would ever consider bringing children back into that school," McManus recalled. "Some in the chancery thought we should. They felt the school was in good condition, that the burned part could be repaired. I thought the trauma had been so terrible that you could never, never carry on education in that building again. You could never bring children back into that burned school and expect them to learn in an atmosphere like that. The place was haunted."

The archdiocese commissioned Chicago architect James L. Barry to design a new school. Before signing the contract, McManus gave Barry just one directive: "Everything that's related to fire safety, put it in there."

Barry designed a three-story reinforced concrete structure with a $1.25 million price tag. The building featured exterior yellow-brick walls accented with large, blue porcelain panels and granite trim. It contained thirty-two classrooms and a kindergarten, and its interior components included ceramic tile walls, marble stairs, and stainless steel handrails. Classrooms surrounded a central core containing a library, visual aids department, two lunchrooms, a book store, washrooms, and maintenance rooms. Interior partition walls were built of concrete block with ceramic tiles. A sprinkler system and smoke detectors were installed and hooked into a central fire alarm panel connected directly to the main fire alarm office via telephone circuits. In short, the school was rock solid, a superb model of fire-resistant construction, a symbol of atonement for what had happened on the site in 1958.

The cost of the new school was paid for by public donations that came in from all over the world, and by local fund-raising efforts, including benefits, carnivals, raffles, and weekly contributions by church parishioners.

By the summer of 1960 the new school was completed. On October 2 of that year, before a large crowd of parishioners, city and church officials, and news reporters, the school was dedicated by Cardinal Meyer, who blessed every classroom with holy water.

In celebrating the dedication Mass in Our Lady of the Angels Church, Meyer had decided early on against making any direct references to the school fire dead. One reason, according to Monsignor McManus, was that on the night of the fire the cardinal had tried to assure parents at St. Anne's Hospital that despite the dreadful circumstances, God still cared for them. Now he wished to strike the same theme at the Mass.

"I remember saying to him directly," McManus recalled years later, " 'I think you ought to mention something about the fire and the way people suffered,' and he said, 'No, I'm not going to do that. You wait and hear how I'm going to handle it.' "

In his homily, Meyer set the fire in a religious perspective, comparing it to the dictates of God's providence. "Be sincere of heart and steadfast, undisturbed in time of adversity," he preached. "Accept whatever befalls you. In crushing misfortune, be patient, for in fire, gold is tested, as are worthy men in the crucible of humiliation.

"Trust God and He will help . . . remind you of the tears of yesterday and the joys of today. . . . It is His image which gives meaning to the generosity of those who have made it possible for us to build this new school. It is His example which gives courage to continue to believe in Divine Providence, despite appearances to the contrary, because of suffering, sin or disaster.

"Here, in this school of Our Lady of the Angels, we understand better the meaning of our Lord's word: 'Suffer the little ones to come unto me . . . for such is the kingdom of heaven.' "

WHEN THE NEW Our Lady of the Angels School opened in the fall of 1960, it marked the first time since December 1, 1958, that children from the parish were together in their own school building. "We were all excited about going back," fire survivor Matt Plovanich remembered. "There was a lot of pride. It was a glistening new school. It was a whole different feeling. We felt so safe. It was so bright. The windows were so large. You were really happy to go back to your school and see how nice it had become."

But the homecoming was also bittersweet. Instead of talking about the fire and discussing their feelings, the children were discouraged by their nuns from ever referring to it. Johnna (Uting) Bovenzo, a survivor from Room 212 who had broken both her ankles after leaping from a second-floor window, recalled that "If we talked about the fire, the nuns wanted to treat it like it never occurred. It was suppressed."

In front of the new school, near the Iowa Street curb, stood a device that had not been there two years earlier: a red fire alarm box. Yet within the school itself there was no visible memorial to the children or sisters who had died in the fire. "The school," said one nun, "is their monument."

DURING THE turbulent 1960s, survivors of the school fire grew into young adulthood. By the end of the decade, many of them had joined the work force as police officers, school teachers, or hourly wage earners. Others entered colleges, professional schools, and religious orders. Some saw combat in Vietnam. They became husbands and wives, mothers and fathers. Families that had lived in Our Lady of the Angels parish gradually drifted away, many moving to the city's far Northwest Side or into the western and northwestern suburbs.

With the exception of a brief flurry of stories about the settlement of court cases and the annual announcement of a memorial Mass celebrated in Our Lady of the Angels Church each December 1, only scant mention of the tragedy appeared in the news media. A collective subconscious seemed to prefer to forget the school fire.

In 1965 Monsignor Cussen retired as pastor of Our Lady of the Angels, a position he had held for thirty years. He was still suffering from the effects of a crippling stroke that had weakened him in 1964, and for the next ten years he lived with his brother. "He never talked much about the school fire," Mort Cussen later recalled, "but I'm quite sure he thought about it a lot."

In October 1975 Monsignor Cussen died in the home of a niece in Tinley Park, a suburb south of Chicago. He was eighty-three. The grief he had tried so hard to hide—even from his own relatives— had finally come to an end. During his funeral mass at Our Lady of the Angels Church, Father Joe McDonnell, an associate pastor at the time of the fire, delivered the eulogy. Not once in his talk did he refer to the school fire or to its lasting physical and emotional impact on Monsignor Cussen.

Thirteen

SURVIVAL

E MOTIONAL EFFECTS of the fire at Our Lady of the Angels
School, like the roots of a giant tree, reached far and deep. Essentially a neighborhood calamity, the school fire was also a micro-
cosm of all great tragedies: swift, cruel, and unexpected. It served
as an unforgettable reminder that fire, undetected at birth and un-
controlled in the early moments of its life, can grow into a savage,
indiscriminate killer. It also left terrible feelings of grief, guilt, and
bitterness.

Thirty years later a troubled Laurie Dann walked into Hubbard
Woods Elementary School in the affluent Chicago suburb of Win-
netka and shot five students, killing one. Those who lived through
the Dann shooting were provided counseling and other mental
health services to help them cope with the shooting's aftermath. But
the Our Lady of the Angels fire occurred at a time when it was not
yet in vogue to send an army of social workers and psychologists
into a community following a traumatic event. The children who
survived the Our Lady of the Angels fire, and the parents of those
who perished, were afforded no such intervention.

A great legacy of the school fire therefore concerns its deep effect on a small and closely knit community. It is a story of ordinary
people uprooted from the daily routines of working-class life and
forced to deal—virtually by themselves—with a terrible disaster. It
is an acknowledgment of human fragility and a testament to the

strength of human perseverance in the face of great personal tragedy.

Treatment of what is now recognized as posttraumatic stress disorder was not an option in 1958. Diagnostically the syndrome was not formally recognized by the psychiatric community until 1989, though research into the phenomenon had begun late in World War II and was expanded in the 1970s after American combat veterans began returning home from Vietnam.

Posttraumatic stress is not a disease. It is a normal reaction by normal people to an abnormal event. According to the American Psychiatric Association's official definition of the disorder, persons may develop the syndrome if they have experienced or witnessed a violent event that involves actual or threatened death or serious injury. A person's response to the event must involve intense fear, helplessness, or horror. Three principal symptoms are persistent re-experiencing of the traumatic event (i.e., flashbacks), persistent avoidance of potentially troubling stimuli associated with the event (shying away from crowded buildings), and increased arousal (rapid heartbeat, feelings of panic and terror) when exposed to stimuli associated with the event.

Commonly, trauma survivors may suffer recurrent troubling thoughts or recollections of the event in question, as well as recurring dreams in which the event is replayed. In rare instances a person may even experience so-called dissociative states lasting from a few seconds to several hours or even days, during which time components of the event are relived and the person behaves as though experiencing the event at that particular moment.

Often a person may mentally revisit the event if he or she is exposed to some type of trigger. In the case of the school fire survivors, these may include the December 1 anniversary dates; fires, whether they be structure fires or campfires; fire and police sirens; old schools; and other disasters, natural or man-made.

"I thought I had gotten over the fire until I saw the movie *Towering Inferno*," recalled Vito Muilli, the former fourth-grader from Room 210. "I had a nervous breakdown right in the theatre, and that was fifteen years later. It put me in shock again because it looked so similar to what happened at the school—people jumping out of windows. My wife was next to me. I was frozen in my seat, squeezing her hand, just crying."

The Catholic archdiocese was in many respects ill-equipped to help parish families psychologically with the fire's aftermath, or to help soothe the widespread grief felt in the neighborhood. Although Catholic Charities provided a great many priests and nuns who infiltrated the neighborhood immediately after the fire, helping families cope with the loss of a child, their primary role was to console, not to provide professional counseling. When the fire shattered the aura of sanctity in which it held itself, the church retreated to a defensive posture, responding the only way it knew how: it tore down the old school, replaced it with a new one, then acted as if the fire had never occurred. It failed to deal with the individual and thus produced a major source of anger and criticism among survivors of the fire.

"They had to have some idea of what we were going through," commented one woman, a sixth-grader in the fire. "They built a new school, but no one talked about the fire with the kids. No one ever came up to us to ask, 'How are you doing? How do you feel? What do you think of this?'

"I really can't buy into the excuse they didn't know how. It's just amazing that nobody thought of helping these people."

Many survivors of the fire developed what is known as "survivor's guilt," an offshoot of posttraumatic stress which causes them to wrestle with the ponderous question, "Why did I survive and not the others?" Taken a step further, a survivor could instead ask, "Why didn't *I* die?"

By leaving it to "God's will" or some other simple explanation, rooted or not in religious metaphor, the children were, at a very young age, forced to assume a simplistic version of what had occurred. But the victims had not died "gloriously," or "magnificently," nor had God swooped down from heaven and scooped them into His bosom. Rather they had died violently in a fast-moving fire. Bad things aren't supposed to happen to good little boys and girls; a church-oriented school ought to be a safe place.

Confusing too was the literal canonization of victims by some nuns in the parish who, fueled by their own repressed grief, explained to the children that "only the good ones were taken." In a child's mind, if only the good ones were taken, survivors could only assume they were not good, and hence were bad. Mary Jane (Nuccio) Cozzi, a fifth-grader who escaped the fire unharmed, recalled: "It's funny how it plays on you, the message they were handing out to us. The ones who died were called the 'lucky ones,' the 'chosen ones.' They were the ones God wanted. Those of us who lived weren't chosen. They were the 'angels.' We were the kids who were left behind.

"We didn't know how to feel. No one explained to us how we were supposed to feel. You were programmed. You were supposed to be sad. You were supposed to pray to the 'angels in heaven.' In retrospect it seems pretty feeble.

"And the parents whose children died were being handed a lot of nonsense too. They were being told their child was now an 'angel in heaven,' but they were angry as hell about it—yet how could they be angry if that's what God wanted for them or chose for them?

"They had to live with this their entire life. It's a struggle. 'Shame on you if you're crying or being angry when God chose your child, when you really are a blessed person because you've got your own personal angel in heaven.' It was so backward, so ludicrous."

In the absence of counseling and organized intervention, many parents came to terms with their loss through their deep religious faith. Such was the case of Nick and Emma Jacobellis, parents of Victor Jacobellis, the nine-year-old who died after jumping from Room 210.

In 1994 the Jacobellises, both white-haired and eighty, were still active, living comfortably in retirement in a yellow-brick bungalow near a lush green forest preserve on the Northwest Side of Chicago. Their home, neatly furnished, was filled with mementos of a full life. Victor's bronzed baseball mitt was set unobtrusively on a table in the living room.

The Jacobellises talked about the fire matter-of-factly, as if it were a distant relative. Their grief had not limited their lives. They appeared to have managed it well.

"We prayed a lot," Mrs. Jacobellis said of the time. "It happened. We knew there was nothing we could do about it. Victor was such a wonderful child. And only in the fourth grade. We love him. We miss him. The hardest part for me came a couple of weeks after, when I went in to clean out his closet in the bedroom. That's when it really hit me. After that I accepted it and went on.

"We stayed in the neighborhood for quite a few years after the fire, until 1970. We didn't want to move. In the beginning everybody was there. By moving I felt we would be abandoning him. By staying there I felt he was close to us.

"We helped raise a lot of money for that new school. It made us feel connected to him. I think he would have wanted us to stay."

For the children who lived through the fire, the event clearly served as a point of demarcation in their early lives. The fire took away something many consider an elemental right of every human being: it stripped them of their innocence, robbed them of their childhoods. It prevented them, as adults, from being able to remember the good times of youth when life was pure, wrought with simple routines and bright shiny bicycles. When survivors are asked to recall their childhoods, instead of a smile one sees watery eyes or a sad look. In order to access the memories of youth, they must first cross the threshold of the school fire.

John Raymond explained: "There are parts of your life that draw big lines, and that one definitely chops off everything else. When I think of my childhood, it goes right back to the fire. I have to go through that to get to my earlier years. I don't think back to when I was five years old on a Radio Flyer or wearing out one gym shoe. I think back to then. It's a barrier."

Group therapy and shared experience has long been touted by mental health professionals as exceptionally helpful to those suffering the effects of trauma. Yet for the children of 1958, talking about the school fire and openly expressing their feelings was not encouraged. Instead the subject was regarded as almost taboo. Hence children and adults alike never learned how to cope with the psychological effects of the fire. Through no fault of their own, survivors kept their emotions locked inside. They were left to form and develop into adulthood seemingly unaffected, yet forever bound to the memories of their unconquered past.

The result is that they are slightly different from the rest of the society in which they exist. Silently they still suffer; the fire is never far away. A few who were left disfigured remain recluses, locked away in their own private cells, sentenced to a life of limitation, their only crime being that they attended school at a time when local government still had not fully addressed the dangers of housing children in unsafe school buildings.

Many survivors can vividly recall the sound of screaming children and the smell of the thick, black smoke that rolled into their classrooms. Some of them who were crowded at the windows admit to claustrophobia; others find it difficult to look at fires or other disasters and accidents on television newscasts. Generally they have a heightened awareness of their vulnerability and mortality. In restaurants, theatres, or multilevel shopping malls, they find themselves instinctively looking for alternate exits. On business or pleasure, they often ask for hotel rooms no higher than the second floor. If they have children, they take more than a casual interest in the conditions of the schools their youngsters attend.

More than a few survivors indicate recurring nightmares related to the fire, especially in the autumn months leading to December. Still others have difficulty enjoying the holiday season, mentally returning to that bleak Christmas of 1958, which came on the heels of the tragedy. To say that the fire remains a difficult subject for them to discuss is an understatement. And even though many years had passed when the major work for this book was under way, many had never recounted their experiences at length. Most surviving firefighters who fought the blaze found it an equally troubling memory. The sights and sounds of that day are buried deep within them.

AGAINST THIS BACKDROP of unfinished business, Linda Maffiola got an idea. Even though she hadn't been in the fire, her life was forever changed by it. It was the day her older brother, Joseph, never came home. Linda was just three and a half years old when the fire occurred, a preschooler unable to comprehend the profound changes taking place in her household. Her parents, devastated by the loss of their son, were consumed by grief. Shortly after the fire her father developed serious physical problems and was hospitalized for a month; he nearly died from an infected kidney. Her mother, severely depressed, broke down after the coroner's inquest at which she was the first parent to testify.

Still, life went on. In 1960 Linda's mother, following the advice of her doctors, had another child, a girl, and that year Linda was enrolled as a kindergartner in the new Our Lady of the Angels School. Parents whose children had died in the fire no longer had to worry about the school burning down, for "OLA" was now the safest school in the city. There Linda studied music and piano and developed a love for literature. When she graduated in 1969 her family packed up and moved away from the neighborhood, relocating to the far Northwest Side of Chicago, where many other parish families had landed.

For Linda, almost three decades passed before she began to address the grief of losing her brother in the fire. It came when her own two children transferred to a grade school in a suburb where she had moved—the school reminded her of the old Our Lady of the Angels School. "Each day when I dropped off my kids," she explained, "as we approached the building I started having flashbacks of the fire. I would have to shake my head and remind myself that this was not 1958, and this school was not OLA."

Linda's family had never talked at length about the fire or the way it had affected them or their community. Not until years later did her father reveal that she had been outside the school on the day of the blaze. "My dad was recalling the events of the day to my younger sister," Linda recalled, "and he mentioned that he and my mother had picked me up from nursery school, and that we had gone together to OLA to search for my brother. Well, I almost fell out of my chair. All my life I just assumed that a relative picked me up from nursery school, that I was shielded from the actual fire. Here thirty-five years later I discover I witnessed the event.

"Unexpectedly I was filled with great peace and comprehension. All my life I had suffered from nightmares and flashbacks of the fire. It finally made sense to me, because I have no conscious recollection of being at the scene. Try as I can, I can't remember a thing about the fire, the search for my brother in the area hospitals, his funeral, and the weeks following. I was told that my brother died in the school fire, which I could not comprehend at all. I was very angry with him for allowing the fire to take his life when he was supposed to be with me, to take care of me and play with me. I was told he was in heaven with 'Jesus and the angels,' and I thought that was totally absurd. I felt I needed him more here on earth than Jesus ever would."

In 1992 Linda Maffiola, a vivacious, dark-haired church musician and former Catholic elementary school teacher, organized the first memorial Mass for the fire to be held in years. It was celebrated at St. Paul of the Cross Church in Park Ridge, a suburb just outside of Chicago, and was offered by the Reverend Carl Morello, a young associate pastor of the church whose cousin, Annette LaMantia, had died in the school fire. "Not only did we remember the victims," said Linda, "we now remembered the survivors."

The next year she organized another memorial Mass, this one to coincide with the fire's thirty-fifth anniversary. It was celebrated at Our Lady of the Angels Church in the old neighborhood and drew an often passionate response from survivors and their families, former parishioners, firefighters, and others who began sharing with Linda their unresolved feelings about the fire.

Moved by the outpouring of emotion, Linda teamed with Terri Schmidt, a social worker, to organize a healing workshop for the survivors. The idea was endorsed by Cardinal Joseph Bernardin of Chicago, who agreed to help finance it. The workshop, held in November 1994, brought together about two hundred people, among them fire survivors, parents, firefighters, nurses, teachers, and former parishioners who had lived in the neighborhood at the time of the fire. It marked the first time they had gathered as a group, and they talked freely about their experiences.

Jane Cozzi, the former fifth-grader, was one survivor who attended the workshop. Cozzi had grown up a half-block south of the school on Avers Avenue. Her fifth-grade class had been assigned to a first-floor classroom in the school annex, and she and her classmates were evacuated without harm. One of her cousins, a girl, was among the eighth-grade students lifted to safety from Room 209 by Father Ognibene. Cozzi's second cousin, James Ragona, age nine, was killed in the blaze, as was her next-door neighbor, Peter Cangelosi, a ten-year-old. Both had been fourth-grade students in Room 210.

"I was trained from a very young age that the show must go on," she said. "We were programmed not to talk about it. So things were suppressed, repressed. There was no outlet.

"As a child I didn't grasp the reality of how enormous this event was. At ten years old, how could you? It was an eerie feeling. When you're a little kid, you don't understand death, you really don't know what's going on. The next thing I knew we were back to school at Our Lady Help of Christians, on half-day schedules, being fed sandwiches, and we thought, 'Hey, this is great, no big deal.'

"Later, they let us go back inside OLA and get our books and coats. We got our jackets, and of course they smelled of smoke. We never wore them again. And why they let us go in there to get them, to see everything, is beyond me. There was stuff everywhere, books, papers.

"For a while it seemed like the mourning never stopped. As a child I never realized the impact. But now as a parent, you think, 'Oh my God! What did those parents go through?' A lot of people were never the same, especially those who suffered a personal loss."

Cozzi, like many child survivors of the fire, did not begin to look at the tragedy from this vantage point until years later. "I didn't deal with any of that until I was a grown woman," she said. "From 1958 to 1990, you could say I was in a vacuum. My best friend was in the fire, with burn marks all over her legs; my next-door neighbor was killed—but nobody ever talked about it. My parents talked about it. They said how blessed we were because none of our kids got hurt, that we were spared, but that was it.

"All I remember was this cloak of sadness. Everyone was sad. This was a sad neighborhood now. You had to be careful of who you were around, what you might say, what you might not say. How could a neighborhood survive that? It didn't. The whole neighborhood started changing, people started moving. It was not the same neighborhood anymore. The whole sense of family and community in the neighborhood was destroyed, and the fire is what destroyed it. People couldn't face those who suffered. They couldn't deal with it. They should have had support groups right then, immediately. They should've got these families together who lost kids right then. They should've brought together these kids who were burned.

"Seeing kids who were scarred—you never knew a person could be burned so badly, that they could be so disfigured. You didn't even want to be around them, to look at them. Yet at the same time you wanted to because you never saw anything like this in your life. These little kids in uniform going to school, all scarred up for life."

Because no one ever discussed the fire with the children, Cozzi said she sensed a message: "What I got from that is, you don't talk about things that are tragic and upsetting. You have to be strong and just go on with your life. You have to bury it because it's over and there's nothing you can do now. You just go on.

"But now we know it will never be over. For us, it was the night that went on forever."

Fourteen

MEMORIES

A COLD unwelcome rain was washing the streets and pelting neatly kept lawns in Lombard, Illinois, a suburban bedroom community west of Chicago. John Trotta, a retired accountant with greying hair, metal-rimmed glasses, and a long, dark cigar clenched firmly between his teeth, stared vacantly through the front picture window of his home. He is a short man, vibrantly articulate, whose voice rises and falls with the passion of the moment. His wife, Lydia, was out, and he had the house to himself. He was dressed casually and wore a pair of leather slippers. Now he had fallen silent and was studying the gloomy, grey scene outside, looking but not seeing.

For more than two hours he had talked about his son, John David, a handsome eighth-grade student who had died in the Our Lady of the Angels fire. John David's last minutes of life had been spent in Room 211, well removed from where the blaze had started.

The father talked about the times they had spent together, the ball games they had gone to, the trivial joys and disappointments they had shared. "There are a lot of happy memories," Trotta finally said, "intermingled with what might have been. It didn't have to be. God only knows what went through the boy's mind at that time. No kid should have to die away from the arms of his parents. You know, we have an old saying that if a little baby dies, it will become a

258

dream. But if a young son dies, it will always be a dagger in your heart."

For all the years since the fire, John Trotta has lived with a dagger in his heart, as have many other fathers and mothers who lost children in the fire. Time has assuaged but not erased their bitterness. It is buried deep within them—a father's anger over the delay in sounding the school's fire alarm, the lapse in calling the Fire Department, the muddled actions of the coroner at the morgue, the inconclusiveness of the inquest, and what Trotta considers the callousness of some church officials in regard to the funerals and the settling of lawsuits.

An edge of bitterness crept into Trotta's voice. "Not one priest from the parish attended my son's funeral, which took place the following Saturday. The mass was at Our Lady of Mt. Carmel Church in Melrose Park. They told us, 'You can have either the funeral at the armory or find your own church.'

"The last time I was at Our Lady of the Angels Church was for Monsignor Cussen's wake. He was a regular Joe. He never made a pitch for one red cent. He kept the church clean, the school clean, but it was an old structure. He made no bones about being human. You could talk to him. He'd appreciate anything you did for him. In the old days it was a good neighborhood, had a good parochial spirit and feeling.

"You don't forget," Trotta continued. "We were a close-knit family. Lydia, I hate to take her to the cemetery. It's like a visit to church. It's a terrible thing to carry with you. You're so helpless to do anything about it.

"At the morgue my guy looked like he got off pretty easy. His hands were behind his head like he was resting. He died of asphyxiation.

"I kept his winter clothes. The other day I tried on his coat. I've kept his baseball mitt. There's no reason to throw it away. His little end table. When I touch it, he touches me too. He had a big sixteen-inch softball. It's still in the drawer. He used to con me about baseball.

"We still miss him. He had a wry, quiet sense of humor. And he was a proud kid. One day he came home from kindergarten. I asked him, 'How'd it go today?' And his eyes lit up and he smiled, 'I'm an assistant shoelace tier. I'm the only one in kindergarten who knows how to tie shoelaces.'

"He was athletically inclined, but not too fast on his feet. I used to tell him, 'No use trying to run away from me, I'll catch you.'

"He was a lot of fun in the privacy of family. Outside, he was shy and reserved. Among Italians we'd call him *figlio della casa*. He was 'a son of the house.' "

Trotta paused a moment, his mind racing back over the years. "At one time there were sixteen hundred kids in that school. The ones that died, you often wonder what careers they'd have followed or what war they'd have died in uselessly."

Trotta went to a closet and returned with a package, neatly wrapped in brown paper. "These were his books," he said. "I'll lay you five to one if I unwrap the package, you can still smell smoke."

Immediately after the fire, police guards had barred the public from entering Our Lady of the Angels School. Trotta was disappointed. He wanted to see his son's classroom, and he expressed his disappointment to Chief Fire Marshal Ray Daley, a longtime family friend.

"One day a fire lieutenant came to our home on Karlov Avenue and rang the bell," Trotta recalled. " 'Mr. Trotta,' he says, 'Chief Daley sent me. He said you wanted to go over to the school.' So we got into the Fire Department car and went to the school. And lo and behold, the side doors were open. No guards around. And the young lieutenant says, 'I'll go up with you. I'd like to see what happened myself.'

"So we went up to my son's room and looked around. There was a hole in the ceiling where the firemen had punched through the roof. My son sat in the front row on the west end of the room, right off the teacher's desk. I knew where he sat. His English book was still open on his desk. There was snow on it. I took all his books, his little missal, everything, and put them in a metal wastebasket I found in the room.

"The basket I've been using ever since, in my office at home. It's my wastebasket now. And I've still got the missal, keep it on my dresser."

Trotta still finds it hard to accept that his son, sitting so close to the front exit stairs of the north wing, was unable to escape. "Maybe it's like Monday morning quarterbacking, but you wonder why they stayed there, like sitting ducks, waiting for help. Instead of waiting, why didn't they take a chance?

"Later on I visited with Sister Helaine. I asked her, 'Sister, what did you do?'

"She said, 'We prayed.'

"What in the hell could I say to that?

"But don't get me wrong. Sister Helaine was a wonderful, intelligent nun. It's just that I feel that no kid—and I am very emphatic about this—should die away from his family.

"This may sound irreligious, but afterward when somebody would come along and say, 'Maybe God wanted the kids,' I'd say, 'Well, God must be pretty damn desperate if He wants innocent kids who die through no fault of their own.'"

In the months and years following the fire, John Trotta pursued his own investigation into the cause of the blaze. "I wanted to know myself what happened, not for any public purposes. I was just damned mad and wanted to find out on my own what I could do.

"I always said if I find the son of a bitch who did it, I'm gonna kill him. I promised my son at the grave. I said, 'If I find out, son, that somebody did this deliberately, I'll avenge you.' Not that my son would have wanted me to do it that way, but this is the way I felt."

When the closed hearing in Family Court was held in 1962 for the Cicero boy suspected of starting the fire, Trotta had a pipeline into the hearing through an attorney who was present.

"After it was over, I asked him, 'What do you think?'"

The attorney said he thought the boy was guilty.

"I says, 'How can we prove it?'

"He says, 'We don't.'

"After the fire, people in the parish used to stop me in the streets. Some of them looked to me for advice. Why, I don't know. But they'd say, 'Mr. Trotta, what should we do? What should we do? We can't find out anything.' I'd say, 'Frankly, I don't know what in the hell we can do. If we sue, it's gonna cost a lot of money. Things have been suppressed, things have been glossed over.' Then the coroner's office makes the price of the inquest transcript prohibitive. The ordinary guy doesn't have four, five, or six hundred dollars to get a transcript. So the people who had kids who died or were injured, they were sort of in a bind."

After the inquest, "I was so mad," he said, "I finally went to my lawyer. I says, 'John, I don't know what to do. I'm bumping my head against a stone wall. Maybe if we file a suit I can get some information, not for the money but just to get the complete truth on this thing.'

"He says, 'Well, I'm not a personal injury man, but I'll take you to a friend.' So we make an appointment with this prominent PI lawyer. He says to my lawyer, 'John, why did you bring this man here? You know we've been told not to handle any of these cases against the archdiocese.'

"Well, that's when I hit the ceiling. Catholic lawyers weren't supposed to handle any of these suits from the fire against the archdiocese. I remember there were five suits, all filed at the same time by the same lawyer. I did some checking up, and I found that other lawyers had siphoned these cases to this fresh, young lawyer just out of law school and used him to sue."

In 1958 the Trottas lived on the first floor of a two-flat on North Karlov Avenue, a few blocks west of Our Lady of the Angels School. On the day of the fire, John Trotta was working in his office at home. "I had a feeling of foreboding," he recalled. "To my sorrow, I have to say I had that same feeling when my mother died.

"I saw my kid at lunch. We had lunch at home. My wife had some errands to do that day, but for some reason she detoured to come home for lunch. The bus was going to take her right to the front of the bank, but she got off the bus at the corner and came home.

"The kid had a slight cold, and I asked him if he wanted to stay home.

" 'No, Poppa,' he said, 'I'll be all right.'

"My son goes back to school. He was wearing an army jacket with a hood that my brother had liberated. He was keen on it because he didn't have to wear earmuffs.

"Well, about ten minutes to three or somewhere close to it, I get a telephone call from one of his schoolmates who had stayed away from school that day because he was ill. He says, 'Is John David home yet?' And I say, 'No.'

" 'Mr. Trotta,' he says, 'the school is on fire!'

"With that I ran out the front door. I ran like hell. I figured I could get there faster if I ran than if I took the car. It was about three and a half blocks to the school."

By the time Trotta arrived at the scene, horror-stricken crowds were massed around the school. What rescue work that could be done had been done, and police were having difficulty controlling the crowd. Ropes were finally secured to hold back the spectators.

"There was a mob of people in front of me," Trotta said, "But I forged closer and got in front of the rope. Ray Daley told them it was okay for me to be there. I'll never forget the look on his face. It was ashen, like he wanted to cry. He knew what was up in those rooms. You could see the emotion in his face."

Trotta watched the grim recovery of bodies. When he finally headed home, he wasn't sure what fate had befallen his son, so with a friend driving the car, he went from one hospital to another, searching vainly for John David.

"What's the use of going to the hospitals," he told his friend. "Drive me to the morgue. I know the guy's there."

Trotta remembered the pandemonium at the morgue. "The parents and relations were there screaming, hollering, crying. And they wouldn't allow those people to go down to look or identify the kids.

"Coroner McCarron, who was in charge of all this, he's over there in a corner, cowering and trembling, all by himself. He had his back to the people, and was looking at the wall. He doesn't know what to do.

"And out of all of this chaos, Monsignor Eddie Pellicore and his assistant, Father Tony Spina, saw me there, and say, 'What's the matter?'

" 'My kid,' I said. 'He's got to be here somewhere.'

"And, fortunately, there was this cop there, Joe Sansone, a friend of mine, who came over and said, 'John, what's the matter?'

" 'The kid, Joe,' and he knew the kid.

"He said, 'They won't let you down?'

"I said, 'No.'

"So he and the monsignor and Tony Spina, we went to the door, and Joe talked to the cop there. 'Let this guy down there,' he said.

"So I went down there, the monsignor with his hand on one of my shoulders and Tony Spina put his hand on my other shoulder. And here they had all these kids laid out on the floor.

"This is the part you don't sleep nights over. I said, 'The kid's gotta be here.'

"And then some young lady, very compassionate, she says they have a few bodies in a little side room over there who came in first.

"And there was the guy.

"So I told the monsignor, I said, 'Don't worry, Eddie.' I used to call him Eddie. He bowled with me. We belonged to the same Knights of Columbus council, and he was chaplain of our Fourth Degree club. I said, 'Don't worry, Eddie, I'll be all right.'

"There was the kid there, in a position just the way he used to sleep with his hands behind his head. There was nothing I could do there anymore. This young lady gave me the things out of his pockets, but . . . after that I went home. My wife and daughter were waiting for me. They had already known because they were publishing the names on TV."

Trotta was close to tears. "You never forget," he said. "There isn't a day you forget. This thing stays with you, weighs heavily on you. I know the wife feels the same way. We go to the cemetery once, twice a week. I stop every time I go by Queen of Heaven. The big monument they have there for all the kids that died, that was erected by Monsignor Joe Cussen.

"Cussen was a helluva guy. It was just that this thing, frankly, broke him. He had a good bunch of priests there then. The parish house was the kind of place a guy could go and feel welcome. It wasn't like that in some parishes where it's easier to see the pope than it is to see the pastor.

"In those days it was a jumping, thriving parish. You used to walk down the street going to church, and you'd be 'hello-ing' everybody. But after the fire the neighborhood changed.

"I was friendly with most of the nuns there—used to do errands for them, drive them to the cemeteries, things like that. In fact, the Wednesday before the fire, Sister Mary Canice Lyng asked me if I would drive her out to Mt. Carmel Cemetery to visit her parents' graves. I did, and then the following Monday she was dead herself. The nuns used me as their chauffeur a lot. I was their 'Uncle John.'

"When John David died he was thirteen, had just been thirteen about ten days, and he was bragging about having finally become a teenager. He was not naive, but he thought the best of everybody.

His sister, Judy, was almost four years older. They worshiped each other. We were an affectionate family."

For months after the fire, John Trotta was in an emotional turmoil. He expressed his bitterness openly, and his feelings were known in the parish.

"For six or seven months after," he admitted, "my wife and daughter didn't know what was going to happen to me. One time we went to an anniversary party of a good friend. I won't mention his name, but he lost his only daughter in the fire. He says to me, 'John, we belong to an exclusive club. We're drinking, having fun, but inside, I'm dying.'"

John Trotta knew exactly what his friend meant.

Some miles south of the Trotta home, John David is buried in the family plot at Queen of Heaven Cemetery. A grey marble monument marks the grave site. It is offset by two angels kneeling in prayer and carries the inscription: "May the angels lead us into paradise."

The marker reads: "Trotta . . . Son, John David. Nov. 21, 1945— Dec. 1, 1958."

IT WOULD BE impossible for a nonsurvivor to know what horrors were imbedded in the minds of children who lived through the Our Lady of the Angels fire. From their experiences they gained an appreciation for life known to few others. It is a lesson they feel compelled to share.

One spring day in 1994, Matt Plovanich talked about that earlier day. He was in his twenty-fifth year with the Chicago Police Department, a detective newly reassigned to the narcotics division after working many years in the organized crime unit.

Plovanich has a sly sense of humor and likes to tell jokes. But beneath the veneer he is deep thinking, contemplative, a bit of a philosopher. His voice is raspy and he speaks in short, clipped sentences. Following in his father's footsteps, he joined the Chicago Police Department in March 1969. One of his brothers is also a cop.

Together with their five children—three girls and two boys— Plovanich and wife live in a spacious, older brick bungalow located in a comfortable, tree-lined neighborhood on Chicago's far Northwest Side. The neighborhood resembles the suburbs that border it more than the city in which it sits. It is clean, quiet, and airy—an enclave that is home to many white Chicago police officers and fire-fighters who, as a condition of their employment, must reside within the city limits.

Despite several brushes with danger as a Chicago police officer, nothing Plovanich has seen matches the peril he experienced as a ten-year-old boy trapped inside Room 207. He could recall precisely the look of utter terror that swept his nun's face when she realized that the occupants of the Cheese Box were trapped inside their tiny corner classroom.

"It really was a panic situation," he said. "We had our backs to the wall. There was no way out. In those days the nuns were always in perfect, rigid control. But when we saw the look on her face after she realized the back door was locked, we knew the Rosary was basically the last rites.

"The nun led us in the Rosary. She said, 'Okay, let's get on our knees. We're going to say the Rosary.'

"And I remember everybody fighting for the good air pocket on the bottom of the floor, huddled in the corner by the back door. We laid as flat as we could with our noses to the floor. The smoke was that thick. And I remember girls panicking and scratching and screaming and clawing.

"I think I reverted into a defense mode, where the horror gets so bad that the body short-circuits so the whole system doesn't explode. It shuts part of your terror mechanism down and you don't get so frightened anymore.

"The initial thrust is to save yourself, just to get out no matter what cost. And then, when you realize that getting out means jumping from a fairly high window and you're too afraid to do it, you pretty much accept the fact that you're gonna die and this is it. I think what happens is the mind will only let a human being go through so much terror and then it just kind of shuts it out and you get into a different state and you're able to accept it a lot better. I found that happened in some of my other incidents on the police force—getting stabbed or having a parachute malfunction on my first jump.

"I just remember thinking of the irony of this whole thing—of going to school and dying. You're supposed to learn in school. You're supposed to be nurtured in school, and school's supposed to be a positive experience, and here I thought, 'This is unbelievable.' I thought, 'All of us, we're all going to die here.' It's just incredible, you know?

"When Mr. Raymond and Father Hund finally got the back door open, they had to start pulling at us because some of the kids were just frozen. We were basically on our last breaths. There wasn't much left. They actually had to go in and pull them to get them to move. Some of the kids were completely panic-stricken. It was that close.

"For many years I asked myself why I didn't struggle more. Why I didn't jump. Why I didn't take more aggressive action. And like I say, I think you just struggle to a certain point and then you just give in to it. It was really like that.

"You think this is pretty hairy but you find this isn't going to be so bad after all. It's a very euphoric feeling. And that's how I reacted to it. I was lying on that floor, in all that smoke, starting to drift off, and all the while I'm thinking, 'It's terribly sad and terribly unbelievable, but we are all gonna die here.'

"My grade—the fifth grade—was hit pretty hard. There were a lot of fifth-graders killed. It was almost a death sentence if you were assigned to those rooms that faced the alley."

A comprehensive review of the school fire shows that the death toll would have been much higher had it not been for the quick action of school personnel and neighbors who rushed into the burning building to help save students before the Fire Department arrived. Matt Plovanich is keenly aware of this. He pondered how his family was spared: "There were two families that lost *two* kids. I mean, how can you figure—we had three kids in there and we lost nobody? And these families lost both children? That's tough. That's really tough.

"After the fire," he continued, "there was a period of protection on the part of my parents. Not overprotection, but protection because they were concerned about us all the time. But the main feeling we had was shared grief for all the families that did lose people. Constantly. Especially those two families that lost two kids. Look at what those poor people went through and look at how God looked favorably upon us. He spared us.

"I've never had flashbacks, but I'm always aware of where exits are. I always have my bearings. Whenever I walk into a new building, I find out where the exits are, mentally planning an escape route, only because, again, when you're in a fire that develops that quickly, you realize once it starts you better have a place to run, a direction, a plan of escape."

Plovanich related how, years later, as a parent, he chose not to send his children to a particular Catholic school because it reminded him too much of the old Our Lady of the Angels School. "We were right on the border of two parishes," he explained, "so I had the option of sending them to one or the other. I walked through the one school and it resembled Our Lady of the Angels so much that I decided to send them to the other one.

"The interior looked like our hallways. Highly varnished woodwork. Wooden desks. The windows were all the same. The pastor to this day is mad at me for making the decision to send my kids to the other school. I told him, 'Father, please, you gotta realize what I went through. This is a real gut-emotional thing, but the plan reminds me too much of Our Lady of the Angels. I just can't send my kids here.' "

Plovanich thought for a moment, then continued. "Death is truly around the corner for us," he said. "We really don't realize how close it is in many cases. The fire just made me appreciate life because I feel that every one of those kids who survived is living on borrowed time. When you look at it, we all should've perished. I remember going to one of our reunions, and this guy who was in the Cheese Box with me looked at me and said, 'Looking back, we should not be here right now.'

"It's kind of inspirational. You think maybe God left you down here for a reason and we shouldn't squander our time down here. We should live a good life and be positive because we are blessed by Him. He did me a big favor."

OGNIBENE in Italian means "every goodness," and if there was one person in Our Lady of the Angels parish at the time of the fire who was considered to have an abundance of good qualities, it was Father Joseph Ognibene.

Ognibene is an unpretentious man who imparts a sense of inner strength. He speaks in a soft monotone, and his once-black hair is now grey. Dressed in a blue sweater and black slacks, he talked in an office inside the rectory of Our Lady Mother of the Church on Chicago's far Northwest Side, where he was pastor. There was still a lean, athletic appearance about him, a carryover from his seminary days when his talents as a ballplayer were highly regarded.

Ognibene had strong emotional ties to many people in Our Lady of the Angels parish, and they to him. The children were especially fond of him. So it was only natural that despite the passage of years—thirty-two of them at the time he was interviewed—he still found it painful to resurrect his memories of the school fire.

"For a long time," he said, "I wanted to black it out, to get it out of my mind, to purge it from my life. Other reporters called me, and I always said no because there was so much written that wasn't true.

"My faith was shaken, I'll be very honest. A lot of times I asked myself, 'Why? Why?' I couldn't say why. I had no answers.

"The fire brought big changes in my life. Until then I was a little boy. I grew up a lot. I think it helped me. In those days we were or-dained at age twenty-six, but we were still like little boys. In our seminary life we had no TV, no newspapers, no radio. We came home for just a week or two. We didn't associate with anyone else. There were no women in our lives. I was thirty-two at the time of the fire.

"I was active in athletics and I knew so many of the kids. I was able to cope with it right away, but I had a hard time whenever I heard things that weren't true. I carried an awful lot of anger inside me. I wouldn't express it, and that wasn't good. I would've been a lot better off if I'd let it out.

"What I'm talking about now comes after an awful lot of reflec-tion, things I was finally able to determine for myself, like 'Why was I always so damn angry?'"

After the fire, priests and nuns from the parish were asked if they wished to remain at Our Lady of the Angels or be transferred to other assignments. Father Ognibene chose to stay, remaining there until 1961.

"In a way," he said, "I thought the fire made us closer as a parish, but at the same time there were a lot people who were very angry. Many people moved out. They disappeared.

"In those days, in that neighborhood, the kids respected the church. We had a good rapport with the kids. They didn't shy away from us. They respected us. We were very active with them. They never defaced the church, never threw eggs at it. It was beautiful. It was probably the closest-knit parish I have ever been to in my entire life. Everybody knew everybody else. They helped each other."

Ognibene paused for a moment, looking pensively at his clasped hands. He continued: "There was a lot of suffering, personal hurt, but there was a lot of kindness and compassion too. I saw people who were having trouble in their marriages brought back together. And families too. So there was still good that came of it. Through death there is resurrection. We saw the worst and we saw the best.

"In the aftermath there was a lot of criticism about the dirty school, the papers at the bottom of the stairwell. It was an old building, but it was a clean building. It was kept up pretty well.

"I got letters galore from all over the world. Some people thought I was the pastor because evidently my name was used in a lot of the syndicated news articles. I opened only one. They called me every name in the book. They said I was probably over in the rectory having 'tea and crumpets' and wasn't concerned with what was going on over in the school. So I decided to just forget it, not to open any more. I can't remember if I burned them or threw them away or what.

"We had police protection. There were police in the house all day and all night long.

"I remember there was a fellow out to kill me. On the day of the fire he ran up to me outside the school, during all the commotion when I was running back and forth, in and out of the school. He grabbed me and asked me about his son. I said, 'He'll be fine. It's okay. Don't worry.'

"Well, the kid died in the fire. As a result, he used that against me. If I would have told him things were bad, he could've gone in the school and saved his son. But because I told him things were fine, he felt he was going to get me for that. We were very close too. His son was going to become a priest because of 'Father Joe.' That's all he ever talked about."

Once, while vacationing in California, Father Ognibene dropped in at a local church rectory to go to confession. "The old monsignor came to the door," he said, "and I told him where I was from. I told him Chicago. He asked where, and I said, 'Our Lady of the Angels.'

"The minute I mentioned that, he said, 'So you're the sons of bitches that caused us all these problems. You're the guys who caused us to have to put out all this money.'

"I guess they had to put sprinkler systems in their schools. So I just said, 'Forget it,' and turned around and said, 'See ya later.' "

Of all the priests and church officials interviewed by the authors, Ognibene was the only one who did not dance around questions about the cause of the fire. He knew the Cicero youth who confessed to starting the blaze and was familiar with the youngster's troubled background. In 1962, when the closed Family Court hearings were held before Judge Cilella, Ognibene was one of those called to testify as a character witness.

"It was an unfortunate accident," Ognibene sighed. "A sick kid playing with matches. I'm sure he had no idea what he was doing would result in what happened. I don't think it was our fault or anybody's fault. I think people under the circumstances did the best they could.

"There were stories saying, 'If Sister So-and-So would've done this, this wouldn't have happened.' That's a bunch of baloney. All that possibly could've been done was done.

"Those nuns were just beautiful people. They loved the children. I crawled through that corridor myself—you couldn't see your hand in front of your face. I'm sure I would've done the same thing. There was no way you could've got through that dense, black smoke. Where would you go? I'm sure they were thinking, 'Let's stay here and hopefully we'll get out the windows. Eventually the Fire Department will come and put out the fire and it will clear up.'

"It was something that happened and it's nobody's fault. Why God allowed it to happen, I have no idea. I saw good come out of it and I saw bad come out of it."

SISTER MARY DAVIDIS DEVINE, the venerable teacher of Room 209, never second-guessed the actions she took when smoke began to curl through the cracks around her classroom's two wooden doors. Of the five larger classrooms on the second floor of the north wing, hers suffered least. Only two fatalities occurred. Still, the numbers gave her little consolation, even though the death toll surely would have been much higher had it not been for her quick thinking and cool head.

In 1995 Sister Davidis was still living, at age eighty-nine, in retirement at the BVM motherhouse in Dubuque, Iowa. Her recollections of the fire, however, came during a 1976 interview, eighteen years after the event. At the time she was seventy years old. She no longer wore a black habit, preferring more conventional clothing.

"If you knew as much on Monday as you know on Tuesday," she remarked, "we'd all be geniuses. Commissioner Quinn told me, 'If you didn't block up the cracks around the doors, you wouldn't have made it out.' "

Sister Davidis remembered how classrooms in the school were extremely crowded that year. "They had put extra rows of desks in Sister Helaine's room and in my room," she said. "My desk was in the corner at the west end. When the pastor would come in to hand out report cards, I had to get up and go down an aisle to meet him because there was just enough room for one person to get by. It was that congested."

After the fire, Sister Davidis did not return to Our Lady of the Angels. "I prayed that I wouldn't have to go back there," she admitted. "Too many memories.

"I try not to think of the fire too much. If I did, it would affect my outlook on the future. But I do remember the children who died. I remember them each morning at Mass, every day."

IN THE FALL of 1976, when Sister Mary Andrienne Carolan was asked to recall her memories of the fire, she arranged for an interview at Immaculata BVM convent, located on the North Side of Chicago near Lake Michigan. She had turned fifty-three and was taking a brief vacation between assignments that had placed her in various teaching and counseling assignments since 1958.

Like Sister Davidis, she had long given up wearing the religious garb of the BVM nuns in favor of civilian dress, and she no longer used the name of Andrienne. "I'm known as Sister Mary Carolan," she said.

Unlike Sister Davidis, however, Sister Carolan had difficulty holding back her emotions as she recalled the day that affected the lives of so many people. She wept as she talked about her former roommate, Sister Mary Clare Therese Champagne, the young nun who died alongside her students in Room 212, and she could not restrain her tears as she described the frightened children at the windows overlooking the street who called to her for rescue.

Her memory of the thick smoke that flowed into the south wing was still keen. "When the smoke came over to our side of the school," she said, "it went 'shish-shish-shish.' You could smell the tar paper. It was the kind of smoke that took your breath away completely.

"In the south wing of the school we had handicapped children. They were in leg braces. You think you have all this strength, and you do things under stress that affect you later in life. I ruined my back that day trying to carry those kids. Father Ognibene was helping us. God bless Joe. He was fantastic.

"I've had three surgical operations on my back. Nothing has helped. But that's beside the point. The children were saved. If I had lost one child in that wing of the school, I'd never have forgiven myself."

Sister Carolan recalled how she returned to her room after leading most of her students safely outside the school, and how several of the children had desperately pinched her legs in order to keep in contact with her in the blinding smoke as they crawled into the hallway and groped for the stairs.

"Later," she said, "a doctor looked at the bruises on my legs. 'What are those?' he asked.

"I said, 'Never mind. Those are my scars of victory.'"

Sister Carolan spoke of the prolonged emotional effect of the tragedy on the BVM community. "It was years before any of us who were in it could talk about it," she said. "I still can't look at fire, even if it's only on television."

Toward the end of her conversation, the nun began recalling the names of children who died or were injured. She remembered Bill Edington, the eighth-grader who fought so gallantly to live, only to succumb eight months after the fire.

"Oh my Billy," she sighed. "He was burned over 80 percent of his body. When I went to see him in the hospital, he said, 'Look, Sister, I can still be a priest. My hands aren't burned.'

"His two hands, from the wrists down, weren't touched. He wanted to go to Quigly Seminary after he graduated. But it wasn't to be."

JOHN RAYMOND was still racked by appalling memories of jumping out of his classroom window and landing on the hard pavement, of looking back up to see other burning children falling to the ground and bouncing off the hard surface of the alley. He has worked hard to distance himself from these memories.

But he also saw his father, James, the school's janitor, destroyed, beaten down by allegations that his negligence contributed to the disaster. John Raymond always believed those accusations were unfounded, and he remained disturbed by his father's lack of vindication.

"It's all hearsay," he said. "I don't want my children to read some day that their grandfather started the Our Lady of the Angels School fire.

"I understood my father's grief," he continued. "I remember him crying at Christmas for all the children who died. And then later they were making accusations and saying, 'Maybe it was your fault.' And he was having a tough time understanding that.

"My father didn't have any help except for an old-timer who used to come around and give him a hand. He would give him a broom and a buck. Today if you had a school that size, there would be four guys working there. But he was working alone. He had to do everything, and you couldn't do it well. It was impossible. But that's how they cut corners in those days."

It wasn't until later that John Raymond learned his father had been made into a scapegoat. "When I was seventeen," Raymond recalled, "I finally realized my father had been taking a lot of shit from people. I heard more and more about this. And soon after, some man on the street said to me, 'I know you. You're the kid who's dad started that fire and killed all those kids.'

"That was the final straw. I went nuts and ran after the guy and started beating him right there on the corner. My friends had to pull me off. There's a ton of people out there who probably think the janitor did it. I shock people when I tell them, 'My father was the janitor. He didn't do it.' "

Raymond admitted he was still angry over the lack of psychological counseling made available to the children. "The archdiocese failed miserably," he said. "The church fell on its face in that respect. They did us an injustice. To this day I feel that way. They never came by. Nobody ever came up to me to ask, 'Hey, how are you doing? How do you feel?'

"All they did was send you a letter telling you to come downtown and pick up some money. Money is not the answer. [Raymond's family received $500 compensation for his injuries.] People were appalled at those first families that sued the church. People were saying, 'They should be happy. Their children are alive.'

"Yeah, they're alive, but they're burnt, and the burns aren't the worst of it. It's what's in their heads that bothers them more than anything. But those families who sued were looked upon as traitors.

"On one occasion, after we went back to school, the nun whom my father brought out of the fire was teaching us religion class, and all of a sudden she just put her head down on the desk and started sobbing and sobbing and sobbing. Finally one of the girls went across the hall and got someone and they took her away and we never saw her again.

"A lot of the kids she had taught died in the fire. The nuns never forgot you. They cared about you. They went through pure hell over this. I don't think a lot of people realize this.

"How the hell are we going to forget this? We're not. Never. Everyone who lived in that neighborhood clings to this."

After the fire, Raymond recalled, "people were going out of their way telling me how special I was, how brave I was. All I knew is when I looked across the street, Wayne Wisz wasn't there anymore. Peggy Sansonetti down the street wasn't there anymore. Larry Dunn wasn't meeting me to go to school anymore. He lived over on Grand Avenue, and he'd walk over to Hamlin and stop by or I'd wait for him. But he wasn't coming by anymore. All these guys, these buddies of mine, were all dead.

"Annette LaMantia, the most beautiful, intelligent girl in the school, she was gone.

"I remember my mom, who graduated from that same school years earlier, saying how the school was meant to be torn down after such an enormous tragedy, that from Day One, God knew when they built it that it would be torn down under such tragic circumstances.

"Even with the new school, you go around there and you can tell it's a sacred place. You can feel something when you drive by there. It's a part of history. It belongs. It has to live. They should never close it. Everybody feels that way about their parish, but this is too special.

"Sometimes you have nightmares when you hear fire stories on the news—apartment fires or house fires where people are trapped

and they die and the firemen find them huddled in corners or in closets. You know the horror these people went through. Your own experience comes right back.

"I think the fire has kept me glued to the past. My friends tell me
they can't believe how I can remember things with such detail.
They're all successful. They think of the future. I always think back
to what could have, should have, might have . . .

"Whenever I see an old red-brick school I think about it. And
there are a lot of old red-brick schools."

THE CHICAGO Fire Department's performance at Our Lady of the
Angels School became an object of popular criticism. Yet a review
of the facts shows that everything humanly possible was done by
firefighters to save those who perished or were injured in the blaze.
The catastrophic scene that greeted them at the school was among
the worst ever encountered by any first-arriving team of firefighters
in the history of the American fire service.

Among the myths associated with the fire are those which
falsely attribute the high loss of life to the Fire Department for not
having ladders long enough to reach the school's high second-floor
classroom windows, and for its delayed response. The first of these
contentions arose immediately after the fire, following the publica-
tion of news photos which showed several ladders on the alley side
of the school that fell short of window ledges. In fact, the short ladders were placed before the Fire Department's arrival by neighbors
and church personnel. All but one of these were too short. The exception was the one ladder thrown up to Room 208 by assistant janitor Mario Camerini, which enabled an estimated twenty-five pupils
to reach safety.

Three ladder companies were at the burning school within seven
minutes of the first alarm, and all windows on the school's north
wing were adequately laddered shortly after. Twenty-two engine
companies, seven ladder companies, and ten squad companies responded to the fire.

Just one Fire Department ladder placed against the building was
indeed too short. This was the twenty-four-foot extension ladder
thrown up to Room 212 by the first-arriving firefighters from Engine 85. Even though this one ladder fell short of the window by

about three feet, it nonetheless enabled firefighters to reach children hanging off the windowsill.

On the second point, the delay, which surely helped to seal the fate of many who died, occurred in transmitting an alarm *to* the Fire Department. For this the men who fought the fire can hardly be blamed. Once the alarm was finally received by the main fire alarm office, it took the first fire company only two and a half minutes to reach the scene. Additional companies were not far behind.

While it may be small consolation, the Chicago Fire Department's record for the number of rescues effected at any single fire in the city was set at Our Lady of the Angels School. Operating under extremely hazardous conditions, firefighters managed to rescue 160 children and nuns within the first thirteen minutes of their arrival. Unofficially the number saved by the Fire Department probably lies around 200.

Today as in 1958, the primary objective in firefighting is to get water on a fire as quickly as possible. With the exceptions of diesel fire apparatus with larger pumping capacities, hydraulic aerial ladders, the introduction of self-contained breathing apparatus in the early 1960s, and better fire-retardant clothing worn by firefighters, almost forty years later little has changed in the way structure fires are fought in this country, particularly in older brick and frame buildings that lack sprinkler systems.

It might be said that entry into the school building was hampered because firefighters in 1958 were not equipped with breathing apparatus. But the smoke conditions present at Our Lady of the Angels were among the worst ever encountered by Chicago firefighters. Even if they had had breathing apparatus, they might not have gained quicker access to those trapped inside the school's blazing classrooms. According to one fire chief who fought the school fire, breathing apparatus "would not have made any difference. That smoke was so bad, all you would've had was a bunch of dead firemen."

LIKE THE SURVIVORS and their families, firefighters who fought the blaze were deeply affected by the tragedy. Most of them rarely discussed their experiences at OLA, choosing instead to follow contemporary norms by keeping their feelings inside.

Joan Hoffman, widow of Engine 85 firefighter Charles Robinson, told how the fire affected her late husband: "He used to wake up at night and head for the windows and yell, 'Hold on. Don't jump. Help's on the way.' I'd have to get up and calm him down."

"There was no such thing as counseling for emergency workers back then," recalled Thomas O'Donnell, who, as a young firefighter with Engine 24, was among the two hundred firemen summoned to the school. "But if there was counseling in those days, I'm sure quite a few guys would've sought it. I saw a lot of firemen cry, and I cried too. I was pretty much a rookie back then, but I saw a lot of hardened firemen take that fire really badly. If it didn't shake you, you weren't a human being."

When he was interviewed for this book, more than three decades had passed since Lieutenant Charles Kamin raced up a ladder to rescue children from the grip of fire that consumed Room 211. But as he lay in bed at night, Kamin would still hear the screams of that December day that refused to go away. He would hear them as if the fire had occurred yesterday. And when he talked about it, his eyes welled with tears.

"I remember those kids screaming," he recalled. "That's what I remember the most. The screaming."

The burns that Kamin sustained that day to his ears and arms had long since healed. But the emotional scars remained. "Those kids," he said, "how the hell I ever picked them up I'll never know. They must've weighed a hundred pounds each. I don't know where I got the strength to pick them up like that by their belts. Under normal circumstances, I couldn't have done that. But I guess that's God's way—you get that superhuman strength.

"After I went into those rooms to get the bodies out, it made it worse. If I hadn't seen them die it would have been different. But I saw them die and that's what sticks with you more than anything else. To see all those kids die in front of you, you can only do so much."

Along with grief, Kamin lived with frustration. He remained angered by the confusion that led up the Fire Department's arrival at the school—first by being given the wrong address, then by having to spend precious time knocking down the locked courtway gate.

"Maybe I could've got another five or six kids out of there if it wasn't for all those damn delays," he said. "People don't realize how long a minute is. A minute is a hell of a long time.

"If I was there two minutes sooner, I could've gotten fifteen to twenty more kids out. If only we didn't have to break that damn gate down. There are so many ifs.

"If it's true that the nuns had to see the sister superior before they pulled the fire alarm, that's stupidity. They should've pulled the alarm and got those kids out of there. I can't see any child or any person staying in their seat. When that fire is burning your butt, you have to move. I can't believe they were so disciplined that the nun would tell them to sit there and they would stay there.

"I just don't know why they held them in those rooms. Even with the heavy smoke they could've tried to go out the door, and then within steps, they're out and down the stairs. But in a situation like that you're second-guessing. The nuns didn't know. It wasn't their fault. They were doing what they thought was right."

Recalling the meeting in Fire Commissioner Quinn's office the day after the fire, Kamin defended the actions of Lieutenant Wojnicki, in charge of first-arriving Engine 85. "Quinn really laid into Wojnicki," Kamin said. "He was really abusive. Quinn called him a 'dumb so-and-so' and asked him why he didn't start getting kids out.

"I felt sorry for Wojnicki. He did a helluva good job. He did exactly what he was supposed to—get water on the fire as soon as he got there. His gang got their line right into that stairwell, right at the base of the fire. As it turned out, he saved a lot of kids just by doing that.

"You do what you think is right. And Wojnicki did what he thought was right. His job was to put out fire, not rescue kids."

Kamin said he never talked much about the fire. Only once in a while would it come up in conversation around the firehouse kitchen. He had never entertained thoughts of leaving the Fire Department. "I didn't want to quit," he said. "It's just one of those things that's part of the job. You never forget. And I never did."

AFTER THE FIRE, Salvatore Imburgia said he seriously considered resigning from the Fire Department. "I didn't think I could take this anymore," he said. "I wasn't afraid. I was never afraid of anything.

That wasn't the point. It's just that I didn't think I could take another disaster like this.

"But I remember talking to this German guy I used to work for on my days off. I was an upholsterer. I said, 'Werner, I think I'm going to resign.' He said, 'Why?' So I told him. And he said, 'Think about it. I salute you and I salute the Chicago Fire Department for what you done there. If you're thinking of quitting, I think you're making a big mistake because we need people like you firemen. You have a job that has to be done.'

"I thought about it for the next couple of days. Finally I said, 'Hey, what the hell. I did the best I could there. I think we all did good. We all tried.' After that I figured this is a good job. I don't want to leave it.

"The fact that this was my neighborhood and my parish made it worse," he said. "These were my people. These were my buddies' kids.

"Oscar Sarno, he used to own a pizza place on Chicago Avenue. He was a good friend of mine. He lost two kids. Another friend of mine was a barber who owned a shop on Chicago Avenue. He lost a child.

"I remember Oscar's daughter being up there in the window. I screamed up to her to jump. She was afraid to jump. She fell back in."

Shortly after the fire, Imburgia was temporarily detailed from Truck 36 to inspect schools as part of the plan implemented by Commissioner Quinn to station a fireman in any school building found to have fire code problems. Imburgia was posted to a West Side Ukrainian church school.

"It was right before Christmas," he recalled, "and I was in the church. These kids were having choir practice. I remember listening to them practicing and it was so beautiful—the music and those little kids singing in the choir. And then I thought about those kids in the fire, and I just broke up. I closed my eyes, and all I could see were those other kids in the fire."

LIEUTENANT JOHN MCCONE was one of six firefighters assigned to Squad 6, among the first-arriving still-alarm companies to reach the school. He too had grown up in Our Lady of the Angels parish and had attended the parish school as a boy.

Squad 6 was returning to its Humboldt Park firehouse from an inhalator call when it was dispatched to the fire. "You didn't know what to do first," McCone recalled, "whether to catch these kids when they were coming down, try to break their fall, or run up the ladder and try to pull them out. They were coming down head first. I tried to catch this one kid and he went right through my arms. I heard his skull hit the sidewalk. It was sickening. But I did manage to stop a couple. And that's when I got my double hernia. You could break their fall a little but you couldn't catch them."

As he talked, McCone, who had risen to the rank of captain, was sipping coffee in the pilot house of the fireboat *Joseph Medill*—Engine 37—moored downtown in the Chicago River. "Emotionally," he said, "it makes you feel like you just didn't do enough. I had kids in school myself at the time. You sit back and say, 'Why didn't I do this? Why didn't I do that? Why didn't I do more?'

"I was forty years old at the time of the fire. I was familiar with the area because I went to school there. I was baptized there in the old church that became the school.

"If I was to venture an opinion, it appeared to me those kids were so well disciplined they wouldn't get up out of their seats because somebody told 'em not to. In my opinion the nuns could've gotten those kids out. But they stayed there until they were told to move, and by that time it was too late."

After the fire, McCone was emotionally distraught. He was transferred to Fire Department headquarters, where he took a desk job handling special assignments for the mayor's office. He was later assigned to the fireboat. Although he rarely discussed the fire, even with members of his own family, his friends in the department said it had a lasting effect on him. "We did as much as humanly possible," he said. "But it was too late. About four minutes too late."

AFTER LEAVING the *Chicago American*, Hal Bruno went on to a highly successful career in journalism. He wrote for *Newsweek* magazine and eventually became director of political coverage for ABC News, working out of the network's Washington, D.C., bureau.

In the weeks following the fire, Bruno was involved in covering the investigation into its cause. The *American* campaigned for the immediate installation of sprinkler systems and enclosure of stairways in city schools. Before Our Lady of the Angels, the paper had run a similar campaign following a series of fatal flophouse fires in Chicago.

"We ran head on into the powers of the church and education lobby, who didn't want to spend the money," Bruno recalled. "It's ironic and infuriating that we could force the city council to protect the bums on skid row, to change the law requiring sprinkler systems in those buildings, but not the children in the schools."

What sticks in his mind more than anything, though, are the anguished faces of parents he saw standing outside the school. About ten years after the fire, Bruno recalled waking up in a cold sweat. He had been dreaming about a woman he saw outside the school. "I saw her for a fleeting second while I was running for the ladder truck," he said. "She was outside looking for her child. I was puzzled as to why I was dreaming about her so many years later.

"By then I was married and had children of my own. So I got up and went into their bedroom to check on them. Then I realized why it had all come back to me that night. My oldest son had just turned eight, and that was the age of the children—eight to ten mostly—who lost their lives at Our Lady of the Angels.

"It's interesting the way things stick in your mind, the psychological impact of what you are seeing without knowing it. Today they have counseling for emergency service people, which we didn't have in those days. Everybody was supposed to be a macho tough guy. The truth is that us 'macho tough guys' were bothered by what we saw and what we had to do at times."

STEVE LASKER was no stranger to horror stories. He carried his camera to thousands of them, including plane crashes and streetcar and automobile accidents in which people were burned and dismembered. All those incidents bothered him, but none so much as what he saw through his camera lens on December 1, 1958.

Lasker shot eighty-four photographs for the *Chicago American* at Our Lady of the Angels, the most notable being that of firefighter Richard Scheidt carrying the Jajkowski boy from a side door of the school. More than thirty years later Lasker talked about the fire while a police radio squawked in the background in his home. He was still working in the news business as a camera operator for WBBM-TV, the CBS affiliate in Chicago.

"When I first got there, I figured some of the kids had panicked and didn't know what to do, that there were a few unfortunate ones. And then they kept a count. I remember somebody kept yelling how many children had been brought out, and the number kept going up. It started at ten or twelve and then nineteen, twenty-eight. It kept going. We thought, 'My God. How many are in there?' And you could hear it in the voices of these firemen. 'There's dozens up there.' We didn't know yet how many rooms had been affected."

Lasker stayed at the school until seven o'clock that evening, then went to the morgue and hospitals. Later that night he and other photographers returned to the neighborhood around the school to collect photographs of the students who had died.

"We'd go to the homes and ask folks for a picture of their son or daughter or whoever it was that had perished. We explained that the newspaper was going to run a memorial the next day on the front page. Some of the people wouldn't hear of it. Others were glad to do it, but they were crying, hysterical. I was crying. I felt terrible. It was for a good cause. Now does that make it right? I don't know."

Lasker never met with the Jajkowski parents, but he did talk with Richard Scheidt. "I didn't know who the fireman was," Lasker said. "I knew his brother, Peter Scheidt. I used to hang out at Engine 45. But I didn't know at the time this fireman in the photo was Peter's brother."

A few days after the fire, Lasker went into Richard Scheidt's firehouse in the Loop. "We had gone down to meet him," he recalled. "Everybody put their arms around me and said, 'Good job' and all that. But I didn't want to talk about it. I was still sick in my brain, not only my stomach.

"Scheidt's reaction was he didn't like publicity. None of the guys liked publicity, except some of the chiefs, the old-timers. The firemen aren't in it for that. They just do their job. This is what they're paid to do. And when it involves children, it hits them hard, as it did me. I just had a little girl in April. So I was looking at it as a parent.

"When I met him, it was not a warm greeting but it wasn't cold either. We were there meeting each other because of a disaster, and I felt it and he felt it. And I said, 'I'm very sorry that it had to be like this.' He said, 'Well, I tried to do the best I could. There was nothing we could do to bring these kids back.' "

RICHARD SCHEIDT himself could never put into words what it was like to enter the fire-scarred rooms inside Our Lady of the Angels School. "It was beyond most people's imaginations," he recalled. "When we got there almost a half-hour after the first alarm, there was still a lot of fire. The smoke was still in the air. When a fire takes off and it's burning and it's got plenty of oxygen and it's allowed to burn for a while, it turns into a monster, and this thing was a monster. That's exactly what it was."

Scheidt recounted his experience at Our Lady of the Angels School while sitting in the kitchen of his home in a suburb southwest of Chicago. He was in his early sixties and had a calm, quiet sincerity about him.

"I remember being on the second floor and looking down at the crowd and seeing the parents looking for their kids," he said. "The silence of the crowds is what really struck me. At most fires there's so much noise—equipment working, men working. But not at this fire. This fire was silent. It was the silence—that's what I remember the most. You just couldn't believe what had happened. Everybody was stunned.

"We went up to the second floor with hose lines, trying to make that hallway. Engine companies were stopped right at the landing with their two-and-a-half-inch lines. They were trying to push back the fire. So that's where we started breaching the walls, right there on the landing. We couldn't get through the hallway so we went through the walls. I never made an effort to get into a building like I did there. We knew they were inside, beyond those walls. We gave it all we had.

"We didn't have masks in those days. We stayed up there in that smoke and that heat and we breached those walls. When we got inside, in those first two rooms on the north side, that's where we found a lot of kids, lying along the floor below the windows.

"They were all dead. In that first room they were piled up on the dais around the nun's desk. And as we removed the bodies from the pile, we noticed the children were not burned. They were asphyxiated. In the next room they were burned very badly."

Scheidt paused for a moment before continuing, his eyes filling with tears.

"The effort, the expenditure of energy to take down that wall was tremendous," he said, "and then to have this hit you in the face, 'Hey, we're too late. We're absolutely too goddamn late.' It was tough.

"I had three brothers who preceded me on the fire department," Scheidt said. "I'd seen death a lot on the job, but not on the scale of this thing. This was something that I don't think any of us who were there were prepared for. I don't think you can ever explain how you feel after something like that. It was the worst fire I have ever been to, and I've been to some goddamn bad ones. But nothing like that one. Never in my wildest dreams . . ."

Epilogue

OFFICIALLY the cause of the Our Lady of the Angels School fire is still listed as "undetermined." The fire remains an open case with Chicago authorities, but because of the passage of time and a lack of interest, it is one that likely will never be solved. The archdiocese of Chicago has long since closed its book on the fire. Officially the church still regards the fire as "accidental." Because of this official curtain of ignorance, the fire has become an enigma whose mystery has deepened with each passing year. Secretiveness has worked against investigators seeking a solution to the case, as though human beings cannot stand being told the truth. Unofficially investigators have long held to the belief that someone intentionally set the school fire—probably never dreaming what the result would be.

Arson is one of the most difficult crimes to prosecute; a successful prosecution virtually requires catching the arsonist in the act. A sad yet interesting footnote to the school fire story is that if it were ever proven legally that the Our Lady of the Angels fire was intentionally set, as we assert, it would go down as the worst case of mass death by arson in American history. As of this writing, that sobering statistic was recorded in 1990, when a thirty-seven-year-old love-spurned Cuban refugee set fire to the Happy Land Social Club in the Bronx, New York, killing eighty-seven people.

Since the school fire, the neighborhood encompassing Our Lady of the Angels parish has changed dramatically. The mass exodus of whites from this and other West Side Chicago neighbor-

hoods was accelerated in part by the actions of unscrupulous real es-
tate agents—both in and out of the community—who by the late
1960s began in earnest a campaign of "panic peddling." Playing
upon the fears of white homeowners, realtors pressured residents
into selling their homes quickly and cheaply as large numbers of
lower- to middle-class African-American families began moving
into the area from the dense, decaying ghetto neighborhoods to the
east. Later, when middle-class black families began moving out, the
neighborhood quickly fell into decay, neglect, and poverty. It now
features boarded-up windows, burned-out and abandoned buildings,
and vacant lots. Gangs, drugs, and violence—more than fire—
threaten the children who live there today.

In 1990, because of a decline in parishioners, the Chicago archdiocese decided to close Our Lady of the Angels Church and merge
it with a neighboring Catholic parish to the west. The parish is now
known as St. Francis of Assisi–Our Lady of the Angels. The new
Our Lady of the Angels School remains open, however, educating
children in both communities. And though its student population has
diminished greatly since the late 1950s, the school nevertheless
stands as an oasis of prayer and learning for the mostly African-
American and Hispanic children who attend it.

As of this writing, at Our Lady of the Angels School there is
no memorial, not the smallest plaque commemorating the victims
or describing what happened on the site in 1958. There does exist
one solemn, visible reminder of the school fire tragedy. It can be
found near the fork of two roads running through Queen of Heaven
Cemetery just outside Chicago, where twenty-five of the school
fire dead lie buried beneath simple, flat grave markers. A long
granite monument, erected in 1960 by Monsignor Cussen, stands
over the markers, and chiseled into the monument and looking
down over the graves is the image of the Virgin Mary, Our Lady of
the Angels. Also chiseled into the granite are the names of three
nuns and ninety-two students. Occasionally, an elderly man or
woman may be seen kneeling and setting flowers over the small
grey markers.

The shrine lies in the shadow of pine trees that rustle gently in
the breeze.

The air in the cemetery smells fresh and clean. The silence is broken by the chattering of birds flitting among the trees and by the noise of a power lawnmower in the distance.

Inscribed at the base of the monument are the words: "Our Lady of the Angels Pray for Us."

Sometimes, when the sun is just right, the words glisten.

	Age	Room
Sister Mary Clare Therese Champagne, BVM	27	212
Sister Mary Seraphica Kelley, BVM	43	210
Sister Mary St. Canice Lyng, BVM	44	208

Name	Age	Room	Name	Age	Room
Michele Altobell	13	211	Barbara Hosking	10	212
Robert Anglim	10	212	Victor Jacobellis	9	210
Karen Baroni	10	212	John Jajkowski	10	212
David Biscan	11	212	Angeline Kalinowski	14	211
Richard Bobrowicz	13	211	Diane Karwacki	9	210
Beverly Ann Burda	13	209	Joseph Anthony King	10	212
Helen Buziak	12	208	Kenneth Kompanowski	14	211
Peter Cangelosi	10	210	Richard Kompanowski	10	210
George Cannella	10	212	Margaret Kucan	10	212
Kathleen Carr	9	210	Patricia Kuzma	10	212
Margaret Chambers	9	210	Annette LaMantia	10	212
Aurelius Chiapetta	14	211	Rose Ann LaPlaca	13	211
Joanne Chiappetta	10	210	Joseph Maffiola	10	212
Joan Chrzas	9	210	Raymond Makowski	12	211
Bernice Cichocki	12	208	Linda Malinski	10	212
Rosalie Ciminello	12	208	John Manganello	10	212
Roseanna Ciochon	9	210	John Joseph Mele	10	212
Jo Ann Ciolino	10	212	Joseph Modica	9	210
Millicent Corsiglia	13	211	James Moravec	13	208
Karen Ann Culp	10	212	Mary Ellen Moretti	12	208
Maria DeGiulio	11	212	Charles Neubert	9	210
Nancy Mary DeSanto	9	210	Lorraine Nieri	12	208
Patricia Drzymala	12	208	Janet Olechowski	12	211
Lawrence J. Dunn	10	212	Yvonne Pacini	9	210
William R. Edington, Jr.	13	211	Antoinette Patrasso	11	212
Mary Ann Fanale	12	208	Eileen Pawlik	13	211
Lucile Filipponio	8	210	Carolyn Marie Perry	10	212
Nancy Rae Finnigan	13	211	Elaine Pesoli	10	210
Ronald Fox	13	211	Mary Ellen Pettenon	9	210
Janet Gasteier	9	210	Edward Pikinski	12	208
Carol Ann Gazzola	13	211	Nancy Pilas	12	211
Lawrence Grasso	13	211	Frank Piscopo	13	212
Frances Guzaldo	12	211	James Joseph Profita	8	210
Kathleen Hagerty	13	211	James Ragona	9	210
Richard Hardy	9	212	Roger Alan Ramlow	13	211
Karen Hobik	13	211	Marilyn Reeb	10	212

	Age	Room		Age	Room
Nancy Riche	12	208	Nancy Smid	10	212
Margaret Sansonetti	10	210	Linda Stabile	9	210
Diane Marie Santangelo	9	210	Mark Stachura	9	210
Joanne Sarno	9	210	Mary Louise Tamburrino	13	211
William Sarno	13	211	Philip Tampone	12	208
Antoinette Secco	10	212	Valerie Ann Thoma	14	209
Kurt Schutt	8	210	John David Trotta	13	211
James Sickel	10	210	Mary Virgilio	14	211
Paul Silvio	10	210	Christine Marie Vitacco	12	208
Susan Smaldone	9	210	Wayne Wisz	10	212

Index

A NOTE ON THE AUTHORS

DAVID COWAN has been a newspaper reporter in Illinois and is now a firefighter and independent journalist. Born into the same neighborhood as Our Lady of the Angels parish, he grew up in Chicago and its suburbs, and studied at Southern Illinois University and Cambridge University (England). He served in the air force and has lived in England and traveled extensively in Western Europe. Mr. Cowan's writings have appeared in major newspapers and magazines.

JOHN KUENSTER is executive editor of Century Publishing Company in Evanston, Illinois, and a former staff writer and columnist for the *Chicago Daily News*. He has spent his life in journalism, earlier as sports editor of the *New World* and as editor of the *Columbian*. He has written extensively for newspapers and magazines, and contributed to books, and has interviewed a wide range of important people, from Harry Truman to Casey Stengel.